La Chapelle

Cité des Sciences

Place du Tertre

D0428286

N

Opéra

Opéra Garnier

Magenta

Ménilmontant

Bourse

Ave de l'Opéra

Marais

Centre Georges Pompidou

Louvre

Louvre

Notre Dame

Île de la Cité

Place des Vosges

République

Hôtel-de-Ville

Place de la Bastille

Île St-Louis

Jardin du Luxembourg

Sorbonne

Blvd Saint-Michel

Panthéon

Bercy

Bibliothèque de France

Seine

USEFUL PHONE NUMBERS

FRANCE
Emergencies (in Paris)

Ambulance	15
Poison Center (Hôpital Fernand Widal)	(01) 40 05 48 48
Dentist, 24-hour	(01) 43 37 51 00
Doctor, 24-hour	(01) 47 07 77 77
Fire	18
Medical Emergencies	(01) 48 28 40 04
Pharmacy, 24-hour	(01) 43 37 51 00
Police	17

Other important numbers:

U.S. Embassy	(01) 43 12 23 47
American Hospital	(01) 46 41 25 25
Hertford British Hospital	(01) 46 39 22 22
Telephone Information	12
Time	36 99
Weather (5 days—all of France)	(08) 36 68 00 00
Railroad Information—SNCF	(01) 53 90 20 20
—RER	(08) 36 68 77 14
Road and traffic conditions	(08) 36 68 10 77

CANADA
Emergencies (in Quebec City)

Ambulance	911
Poison emergencies	(1) (800) 463-5060
Fire	911
Police	911

Other important numbers:

U.S. Consulate (Montreal)	(514) 692-2095
(Quebec)	(418) 398-9695
Weather Environment (Canada)	(1) (900) 565-5555
(call costs $1.95/min., 2 min. minimum)	
Weather (Montreal)	(514) 283-3010
(Quebec)	(418) 648-7766
Railroads (from U.S.)	(1) (800) 872-7245
Road and traffic conditions (Montreal)	(514) 873-4121
(Quebec)	(418) 648-7766
Quebec Province Tourist Information	(1) (800) 363-7777

FRENCH
AT A GLANCE

PHRASE BOOK & DICTIONARY FOR TRAVELERS

BY GAIL STEIN, M.A.
Teacher of French
Department of Foreign Languages
Martin Van Buren High School, New York

HEYWOOD WALD, Coordinating Editor
Former Chairman, Department of Foreign Languages
Martin Van Buren High School, New York

Fourth Edition

BARRON'S

© Copyright 2003, 2000, 1992, 1984 by Barron's Educational Series, Inc.

All inquiries should be addressed to:
Barron's Educational Series, Inc.
250 Wireless Boulevard
Hauppauge, New York 11788
http://www.barronseduc.com

ISBN-13: 978-0-7641-2512-6
ISBN-10: 0-7641-2512-5

Library of Congress Cataloging-in-Publication Data

Stein, Gail.
    French at a glance : phrase book & dictionary for travelers / by Gail Stein ;
Heywood Wald, coordinating editor. — 4th ed.
        p. cm.
    Includes index.
    ISBN 0-7641-2512-5 (alk. paper)
      1. French language—Conversation and phrase books—English.   2. French
language—Dictionaries—English.   3. English language—Dictionaries—
French.   I. Wald, Heywood.   II. Title

PC2121.S67   2003
448.3′421—dc21   2003045365

PRINTED IN CHINA
19 18 17 16 15 14 13 12 11

CONTENTS

PREFACE

So you're taking a trip to one of the many fascinating countries of the world. That's exciting! This phrase book, part of Barron's popular *At a Glance* series, will prove an invaluable companion.

In these books we present the phrases and words that a traveler most often needs for a brief visit to a foreign country, where the customs and language are often different. Each phrase book highlights the terms particular to that country, in situations that the tourist is most likely to encounter. Travel tips found throughout the book have been updated. With a specially developed key to pronunciation, this book will enable you to communicate quickly and confidently in colloquial terms. It is intended not only for beginners with no knowledge of the language, but also for those who have already studied it and have some familiarity with it.

Some of the unique features and highlights of the Barron's series are:

■ Easy-to-follow *pronunciation keys* and complete phonetic transcriptions for all words and phrases in the book.

■ Compact *dictionary* of commonly used words and phrases—built right into this phrase book so there's no need to carry a separate dictionary.

■ Useful phrases for the *tourist*, grouped together by subject matter in a logical way so that the appropriate phrase is easy to locate when you need it.

■ Special phrases for the *business traveler*, including banking terms, trade and contract negotiations, a computer mini-dictionary, computer terms, a list of helpful websites, and secretarial services.

■ Thorough section on food and drink, with comprehensive food terms you will find on menus.

■ *Emergency phrases* and terms you hope you won't need: legal complications, medical problems, theft or loss of valuables, replacement or repair of watches, camera, etc.

■ *Sightseeing itineraries*, with shopping tips, practical travel tips, and regional food specialties to help you get off the beaten path and into the countryside, to the small towns and cities, and to the neighboring areas.

■ A *reference section* providing important signs, conversion tables, holidays, abbreviations, telling time, days of week, and months of year.

■ A brief *grammar section*, with the basic elements of the language quickly explained.

Enjoy your vacation and travel with confidence. You have a friend by your side.

Travel Tips There are many theories on how to survive jet lag—the adjustment to a long trip into a different time zone. Some multinational corporations take jet lag so seriously they do not allow employees to make business decisions on the first day abroad. Most experts agree on several techniques: Eat lightly for several days before departing, avoid dehydration while flying by drinking plenty of nonalcoholic liquids; take frequent strolls around the plane to keep your blood circulating; if possible, get some rest on the flight; use ear plugs, an eye mask, and an inflatable neck collar to make sleep easier. If you arrive early in the morning, take an after-lunch nap, get up for some exercise and dinner, then go to bed at the regular new time. If you arrive at your destination in the afternoon or later, skip the nap and try to sleep late the next morning. In countries where massage or saunas are standard hotel service, indulge yourself on the evening of arrival to help you sleep soundly that night.

ACKNOWLEDGMENTS

We would like to thank the following individuals and organizations for their assistance on this project:

Nora Brossard, Assistant Director Public Relations, French National Tourist Office, New York, New York; Professor Pierre François, SUC New Paltz, New York; Marie-Charlotte Iszkowski, Foreign Service Institute, Washington, D.C.; Michel Lalou, Phonelab, New York, New York; George Lang, George Lang, Inc., New York, New York; Dr. Gladys Lipton, Coordinator of Foreign Languages and ESOL; Marek Pukteris, Quebec Tourist Information Center; Anne Arundel County Public Schools, Annapolis, Maryland; François Mead, Alliance Française, New York, New York; Professor Henry Urbanski, Chairman, Department of Foreign Languages, SUC New Paltz, New York; Herta Erville; and Andrée Katz.

Also, Air France, Association of American Travel Writers, French National Tourist Office, *New York Times*, *Signature Magazine*, *Travel-Holiday Magazine*, *Travel and Leisure Magazine*, U.S. Tour Operators, and U.S. Travel Data Center.

QUICK PRONUNCIATION GUIDE

Although all the phrases in this book are presented with an easy-to-use key to pronunciation, you will find speaking French quite a bit easier if you learn a few simple rules. Below are some tables that give the sounds represented by each French letter along with the symbols used to indicate them in this book. Although a French sound is quite different from ours, with a little practice and repetition you will be able to make yourself understood by native French speakers.

After studying the phonetic pronunciation system below, begin to practice the vocabulary words and then progress to the longer phrases. Bonne chance! *Bohn shah<u>n</u>ss*

STRESS

As an aid to pronunciation, words in this book have been divided into syllables. Since all French syllables have approximately the same amount of stress, pronounce each syllable with equal emphasis and put a slightly stronger emphasis on the last syllable of a word group.

CONSONANTS

In French, final consonants are usually silent, except for final C, R, F, and L (as in CaReFuL), which are usually pronounced.

FRENCH LETTER	ENGLISH SOUND	SYMBOL	EXAMPLE
b, d, f, k, l, m, n	same as English		
p, t, v, z	same as English		
c (before e, i, y)	SS (S at beginning of word)	S	cigare *see-gahr*
ç (before a, o, u)	SS (S at beginning of word)	S	garçon *gahr-ssoh<u>n</u>*
c (before a, o, u)	K	K	comme *kohm*

FRENCH LETTER	ENGLISH SOUND	SYMBOL	EXAMPLE
g (before e, i, y)	S as in pleasure	ZH	rouge *roozh*
ge (before a, o)	S as in pleasure	ZH	mangeons *mahn-zhohn*
g (before a, o, u)	G	G	gant *gahn*
gn	nyuh as in onion	NY	oignon *oh-nyohn*
h	always silent		hôtel *oh-tehl*
j	S as in pleasure	ZH	je *zhuh*
qu, final q	K	K	cinq *sank*
r	Say the R at the top back of the mouth as if you were gargling or spitting.	R	rue *rew*
ss	S	SS	poisson *pwah-ssohn*
s	beginning of word	S	six *sees*
	next to consonant	SS	disque *deessk*
s	between vowels	Z	poison *pwah-zohn*
th	T	T	thé *tay*
x	S in these words only	SS	six *seess*, dix *deess*, soixante *swah-ssahnt*
x	X	KSS	excellent *ehkss-eh-lahn*
x	X	GS	exemple *ehg-sahn-pluh*

NOTE: When combined with a word beginning with a vowel or *h*, *x* has a *z* sound. Beford a word beginning with a consonant, it is silent.

VOWELS

FRENCH LETTER	ENGLISH SOUND	SYMBOL	EXAMPLE
a, à, â	A as in yacht or A in after	AH	la *lah*
é, final er, final ez, et	A as in day	AY	musée *mew-zay*
e + 2 consonants e + final pronounced consonant e, ê, è	E as in ever	EH	sept *seht*
e	sometimes like E of early with no R sound	UH	le *luh*
i (î), y	EE as in meet	EE	île *eel*
i + vowel or ll	Y as in yes	EE	famille *fah-mee*
o + final pronounced consonant	O as in love	OH	homme *ohm*
ô, o before se, o last sound in word, au, eau	O as in open	OH	au *oh*
ou	OO as in tooth	OO	où *oo*
oy, oi	WA as in watch	WAH	trois *trwah*
U	There is none. Round lips and say E and U at same time.	EW	du *dew*
U + vowel	WEE as in wee	WEE	huit *weet*

NASAL SOUNDS

Nasal sounds are produced through the mouth and the nose at the same time. Nasal sounds occur when N or M follows a vowel in the same syllable. There is NO nasal sound for VOWEL + NN, VOWEL + MM, VOWEL + N + VOWEL, VOWEL + M + VOWEL. NOTE: <u>n</u> means there is a nasalized pronunciation of the "N" sound. The tip of the tongue does not touch the roof of the mouth.

FRENCH LETTER	ENGLISH SOUND	SYMBOL	EXAMPLE
AN, AM, EN, EM	similar to on	AH<u>N</u>	France *Frah<u>nss</u>*
IN, IM, AIN, AIM	similar to an	A<u>N</u>	pain *pa<u>n</u>*
IEN	similar to <u>yan</u> of <u>Yan</u>kee	YA<u>N</u>	bien *bya<u>n</u>*
ON, OM	similar to <u>on</u> of <u>long</u>.	OH<u>N</u>	bon *boh<u>n</u>*
UN, UM	similar to <u>un</u> of <u>un</u>der.	UH<u>N</u>	un *uh<u>n</u>*

LIAISON and ELISION

Liaison and elision are two linguistic devices that add to the beauty and fluidity of the French language.

Liaison means linking. In French, the final consonant of a word is usually not pronounced. Sometimes, however, when the final consonant of one word is followed by a beginning vowel or H of the next word, liaison occurs.

EXAMPLE:

Nous arrivons. *noo zah-ree-voh<u>n</u>*

With the following words in French, the final vowel is dropped if the next word starts with a vowel or H. The dropped vowel is replaced by an apostrophe. This is called elision.

EXAMPLE:

la auto = l'auto *(loh-toh)*

le homme = l'homme *(lohm)*

THE BASICS FOR GETTING BY

MOST FREQUENTLY USED EXPRESSIONS

The expressions in this section are the ones you'll use again and again—the fundamental building blocks of conversation, the way to express your wants or needs, and some simple question forms that you can use to construct all sorts of questions. It's a good idea to practice these phrases until you know them by heart.

Sir	**Monsieur**	*muh-ssyuh*
Madame	**Madame**	*mah-dahm*
Miss (Ms.)	**Mademoiselle**	*mahd-mwah-zehl*
I'm American.	**Je suis américain/ américaine (f.)**	*zhuh swee zah- may-ree-kan/ ah-may-ree-kehn*
Do you speak English?	**Parlez-vous anglais?**	*pahr-lay voo ahn-gleh*
I speak a little French.	**Je parle un peu le français.**	*zhuh pahrl uhn puh luh frahn-seh*
Do you understand me?	**Vous me comprenez?**	*voo muh kohn-pruh-nay*
I understand.	**Je comprends.**	*zhuh kohn-prahn*
I don't understand.	**Je ne comprends pas.**	*zhuh nuh kohn-prahn-pah*
What did you say?	**Qu'est-ce que vous avez dit?**	*kehs-kuh voo zah-vay dee*

Please repeat.	**Répétez, s'il vous plaît.**	*ray-pay-tay seel voo pleh*
How do you say ____ in French?	**Comment dit-on ____ en français?**	*kohn-mahn dee-tohn ahn frahn-seh*
What does this/ that mean?	**Qu'est-ce que ça veut dire?**	*kehs-kuh sah vuh deer*
My name is ____.	**Je m'appelle ____.**	*zhuh mah-pehl*
What is your name?	**Comment vous appelez-vous?**	*kohn-mahn voo zah-play voo*
What is your name, address, phone number?	**Quelles sont vos coordonnées?**	*kehl sohn voh koh-ohr-doh-nay*
How are you?	**Comment allez-vous?**	*kohn-mahn tah-lay voo*
Very well, thanks.	**Très bien, merci.**	*treh byan mehr-see*
And you?	**Et vous?**	*ay voo*
How's everything?	**Ça va?**	*sah vah*
Everything's fine.	**Ça va.**	*sah vah*
I'm lost.	**Je me suis égaré(e).**	*zhuh muh swee zay-gah-ray*
I'm looking for ____	**Je cherche ____**	*zhuh shehrsh*
Where is ____?	**Où est ____?**	*oo eh*
■ the exit	**la sortie**	*lah sohr-tee*
■ the taxi stand	**l'arrêt de taxis**	*lah-reh duh tahk-ssee*

▪ the bus stop	**l'arrêt de bus**	*lah-reh duh bewss*
▪ the metro station	**l'arrêt de métro**	*lah-reh duh may-troh*
▪ the train station	**la gare**	*lah gahr*
Where are ____?	**Où sont ____?**	*oo sohn*
▪ the bathrooms	**les toilettes**	*lay twah-leht*
▪ the telephones	**les téléphones**	*lay tay-lay-fohn*
▪ the taxis	**les taxis**	*lay tahk-ssee*
It's ____.	**C'est ____.**	*seh*
▪ to the left	**à gauche**	*ah gohsh*
▪ to the right	**à droite**	*ah drwaht*
▪ straight ahead	**tout droit**	*too drwah*
What's that?	**Qu'est-ce que c'est?**	*kehs-kuh seh*
I (don't) know.	**Je (ne) sais (pas).**	*zhuh (nuh) seh (pah)*

Do you have ____?	**Avez-vous ____?**	*ah-vay-voo*
I'd like ____.	**Je voudrais ____.**	*zhuh voo-dreh*
I need ____.	**Il me faut ____.**	*eel muh foh*
Please bring me ____.	**Apportez-moi, s'il vous plaît ____.**	*ah-pohr-tay mwah seel voo pleh*
Please give me ____.	**Donnez-moi, s'il vous plaît ____.**	*doh-nay mwah seel voo pleh*
Please show me ____.	**Montrez-moi, s'il vous plaît ____.**	*mohn-tray mwah seel voo pleh*
How much is it?	**C'est combien?**	*seh kohn-byan*
I'm hungry.	**J'ai faim.**	*zhay fan*
I'm thirsty.	**J'ai soif.**	*zhay swahf*
I'm tired.	**Je suis fatigué(e).**	*zhuh swee fah-tee-gay*
Good-bye.	**Au revoir.**	*oh ruh-vwahr*
See you later.	**À tout à l'heure.**	*ah toot ah luhr*
See you tomorrow.	**À demain.**	*ah duh-man*

QUESTIONS

Where is (are) ____?	**Où est (sont) ___?**	*oo eh (sohn)*
When?	**Quand?**	*kahn*

At what time?	**À quelle heure?**	*ah kehl uhr*
How much/many?	**Combien?**	*koh<u>n</u>-bya<u>n</u>*
Who?	**Qui?**	*kee*
What?	**Que?/Quoi?**	*kuh/kwah*
Why?	**Pourquoi?**	*poor-kwah*
How?	**Comment?**	*koh<u>n</u>-mah<u>n</u>*
Which?	**Quel/Quelle/ Quels/Quelles**	*kehl*
Which one(s)?	**Lequel/Laquelle/ Lesquel/Lesquelles**	*luh/lah/lay-kehl*

EXCLAMATIONS, SLANG, COLLOQUIALISMS

Wow!	**Oh là là!**	*oh lah lah*
Darn!	**Zut!**	*zewt*
Well!	**Eh bien!**	*eh bya<u>n</u>*
Great!	**Chouette!**	*shoo-eht*
Wonderful!	**Formidable!**	*fohr-mee-dahbl*
Fantastic!	**Génial!**	*zhay-nyahl*
My goodness!	**Mon Dieu!**	*moh<u>n</u> dyuh*
That's it!	**C'est ça!**	*seh sah*
That's awful!	**C'est affreux!**	*seh tah-fruh*

It's marvelous!	**C'est magnifique!**	*seh mah-nyee-feek*
Cheers!	**Santé!**	*sah<u>n</u>-tay*
Quiet!	**Silence!**	*see-lah<u>n</u>ss*
That's enough!	**Ça suffit!** **C'est assez!**	*sah sew-fee* *seh tah-say*
Too bad!	**Tant pis!**	*tah<u>n</u> pee*
So much the better!	**Tant mieux!**	*tah<u>n</u> myuh*
Never mind!	**N'importe!**	*na<u>n</u>-pohrt*
Of course!	**Bien sûr!**	*bya<u>n</u> sewr*
OK.	**D'accord.**	*dah-kohr*
With pleasure.	**Avec plaisir.**	*ah-vehk pleh-zeer*
Let's go!	**Allons-y!**	*ah-loh<u>n</u>-zee*
What a shame!	**Quel dommage!**	*kehl doh-mahzh*
How annoying!	**Que c'est ennuyeux!**	*kuh seh tah<u>n</u>-nwee-yuh*
Nonsense!	**C'est ridicule!**	*seh ree-dee-kewl*
What a drag!	**Quelle barbe!**	*kehl bahrb*
You're kidding!	**Vous rigolez!**	*voo ree-goh-lay*
Good luck!	**Bonne chance!**	*bohn shah<u>n</u>ss*

PROBLEMS, PROBLEMS, PROBLEMS (EMERGENCIES)

Hurry up!	**Dépêchez-vous!**	*day-peh-shay-voo*
Look!	**Regardez!**	*ruh-gahr-day*
Watch out!	**Attention!**	*ah-tah<u>n</u>-syoh<u>n</u>*
Be careful!	**Soyez prudent(e)!**	*swah-yay prew-dah<u>n</u>(t)*
Calm down!	**Calmez-vous!**	*kahl-may voo*
Take it easy!	**Allez-y doucement!**	*ah-lay zee dooss-mah<u>n</u>*
Listen!	**Écoutez!**	*ay-koo-tay*
Wait!	**Attendez!**	*ah-tahn-day*

I have lost ____.	**J'ai perdu ____.**	*zhay pehr-dew*
What's the matter?	**Qu'est-ce qu'il y a?**	*kehs-keel yah*
What's the matter with you?	**Qu'est-ce que vous avez?**	*kehs-kuh voo zah-vay*
What do you want?	**Que voulez-vous?**	*kuh voo-lay voo*
Stop bothering me.	**Laissez-moi tranquille!**	*leh-say mwah trahn-keel*
It's none of your business!	**Ce n'est pas votre affaire!**	*suh neh pah vohtr ah-fehr*
Go away!	**Allez-vous-en!**	*ah-lay voo zahn*
Get out!	**Sortez!**	*sohr-tay*
I'm going to call the police!	**Je vais appeler la police!**	*zhuh veh zah-play lah poh-leess*
Help, police!	**Au secours, police.**	*oh skoor, poh-leess*
Someone has stolen ____.	**Quelqu'un a volé ____.**	*kehl-kuhn ah voh-lay*
▪ my car	**ma voiture**	*mah vwah-tewr*
▪ my passport	**mon passeport**	*mohn pahss-pohr*
▪ my purse	**mon sac**	*mohn sahk*
▪ my suitcase	**ma valise**	*mah vah-leez*
▪ my wallet	**mon portefeuille**	*mohn pohr-tuh-fuhy*
▪ my watch	**ma montre**	*mah mohntr*
This person is bothering me.	**Cette personne m'embête.**	*seht pehr-sohn mahn-beht*
That person is following me.	**Cette personne me suit.**	*seht pehr-sohn muh swee*

Stop that person!	**Arrêtez cette personne!**	*ah-ruh-tay seht pehr-sohn*
I haven't done anything.	**Je n'ai rien fait.**	*zhuh nay ryan feh*
It's a lie!	**C'est un mensonge!**	*seh tuhn mahn-sohnzh*
It's not true!	**Ce n'est pas vrai!**	*seh neh pah vreh*
I'm innocent.	**Je suis innocent(e).**	*zhuh swee zee-noh-sahn(t)*
I want a lawyer.	**Je voudrais parler à un(e) avocat(o).**	*zhuh voo-dreh pahr-lay ah uhn ah voh kah(t)*
I want to go _____.	**Je voudrais aller ____.**	*zhuh voo-dreh zah-lay*
■ to the American Consulate	**au consulat américain**	*oh kohn-sew-lah ah-may-ree-kan*
■ to the American Embassy	**à l'ambassade américaine**	*ah lahn-bah-sahd ah-may-ree-kehn*
■ to the police station	**au commissariat de police**	*oh koh-mee-sah-ryah duh poh-leess*
I need help, quick!	**Vite. Aidez-moi!**	*veet eh-day mwah*
Can you help me, please?	**Pouvez-vous m'aider s'il vous plaît?**	*poo-vay voo meh-day seel voo pleh*
Does anyone here speak English?	**Il y a quelqu'un ici qui parle anglais?**	*eel yah kehl-kuhn ee-see kee pahrl ahn-gleh*
I need an interpreter.	**Il me faut un interprète.**	*eel muh foh tuhn an-tehr-preht*

NUMBERS

You will use numbers the moment you land in France, whether it be to exchange money at the airport, purchase a bus ticket for a ride into town, or describe the length of your stay to a customs official. We list here first the cardinal numbers, then the ordinal numbers, fractions, and other useful numbers.

CARDINAL NUMBERS

0	**zéro**	*zay-roh*
1	**un**	*uhn*
2	**deux**	*duh*
3	**trois**	*trwah*
4	**quatre**	*kah-truh*
5	**cinq**	*sank*
6	**six**	*seess*
7	**sept**	*seht*
8	**huit**	*weet*
9	**neuf**	*nuhf*
10	**dix**	*deess*
11	**onze**	*ohnz*
12	**douze**	*dooz*
13	**treize**	*trehz*
14	**quatorze**	*kah-tohrz*
15	**quinze**	*kanz*
16	**seize**	*sehz*
17	**dix-sept**	*dee-seht*

18	**dix-huit**	*dee-zweet*
19	**dix-neuf**	*deez-nuhf*
20	**vingt**	*va<u>n</u>*
21	**vingt et un**	*va<u>n</u>-tay-uh<u>n</u>*
22	**vingt-deux**	*va<u>n</u>-duh*
23	**vingt-trois**	*va<u>n</u>-trwah*
24	**vingt-quatre**	*va<u>n</u>-kah-truh*
25	**vingt-cinq**	*va<u>n</u>-sa<u>n</u>k*
26	**vingt-six**	*va<u>n</u>-seess*
27	**vingt-sept**	*va<u>n</u>-seht*
28	**vingt-huit**	*va<u>n</u>-tweet*
29	**vingt-neuf**	*va<u>n</u>-nuhf*
30	**trente**	*trah<u>n</u>t*
31	**trente et un**	*trah<u>n</u>-tay-uh<u>n</u>*
32	**trente-deux**	*trah<u>n</u>t-duh*
40	**quarante**	*kah-rah<u>n</u>t*
41	**quarante et un**	*kah-rah<u>n</u> tay uh<u>n</u>*
42	**quarante-deux**	*kah-rah<u>n</u>t-duh*
50	**cinquante**	*sa<u>n</u> kah<u>n</u>t*
51	**cinquante et un**	*sa<u>n</u>-kah<u>n</u>-tay-uh<u>n</u>*
52	**cinquante-deux**	*sa<u>n</u>-kah<u>n</u>t-duh*
60	**soixante**	*swah-ssah<u>n</u>t*
61	**soixante et un**	*swah-ssah<u>n</u>-tay-uh<u>n</u>*
62	**soixante-deux**	*swah-ssah<u>n</u>t-duh*
70	**soixante-dix**	*swah-ssah<u>n</u>t-deess*
71	**soixante et onze**	*swah-ssah<u>n</u>-tay-oh<u>n</u>z*

72	**soixante-douze**	*swah-ssah<u>nt</u>-dooz*
73	**soixante-treize**	*swah-ssah<u>nt</u>-trehz*
74	**soixante-quatorze**	*swah-ssah<u>nt</u>-kah-tohrz*
75	**soixante-quinze**	*swah-ssah<u>nt</u>-ka<u>n</u>z*
76	**soixante-seize**	*swah-ssah<u>nt</u>-sehz*
77	**soixante-dix-sept**	*swah-ssah<u>nt</u>-dee-seht*
78	**soixante-dix-huit**	*swah-ssah<u>nt</u>-dee-zweet*
79	**soixante-dix-neuf**	*swah-ssah<u>nt</u>-deez-nuhf*
80	**quatre-vingts**	*kah-truh-va<u>n</u>*
81	**quatre-vingt-un**	*kah-truh-va<u>n</u>-uh<u>n</u>*
82	**quatre-vingt-deux**	*kah-truh-va<u>n</u>-duh*
90	**quatre-vingt-dix**	*kah-truh-va<u>n</u>-deess*
91	**quatre-vingt-onze**	*kah-truh-va<u>n</u>-oh<u>n</u>z*
92	**quatre-vingt-douze**	*kah-truh-va<u>n</u>-dooz*
100	**cent**	*sah<u>n</u>*
101	**cent un**	*sah<u>n</u>-uh<u>n</u>*
102	**cent deux**	*sah<u>n</u>-duh*
110	**cent dix**	*sah<u>n</u>-deess*
120	**cent vingt**	*sah<u>n</u>-va<u>n</u>*
200	**deux cents**	*duh-sah<u>n</u>*
201	**deux cent un**	*duh-sah<u>n</u>-uh<u>n</u>*
330	**trois cent trente**	*trwah-sah<u>n</u>-trah<u>nt</u>*

1000	**mille**	*meel*
1001	**mille un**	*meel-uh<u>n</u>*
1100	**mille cent**	*meel-sah<u>n</u>*
	onze cents	*oh<u>n</u>z-sahn*
1200	**mille deux cents**	*meel-duh-sah<u>n</u>*
	douze cents	*dooz-sah<u>n</u>*
1350	**mille trois cent cinquante/treize cent cinquante**	*meel-trwah-sah<u>n</u>-sa<u>n</u>-kah<u>n</u>t/trehz-sah<u>n</u>-sa<u>n</u>-kah<u>n</u>t*
2000	**deux mille**	*duh-meel*
5000	**cinq mille**	*sa<u>n</u>k-meel*
10,000	**dix mille**	*doo-meel*
100,000	**cent mille**	*sah<u>n</u>-meel*
1,000,000	**un million**	*uh<u>n</u>-mee-lyoh<u>n</u>*
200_	**deux mille___**	*duh meel*

ORDINAL NUMBERS

first	**premier/première (1er)**	*pruh-myay/pruh-myehr*
second	**deuxième (2e)**	*duh-zyehm*
third	**troisième**	*trwah-zyehm*
fourth	**quatrième**	*kah-tree-yehm*
fifth	**cinquième**	*sa<u>n</u>-kyehm*
sixth	**sixième**	*see-zyehm*
seventh	**septième**	*seh-tyehm*
eighth	**huitième**	*wee-tyehm*
ninth	**neuvième**	*nuh-vyehm*
tenth	**dixième**	*dee-zyehm*

QUANTITIES

a half	**une moitié**	*ewn mwah-tyay*
half a	**un/une demi/e**	*uh<u>n</u>/ewn duh-mee*
half of	**la moitié de**	*lah mwah-tyay duh*
a quarter	**un quart**	*uh<u>n</u> kahr*
three-quarters	**trois quarts**	*trwah kahr*
a third	**un tiers**	*uh<u>n</u> tyehr*
two-thirds	**deux tiers**	*duh tyehr*
a bag of	**un sac de**	*uh<u>n</u> sahk duh*
a bottle of	**une bouteille de**	*ewn boo-tehy duh*
a box (can) of	**une boîte de**	*ewn bwaht duh*
a cup of	**une tasse de**	*ewn tahss duh*
a dozen of	**une douzaine de**	*ewn doo-zehn duh*
a kilo of	**un kilo de**	*uh<u>n</u> kee-loh duh*
a liter of	**un litre de**	*uh<u>n</u> leetr duh*
a package of	**un paquet de**	*uh<u>n</u> pah-keh duh*
a pair of	**une paire de**	*ewn pehr duh*
a pound of	**une livre de** **cinq cents grammes de**	*ewn lee-vruh duh sank sahn grahm duh*
a slice of	**une tranche de**	*ewn trahnsh duh*
a little bit of	**un peu de**	*uh<u>n</u> puh duh*
a lot of	**beaucoup de**	*boh-koo duh*
enough of	**assez de**	*ah-ssay duh*
too much of	**trop de**	*troh duh*

Travel Tips   There was a time when buying an airline ticket was simple. Since the airline industry was deregulated, however, travelers must shop and compare prices, buy charter or discount tickets far in advance, join frequent flier clubs to become eligible for free tickets, and do research on the Internet. Read the fine print in ads and ask questions when making reservations. Often, discount fare tickets cannot be exchanged for cash or another ticket if travel plans must be changed. If you must change plans en route, talk to an airline ticket agent. Sometimes they have soft hearts!

WHEN YOU ARRIVE

PASSPORT AND CUSTOMS

In France at last! Your vacation can't begin until you've shown your passport to the proper authorities and passed through customs.

The following chart shows what duty-free items visitors from the United States or those coming from the Economic Community (EC) countries may bring into France.

DUTY-FREE ITEMS	FROM U.S.* & NON-EC COUNTRIES	FROM EC COUNTRIES
cigarettes	200 *or*	"Reasonable amounts" of tobacco, alcohol, and perfumes destined for personal use
cigars	50 *or*	
tobacco	250 grams	
table wine	2 liters *and*	
spirits	1 liter	
perfume	60 ml	
toilet water	250 ml	
other goods	183 euros	
	91 euros	
	under age 15	

*Goods purchased in a duty-free shop within the U.S.

And when you return to the United States:

DUTY-FREE ITEMS FROM EUROPE
$400 worth of foreign goods if you have been out of the U.S. for at least 48 hours and have not used the $400 allowance or any part of it in the past 30 days
1 liter of alcohol if you are 21 or older 200 cigarettes *and* 100 non-Cuban cigars works of art and antiques (objects over 100 years old)

Generally all items for personal use enter duty-free in France and most tourists have little trouble passing through customs. Baggage in hand, you must follow the sign that applies to you: Articles à déclarer or Rien à déclarer (Nothing to declare). Good luck! You're on your way!

ARTICLES À DÉCLARER	RIEN À DÉCLARER

My name is _____.	**Je m'appelle** _____.	*zhuh mah-pehl*
I'm American, Canadian, British, Australian.	**Je suis américain(e), canadien(ne), anglais(e), australien(ne).** *zhuh swee zah-may-ree-kuhn (kehn), kah-nah-dyan (dyehn), ahn-gleh (glehz), ohs-trah-lyan (yehn)*	
My address is _____.	**Mon adresse est** _____.	*mohn nah-drehss eh*
I'm staying at _____.	**Je reste à** _____.	*zhuh rehst ah*
Here is (are) _____.	**Voici** _____.	*vwah-ssee*
my documents	**mes papiers**	*may pah-pyay*
my passport	**mon passeport**	*mohn pahss-pohr*
my identification card	**ma carte d'identité**	*mah kahrt dee-dahn-tee-tay*
I'm _____.	**Je suis** _____.	*zhuh swee*
on a business trip	**en voyage d'affaires**	*zahn vwah-yahzh dah-fehr*
on vacation	**en vacances**	*zahn vah-kahnss*
I'll be staying here _____.	**Je resterai ici** _____.	*zhuh rehss-tray ee-ssee*
a few days	**quelques jours**	*kehl-kuh zhoor*
a few weeks	**quelques semaines**	*kehl-kuh suh-mehn*

■ a week	**une semaine**	*ewn suh-mehn*
■ two weeks	**quinze jours**	*ka_n_z zhoor*
■ a month	**un mois**	*uh_n_ mwah*

I'm traveling _____. **Je voyage _____.** *zhuh vwah-yahzh*

■ alone	**seul**	*suhl*
■ with my husband	**avec mon mari**	*ah-vehk moh_n_ mah-ree*
■ with my wife	**avec ma femme**	*ah-vehk mah fahm*
■ with my family	**avec ma famille**	*ah-vehk mah fah-mee*
■ with my friends	**avec mes ami(e)s**	*ah-vehk may zah-mee*

Here are my bags. **Voici mes bagages.** *vwah-ssee may bah-gahzh*

I have nothing to declare. **Je n'ai rien à déclarer.** *zhuh nay rya_n_ ah day-klah-ray*

I have only _____. **J'ai seulement _____.** *zhay suhl-mah_n_*

■ a carton of cigarettes	**une cartouche de cigarettes** *ewn kahr-toosh duh see-gah-reht*
■ a bottle of whisky	**une bouteille de whisky** *ewn boo-tehy duh wheess-kee*

They're gifts. **Ce sont des cadeaux.** *suh soh_n_ day kah-doh*

It's for my personal use. **C'est pour usage personnel.** *seh poor ew-zazh pehr-soh-nehl*

Do I have to pay duty? **Dois-je payer des droits de douane?** *dwahzh peh-yay day drwah duh dwahn*

May I close my bag now? **Puis-je fermer ma valise maintenant?** *pweezh fehr-may mah vah-leez ma_n_t-nah_n_*

Travel Tips Students traveling abroad should inquire about the International Student Identity Card issued by the Council on International Educational Exchange and the Youth International Educational Exchange Card issued by the Federation of International Youth Travel Organizations. These agencies offer many enticing discounts to students at a very reasonable price.

IDENTITY CARD

Upon entering the country you will be required to fill out an identity card, usually with the following information.

Nom de famille _____   Last name _____

Prénom _____   First name

Nationalité _____   Nationality _____

Date de naissance _____   Birthdate _____

Profession _____   Profession _____

Adresse _____   Address _____

Passeport (de) _____   Passport (from) _____

BAGGAGE AND PORTERS

If you can find a porter to help you with your luggage, it is customary to give him/her a tip the equivalent of $1.00 per bag. It will probably be simpler and less expensive, however, to avail yourself of the handcarts now in use at most airports and railroad stations. You can usually wheel them right through customs and into the street.

Where can I find a baggage cart?	**Où puis-je trouver un chariot à bagages?** *oo pweezh troo-vay uhn shah-ryoh ah bah-gahzh*
(I need a) porter.	**(Il me faut un) porteur.** *(eel muh foh tuhn) pohr-tuhr*
Please take our (my) bags.	**Prenez nos (mes) valises, s'il vous plaît.** *pruh-nay noh (may) vah-leez seel voo pleh*
■ that big one	**cette grande** *seht grahnd*
■ these two little ones	**ces deux petites** *say duh puh-teet*
Put them here (there).	**Mettez-les ici (là).** *meh-tay lay zee-ssee (lah)*
Be careful with that one!	**Faites attention avec celle-là!** *feht zah-tahn-syohn ah-vehk sehl lah*
I'll carry this one myself.	**Je porterai celle-ci moi-même.** *zhuh pohr-tray sehl see mwah mehm*

I'm missing a suitcase.	**Il me manque une valise.** *eel muh mahnk ewn vah-leez*
Thank you (very much).	**Merci (beaucoup).** *mehr-ssee (boh-koo)*
This is for you.	**C'est pour vous.** *seh poor voo*

AIRPORT TRANSPORTATION

Where can I get a taxi?	**Où puis-je trouver un taxi?** *oo pweezh troo-vay uhn tahk-ssee*
What buses go into the city?	**Quels bus vont en ville?** *kehl bews vohn tahn veel*
Where is the bus stop?	**Où est l'arrêt de bus?** *oo eh lah-reh duh bews*
How much is the fare?	**Quel est le tarif?** *kehl eh luh tah-reef*
Where can I rent a car?	**Où puis-je louer une voiture?** *oo pweezh loo-ay ewn vwah-tewr*

Travel Tips   Luggage is sometimes lost or arrives long after you do. To avoid problems, some people travel light and carry everything with them. At the very least, take one complete change of clothing, basic grooming items, and any regular medication aboard with you. Because airlines will not replace valuable jewelry when paying for lost luggage, it should be carried on your person. Safer yet, select one set of basic, simple jewelry that can be worn everywhere—even in the shower—and wear it during your whole trip. Remember, carry-on bags must be small enough to fit in overhead compartments or to slide under your seat.

BANKING AND MONEY MATTERS

BANKS

Banks generally open between 8:15 and 9:00 and close between 3:00 and 4:45. Some banks close between noon and 1:30, especially during the summer, for a longer lunch break. All banks close at noon the day preceding a holiday. Banks will change foreign currency at the most favorable rate of exchange. *Bureaux de change* at airports or railway stations give a less favorable exchange rate. Some *bureaux de change* on the streets of Paris give very favorable exchange rates. Many hotels will exchange money and travelers' checks, but the rate will be the least favorable.

The current exchange rates are available in the banks that exchange money, and are also published daily in the newspapers.

BANKING TERMS

amount	**le montant**	*luh mohn-tahn*
bad check	**le chèque sans provision**	*luh shehk sahn proh-vee-zyohn*
banker	**le banquier**	*luh bahn-kyay*
bill	**le billet**	*luh bee-yeh*
borrow (to)	**emprunter**	*ahn-pruhn-tay*
cashier	**le caissier**	*luh kehss-yay*
capital	**le capital**	*luh kah-pee-tahl*
cash register	**la caisse**	*lah kehss*
checkbook	**le carnet de chèques**	*luh kahr-neh duh shehk*

endorse (to)	**endosser**	*ahn-doh-ssay*
interest rate	**le taux d'intérêt**	*luh toh dan-tay-reh*
investment	**le placement**	*luh plahss-mahn*
lend (to)	**prêter**	*preh-tay*
make change (to)	**faire de la monnaie**	*fehr duh la moh-neh*
money	**l'argent (m.)**	*lahr-zhahn*
mortgage	**l'hypothèque (f.)**	*lee-poh-tehk*
open an account (to)	**ouvrir un compte**	*oo-vreer uhn kohnt*
premium	**la prime**	*lah preem*
profit	**le bénéfice**	*luh bay-nay-feess*

safe	**le coffre-fort**	*luh koh-fruh fohr*
signature	**la signature**	*lah see-nyah-tewr*
window	**le guichet**	*luh gee-sheh*

The franc, the old unit of French currency, has been replaced by the **euro,** the approximate equivalent of one U.S. dollar, which is used throughout Europe.

The euro is the official monetary currency not only of France but of the entire European Union, which means that you can use the same currency throughout Western Europe. The euro is issued in the following denominations: notes—5, 10, 20, 50, 100, 200, and 500; coins—1, 2, 5, 10, 20, 50 cents, 1 and 2 euros.

EXCHANGING MONEY

Where can I (change) _____?	**Où puis-je (changer) _____?** *oo pweezh (shahn-zhay)*
▪ money	**de l'argent** *duh lahr-zhahn*
▪ dollars	**des dollars** *day doh-lahr*
▪ travelers' checks	**des chèques de voyage** *day shehk duh vwah-yahzh*
▪ cash a personal check	**toucher un chèque personnel** *too-shay uhn shehk pehr-soh-nehl*

Where is _____?	**Où se trouve _____?** *oo suh troov*
▪ a bank	**une banque** *ewn bahnk*
▪ a money exchange	**un bureau de change** *uhn bew-roh duh shahnzh*

| At what time do they open (close)? | **Ça ouvre (ferme) à quelle heure?** *sah oo-vruh (fehrm) ah kehl uhr* |

| Where is the banking window? | **Où est le guichet?** *oo eh luh gee-sheh* |

Do you have an ATM machine?	**Avez-vous un distributeur (un guichet) automatique de billets?** *ah-vay voo uh<u>n</u> dee-sstree-bew-tuhr (uh<u>n</u> gee-sheh) oh-toh-mah-teek duh bee-yeh*
How do you use it?	**On s'en sert comment?** *oh<u>n</u> sah<u>n</u> sehr koh-mah<u>n</u>*
What's the current exchange rate?	**Quel est le cours (du change) le plus récent?** *kehl eh luh koor (dew shahnzh) luh plew ray-sahn*
I'd like to cash this check.	**Je voudrais toucher ce chèque.** *zhuh voo-dreh too-shay suh shehk*
Where do I sign?	**Où dois-je signer?** *oo dwahzh see-nyay*
I'd like the money _____.	**Je voudrais l'argent _____.** *zhuh voo-dreh lahr-zhah<u>n</u>*
▨ in (large) bills	**en (grosses) coupures** *ah<u>n</u> (grohss) koo-pewr*
▨ in small change	**en petite monnaie** *ah<u>n</u> puh-teet moh-nay*
Do you accept credit cards?	**Acceptez-vous les cartes de crédit?** *ahk-ssehp-tay voo lay kahrt duh kray-dee*

TIPPING

In many instances, service charges are included in the price of the service rendered. These generally amount to 15% and should be indicated on the bill.

A customer may leave some small change, in addition to any charge that has been included, if the service has been satisfactory. At times, a set amount should be given.

The following table is merely a suggested guide. Tips will vary from time to time due to inflation and other factors. It is therefore advisable to ask some knowledgeable person such as the hotel concierge or tour director, once you get to the country, for proper tipping information, or you should check the rate of exchange.

SERVICE	TIP
Waiter	12–15%
Bellboy, porter	the equivalent of $1.00 per bag
Chambermaid	the equivalent of $1.00 per person per day
Usher	the equivalent of $1.00 per person
Taxi driver	10–15% of the fare
Guide	10%
Barber, hairdresser	10–15%
Shoeshine	small change
Bathroom attendant	small change

TIPPING AT HOTELS

Check to see whether the service charge (usually 15%) is included in the room price. The words **service compris** or **toutes taxes comprises** indicate that your tipping obligations have been fulfilled except for the bellboy carrying your luggage and the concierge, who may perform special services for you. Should any other employee go out of his/her way to help you, then a small additional tip would be in order.

AT THE HOTEL

LODGING

Accommodations are varied and plentiful, and are available in different price ranges. If you have not made a reservation and are looking for a place to stay, it is best to go to a tourist information center called **le Syndicat d'Initiative (SI)** or **Office du Tourisme (OT)**. Someone there will gladly help you find a room to suit your needs and your budget. You will find yourself staying at one of the following.

HOTEL

Although there are hotel rooms in every price range, it is best to make an advance reservation. Festivals, exhibitions, shows, and trade fairs attract many visitors and rooms are quickly filled. The French government rates hotels by using a star system ranging from * (inexpensive) to ***** (expensive) (*luxe*). A hotel receives its rating based on room price and the conveniences it provides: size of room, telephone availability, bathroom facilities. A continental breakfast, consisting of rolls, butter and jam, and coffee or tea is often included in the price of the room. English is spoken in the larger, more exclusive hotels, and American-style breakfasts are usually available there.

CHÂTEAU-HOTEL

Running the gamut from a simple bed-and-breakfast to the most luxurious accommodations available, these aristocratic mansions offer an interesting change from the typical hotel setting.

MOTEL

Motels have recently appeared in France. They are located near main roads outside towns and cities and at the airport.

PENSION

Pensions resemble rooming houses where the visitor pays for a room and all or part of his meals.

AUBERGE (LOGIS)

This is usually a small, modest, and inexpensive country inn found off the main roads in rural areas. An **auberge de jeunesse** is a relatively inexpensive youth hostel that is set up dormitory fashion.

CHAMBRES D'HÔTE

In towns or villages rooms are made available in the homes of local families, who will supply bed and breakfast for a fee.

GÎTES RURAUX

If you visit the countryside, you may rent a gîte, a private residence—house or apartment.

You should be aware that in France, especially outside of Paris, it is customary and expected that a guest eat dinner at his hotel. Many smaller hotels will charge you for dinner whether you eat it or not, or refuse to rent the room unless you eat in the hotel. You may inquire about this at the desk.

Travel Tips Touring on a budget? Then it pays to do your homework. Look for hotels or bed-and-breakfast establishments that include a morning meal in the price of a room. Carry nutrition bars from home in your tote bag for snacking when only expensive airport or restaurant food is available. Use public transportation whenever possible. Rail and air passes are sold for Europe and other regions but often can only be purchased in the United States before departure. If you must rent a car and have booked one from home, double-check local prices. Sometimes better deals can be arranged on the spot. When you first arrive in a country, check with a visitors' bureau. Agents there will explain discount cards or money-saving packets offered by local governments or merchants. The discount plans often cover transportation, food, lodging, museums, concerts, and other entertainment.

GETTING TO YOUR HOTEL

I'd like to go to the _____ Hotel.	**Je voudrais aller à l'hôtel _____.** *zhuh voo-dreh zah-lay ah loh-tel*
Is it near (far)?	**C'est près (loin) d'ici?** *seh preh (lwan) dee-ssee*
Where can I get a taxi?	**Où puis-je trouver un taxi?** *oo pweezh troo-vay uhn tahk-see*
Where is the nearest bus (métro) stop?	**Où est l'arrêt de bus (métro) le plus proche?** *oo eh lah-reh duh bews (duh may-troh) luh plew prohsh*
How much is the fare?	**Quel est le tarif?** *kehl eh luh tah-reef*

CHECKING IN

When you register, it will be necessary to fill out a form (*une fiche*) with your name, address, and passport number at the registration desk of any establishment.

I'd like a single (double) room for tonight _____.	**Je voudrais une chambre à un lit (à deux lits) pour ce soir _____.** *zhuh voo-dreh zewn shahn-bruh ah uhn lee (ah duh lee) poor suh swahr*
▧ with a shower	**avec douche** *ah-vehk doosh*
▧ with a bath	**avec salle de bains** *ah-vehk sahl duh ban*
▧ with a balcony	**avec balcon** *ah-vehk bahl-kohn*
▧ facing the ocean	**qui donne sur l'océan** *kee dohn sewr loh-ssay-ahn*
▧ facing the street	**qui donne sur la rue** *kee dohn sewr lah rew*
▧ facing the courtyard	**qui donne sur la cour** *kee dohn sewr lah koor*

Does it have _____?	**Il y a _____?** *eel yah*
▪ air conditioning	**la climatisation** *lah klee-mah-tee-zah-ssyohn*
▪ a hair dryer	**un sèche-cheveux** *uhn sehsh-shuh-vuh*
▪ a television	**une télévision** *ewn tay-lay-vee-zyohn*
▪ a safe	**un coffre-fort** *uhn kohfr-fohr*
▪ a private bathroom	**une douche et des toilettes privées** *ewn doosh ay day twah-leht pree-vay*
▪ a mini-bar	**un mini-bar** *uhn mee-nee bahr*
I (don't) have a reservation.	**J'ai (Je n'ai pas de) une réservation.** *zhay (zhuh nay pah duh) ewn ray-zehr-vah-syohn*
May I see the room?	**Puis-je voir la chambre?** *pweezh vwahr lah shahn-bruh*
I (don't) like it.	**Elle me plaît.** *ehl muh pleh* **Elle ne me plaît pas.** *ehl nuh muh pleh pah*
Do you have something _____?	**Avez-vous quelque chose _____?** *Ah-vay voo kehl-kuh shohz*
▪ better	**de meilleur** *duh meh-yuhr*
▪ larger	**de plus grand** *duh plew grahn*
▪ smaller	**de plus petit** *duh plew puh-tee*
▪ cheaper	**de meilleur marché** *duh meh-yuhr mahr-shay*
On what floor is it?	**C'est à quel étage?** *seht ah kehl ay-tahzh*
Is there an elevator?	**Il y a un ascenseur?** *eel yah uhn nah-sahn-suhr*

How much do you charge for ____?	**Quel est le tarif ____?** *kehl eh luh tah-reef*
▓ the American plan	**pension complète** *pahn ssyohn kohn-pleht*
▓ bed and breakfast	**petit déjeuner compris** *puh tee day-zhuh-nay kohn-pree*
▓ breakfast and dinner	**en demi-pension** *ahn duh-mee pahn-ssyohn*
▓ the room without meals	**pour la chambre sans repas** *poor lah shahn bruh sahn ruh pah*

Is it necessary to eat here?	**Faut-il manger ici?** *foh-teel man-zhay ee-see*
Is everything included?	**Tout est compris?** *too teh kohn-pree*
I'll take this room.	**Je prends cette chambre.** *Zhuh prahn seht shahn-bruh*
What is my room number?	**Quel est le numéro de ma chambre?** *kehl eh luh new-may-roh duh mah shahn-bruh*

May I please have my key?	**Pourrais-je avoir la clef?** *poo-rehzh ah-vwahr lah klay*
Is there a reduction for children?	**Accordez-vous des réductions aux enfants?** *ah-kohr-day voo day ray-dewk-ssyohn oh zahn-fahn*
Could you put another bed in the room?	**Pourriez-vous mettre un autre lit dans la chambre?** *poo-ree-yay voo meh-truh uhn noh-truh lee dahn lah shahn-bruh*
Is there a charge? How much?	**Faut-il payer cela? Combien?** *foh teel peh-yay suh-lah? kohn-byan*

OTHER ACCOMMODATIONS

I'm looking for _____.	**Je cherche _____.** *zhuh shehrsh*
▥ a boarding house	**une pension** *ewn pahn-ssyohn*
▥ a private house	**une maison particulière** *ewn meh-zohn pahr-tee-kew-lyehr*
I want to rent an apartment.	**Je voudrais louer un appartement.** *zhuh voo-dreh loo-ay uhn nah-pahr-tuh-mahn*
I need a living room, bedroom, and kitchen.	**Il me faut un salon, une chambre à coucher, et une cuisine.** *eel muh foh tuhn sah-lohn, ewn shahn-bruh ah koo-shay, ay ewn kwee-zeen*
Do you have a furnished room?	**Avez-vous une chambre meublée? (garnie?)** *ah-vay voo zewn shahn-bruh muh-blay (gahr-nee)*
How much is the rent?	**C'est combien le loyer?** *seh kohn-byan luh lwah-yay*

I'll be staying here for _____.	**Je resterai ici _____.**	*zhuh rehss-tray ee-ssee*
one week	**une semaine**	*ewn suh-mehn*
two weeks	**quinze jours**	*kah<u>n</u>z zhoor*
one month	**un mois**	*uh<u>n</u> mwah*
the whole summer	**tout l'été**	*too lay-tay*

I want a place that's centrally located near public transportation.

Je voudrais (avoir) une résidence située au centre ville près des transports publics. *zhuh voo-dreh (zah-vwahr) ewn ray-zee-dah<u>n</u>ss see-tew-ay oh sah<u>n</u>-truh veel preh deh trah<u>n</u>ss-pohr pew-bleek*

Is there a youth hostel around here?

Il y a une auberge de jeunesse par ici? *eel yah ewn oh bohrzh duh zhuh-nehss preh dee-ssee*

ORDERING BREAKFAST

The French or continental breakfast is usually simple—coffee or hot chocolate and a croissant or brioche with jam or marmalade. At the larger hotels you will be able to order an English-style breakfast (juice, eggs, bacon, toast). You may enjoy having breakfast in your room.

We'll have breakfast in the room.	**Nous prendrons le petit déjeuner dans la chambre.**	*noo prah<u>n</u>-droh<u>n</u> luh puh-tee day-zhuh-nay dah<u>n</u> lah shah<u>n</u>-bruh*
Please send up _____.	**Faites monter _____, s'il vous plaît.**	*feht moh<u>n</u>-tay _____ seel voo pleh*
We'd like _____.	**Nous voudrions _____.**	*noo voo-dree-yoh<u>n</u>*
one (two) coffee(s)	**un (deux) café(s)**	*uh<u>n</u> (duh) kah-fay*

■ tea	**un thé** *uhn tay*
■ hot chocolate	**un chocolat** *uhn shoh-koh-lah*
■ a (some) croissant(s)	**un (des) croissant(s)** *uhn (day) krwah-ssahn*
■ fruit	**des fruits** *day frwee*
■ fruit juice	**du jus de fruit** *dew zhew duh frwee*
■ scrambled (fried) (boiled) eggs	**des oeufs brouillés (au plat) (à la coque)** *day zuh broo-yay (oh plah) (ah lah kohk)*
■ toast	**du pain grillé** *dew pan gree-yay*
■ jam	**de la confiture** *duh lah kohn-fee-tewr*
■ butter	**du beurre** *dew buhr*
We'll eat breakfast downstairs.	**On descend prendre le petit déjeuner.** *ohn deh-sahn prahn-druh luh puh-tee day-zhuh-nay*

NOTE: See Food section (page 105) for more phrases for ordering meals.

HOTEL SERVICES

Where is (are) ____?	**Où est (sont) ____?** *oo eh (sohn)*
■ the dining room	**la salle à manger** *lah sahl ah mahn-zhay*
■ the restrooms	**les toilettes** *lay twah-leht*
■ the elevator	**l'ascenseur** *lah-ssahn-ssuhr*
■ the phone	**le téléphone** *luh tay-lay-fohn*
I need ____.	**Il me faut ____.** *eel muh foh*
■ a bellboy	**un chasseur** *tuhn shah-ssuhr*
■ a chambermaid	**une femme de chambre** *tewn fahm duh shahn-bruh*

Please give me ____.	**Veuillez me donner ____.**	*vuh-yay muh doh-nay*
a towel	**une serviette**	*ewn sehr vyeht*
a bar of soap	**une savonnette**	*ewn sah-voh-neht*
some hangers	**des cintres**	*day sa<u>n</u>-truh*
a pillow	**un oreiller**	*uh<u>n</u> noh-reh-yay*
a blanket	**une couverture**	*ewn koo-vehr-tewr*
some ice	**de la glace**	*duh lah glahss*
ice cubes	**des glaçons**	*day glah-ssoh<u>n</u>*
some ice water	**de l'eau glacée**	*duh loh glah ssay*
an ashtray	**un cendrier**	*uh<u>n</u> sah<u>n</u>-dree-yay*
toilet paper	**un rouleau de papier hygiénique**	*uh<u>n</u> roo-loh duh pah-pyay ee-zhyay-nook*
a bottle of mineral water	**une bouteille d'eau minérale**	*ewn boo-tehy doh mee-nay-rahl*
an electric adaptor	**un transformateur**	*uh<u>n</u> trah<u>n</u>ss-fohr-mah-tuhr*

NOTE: Electric current is usually 220 volts. A European-style adaptor plug or an adaptable appliance is necessary for electric hair dryers or clocks. Large international hotels may have an adaptor plug at the reception desk, but smaller hotels or pensions are unlikely to be able to provide one.

Just a minute.	**Un moment.**	*uh<u>n</u> moh-mah<u>n</u>*
Come in.	**Entrez.**	*ah<u>n</u>-tray*
Put that on the table.	**Mettez ça sur la table.**	*meh-tay sah sewr lah tah-bluh*
Please wake me tomorrow at ____.	**Réveillez-moi demain matin à ____, s'il vous plaît.**	*ray-veh-yay mwah duh-ma<u>n</u> mah-ta<u>n</u> ah ____ seel voo pleh*

There is no _____.	**Il n'y a pas _____.**	*eel nyah pah*
▨ running water	**d'eau courante**	*doh koo-rahnt*
▨ hot water	**d'eau chaude**	*doh shohd*
▨ electricity	**d'électricité**	*day-lehk-tree-ssee-tay*

The _____ doesn't work.	**_____ ne fonctionne pas.**	*nuh fohnk-ssyohn pah*
▨ air conditioner	**le climatiseur**	*luh klee-mah-tee-zuhr*
▨ fan	**le ventilateur**	*luh vahn-tee-lah-tuhr*
▨ faucet	**le robinet**	*luh roh-bee-neh*
▨ lamp	**la lampe**	*lah lahnp*
▨ radio	**la radio**	*lah rah-dyoh*
▨ socket	**la prise de courant**	*lah preez duh koo-rahn*
▨ switch	**le commutateur**	*luh koh-mew-tah-tuhr*
▨ television	**la télévision**	*lah tay-lay-vee-zyohn*

Can you fix it?	**Pouvez-vous la réparer?**	*poo-vay voo lah ray-pah-ray*
▨ now	**maintenant**	*mant-nahn*
▨ as soon as possible	**aussitôt que possible**	*oh-ssee-toh kuh poh-ssee-bluh*

The room is dirty.	**La chambre est sale.**	*lah shahn-bruh eh sahl*

Are there any _____ for me?	**Il y a _____ pour moi?**	*eel yah _____ poor mwah*
▨ letters	**des lettres**	*day leh-truh*
▨ messages	**des messages**	*day meh-ssahzh*
▨ packages	**des colis**	*day koh-lee*
▨ postcards	**des cartes postales**	*day kahrt pohss-tahl*

Can you make a phone call for me?	**Pouvez-vous faire un coup de téléphone pour moi?** *poo-vay voo fehr uhn koo duh tay-lay-fohn poor mwah*
I'd like to put this in the hotel safe.	**Je voudrais mettre ceci dans le coffre-fort de l'hôtel.** *zhuh voo-dreh meh-truh ssuh-ssee dahn luh koh-fruh-fohr duh loh-tehl*

CHECKING OUT

I'd like the bill, please.	**Je voudrais la note, s'il vous plaît.** *zhuh voo-dreh lah noht seel voo pleh*
I'm leaving today (tomorrow).	**Je pars aujourd'hui (demain).** *zhuh pahr oh-zhoor-dwee (duh-man)*
Please send someone up for the baggage.	**Faites monter quelqu'un pour les valises, s'il vous plaît.** *feht mohn-tay kehl-kuhn poor lay vah-leez seel voo pleh*

Travel Tips Packing for a trip abroad is an art. Porters may sometimes be hard to find, so never take more luggage than you can handle alone. Wrap shampoo, mouthwash, or anything that can leak in recycled plastic bags or small plastic bottles. To prevent wrinkling, pack suits, dresses, etc. in dry cleaning bags.

GETTING AROUND TOWN

In villages or out in the country you may want to stroll around to do your sightseeing. Although walking in the city is also rewarding, you'll want to be familiar with the types of public transportation available.

For information on plane, train, or boat travel, see pages 58–64.

The **R.A.T.P.** (**Régie Autonome des Transports Parisiens**) directs the entire Parisian bus and subway system. In addition to the **métropolitain** (subway), commonly referred to as the **métro**, the R.A.T.P. also provides service on the **R.E.R.** (**Réseau Express Régional**), the local suburban system.

THE SUBWAY (UNDERGROUND)

Le métro (the subway) is the clean, inexpensive, and efficient underground train system in Paris. Above ground, a big yellow **M** within a circle, or easily recognizable curly, green railings and an archway indicate the métro, which can take you within walking distance of almost any tourist attraction in the city. Trains run very frequently—about every five minutes.

There are 13 numbered subway lines, indicated by different colors on the free subway maps available in most stations, hotel lobbies, and department stores. Each métro station also displays a map with a **plan du quartier**, a detailed map of the surrounding area. The métro is easy to navigate if you know the name of the last station, in both directions, on the line you plan to take, since all subway lines are identified on signs by their final destination. Transfers from one line to another are free and connections are indicated by orange **correspondance** signs. You may transfer as often as you like on one ticket, provided that you do not exit to the street. Exits are clearly marked by blue **SORTIE** signs.

Each métro ride costs one ticket. For convenience and economy, a book of 10 tickets (**un carnet**) is available for regular riders. Frequent riders may wish to purchase an orange card (**une carte orange**), which permits unlimited rides for a month. **Paris Visite** three-day or five-day tourist tickets are available in advance from U.S. travel agents and are valid for unlimited travel on the bus, métro, and R.E.R. They also give discounts on certain sightseeing trips.

French métro tickets are a little tricky to use. Slide the ticket into the automatic ticket machine and then wait for it to quickly pop up. It is essential that you keep your ticket until you reach the point that says **Limite de Validité des Billets** for two reasons: An inspector may ask to see your ticket at any time and you risk a fine if you cannot furnish it, and you will need the ticket in the event that you would like to transfer to the R.E.R. within Paris. For trips to the suburbs, a special R.E.R. ticket will have to be purchased.

French subways are generally open from 5:00 A.M. to 2:00 A.M.

Is there a subway in this city?	**Y a-t-il un métro dans cette ville?** *ee ah teel uhn may-troh dahn seht veel*
Where is the nearest subway station?	**Où se trouve la station de métro la plus proche?** *oo suh troov lah stah-ssyohn duh may-troh lah plew prohsh*
How much is the fare?	**Quel est le prix du trajet?** *kehl eh luh pree dew trah-zheh*
Where can I buy a ticket?	**Où puis-je acheter un billet?** *oo pweezh ahsh-tay uhn bee-yeh*
Which line goes to ____?	**Quelle ligne va à ____?** *kehl lee-nyuh vah ah*
Does this train go to ____?	**Ce train va à ____?** *suh tran vah ah*
How many more stops are there?	**Il reste combien d'arrêts?** *eel rehsst kohn-byan dah-reh*

What's the next station?	**Quelle est la prochaine station?** *kehl eh lah proh-shehn stah-ssyohn*
Where should I get off to go to _____?	**Où dois-je descendre pour aller à _____?** *oo dwahzh day-sahn-druh poor ah-lay ah*
Do I have to change trains?	**Faut-il prendre une correspondance?** *foh teel prahn-druh ewn koh-rehss-pohn-dahnss*
Please tell me when we get there.	**S'il vous plaît, dites-moi quand nous y arrivons.** *seel voo pleh, deet mwah kahn noo zee ah-ree-vohn*

Défense de cracher	No spitting

In the trains, buses, and metro, certain seats with numbers are reserved. You may sit in one of those seats if there are enough seats vacant. A war veteran may come up to you and show you his ID card, and in that case, you have to give him your seat. You may see the following notices posted:

LES PLACES NUMÉROTÉES SONT RÉSERVÉES:	NUMBERED SEATS ARE RESERVED FOR:
1. Aux invalides de guerre	Disabled veterans
2. Aux invalides civils	Handicapped persons
3. Aux femmes enceintes	Pregnant women
4. Aux personnes accompagnées d'enfants de moins de 4 ans	Persons with children under 4 years of age

THE BUS (STREETCAR, TRAM)

Green Parisian buses post their route and destination in the front of the bus and their major stops on the sides of the bus. The routes of each line are indicated on a sign at each stop. A free bus map **Autobus Paris—Plan du Réseau** is available at tourist offices and some métro information booths. Since tickets may not be purchased on buses, they must be bought ahead of time at a métro station or **bureau de tabac** (tobacco shop). The same ticket is used for buses as for the métro. Regular tickets are validated by inserting them into a canceling machine at the driver's seat. A **carte orange**, on the other hand, is merely shown to the driver. Once again, it is important to keep your ticket until the end of the ride.

Most buses operate from 6 A.M. to 8:30 P.M., although some do run throughout the night.

European Express and Europabus serve major European cities. They are less expensive, but slower, than trains. If you plan to travel around the city by bus, you can purchase a discount book of tickets (**un carnet**).

Défense de parler au conducteur	Do not speak to the driver

Where is the bus stop? (bus terminal?)	**Où est l'arrêt de bus? (le terminus?)** *oo eh lah-reh duh bewss (luh tehr-mee-newss)*
How often do the buses run?	**Quelle est la fréquence des bus?** *kehl eh lah fray-kahnss day bewss*
I want to go to _____.	**Je voudrais aller à _____.** *zhuh voo-dreh zah-lay ah*
In which direction do I have to go?	**Dans quel sens dois-je aller?** *dahn kehl sahnss dwahzh ah-lay*

Which bus do I take to get to _____?	**Quel bus faut-il prendre pour aller à _____?** *kehl bewss foh teel prahn-druh poor ah-lay ah*
Is it far from here?	**C'est loin d'ici?** *seh lwan dee-ssee*
How many stops are there?	**Il y a combien d'arrêts?** *eel yah kohn-byan dah-reh*
Do I have to change?	**Faut-il changer de bus?** *foh teel shahn-zhay duh bewss*
Do you go to _____?	**Vous allez à _____?** *voo zah-lay ah*
Where do I get off?	**Où dois-je descendre?** *oo dwahzh day-sahn-druh*
Could you tell me when to get off?	**Pourriez-vous me dire quand je dois descendre?** *poo-ree-yay voo muh deer kahn zhuh dwah day-sahn-druh*

TAXIS

Taxis, except for certain ones that make trips to and from the airport and give a flat rate, are metered. Taxi rates vary according to time of day and geographical area. A 15% tip is customary. Taxis may refuse to accept more than three passengers. Look for the sign **Stationnement de Taxis** indicating a taxi stand. You cannot hail a taxi on the street within 100 meters of a stand. There is a supplement (indicated on the meter) after 11:00 P.M.

Is there a taxi stand around here?	**Il y a une station de taxis près d'ici?** *eel yah ewn stah-ssyohn duh tahk-ssee preh dee-ssee*
Where can I get a taxi?	**Où puis-je trouver un taxi?** *oo pweezh troo-vay uhn tahk-ssee*
Taxi! Are you available?	**Taxi! Etes-vous libre?** *tahk-ssee eht voo lee-bruh*

Take me (I want to go) _____.	**Conduisez-moi (Je voudrais aller)** _____.	*kohn dwee-zay mwah (zhuh voo-dreh zah-lay)*
▪ to the airport	**à l'aéroport**	*ah lahy-roh-pohr*
▪ to this address	**à cette adresse**	*ah seht ah-drehss*
▪ to the hotel _____	**à l'hôtel**	*ah loh-tehl*
▪ to the train station	**à la gare**	*ah lah gahr*
▪ to _____ Street	**à la rue** _____	*ah lah rew*
▪ to _____ Avenue	**à l'avenue** _____	*ah lahv-new*
▪ to _____ Boulevard	**au boulevard** _____	*oh bool-vahr*

Do you know where it is?

Savez-vous où ça se trouve?
sah-vay voo oo sah suh troov

How much is it to _____?

C'est combien pour aller à _____?
seh kohn-byan poor ah-lay ah

I'm in a hurry.

Je suis pressé(e)! *zhuh swee preh-ssay*

Don't go so fast.

Ne conduisez pas si vite, s'il vous plaît. *nuh kohn-dwee-zay pah see veet seel voo pleh*

Stop here at the corner.	**Arrêtez-vous ici, à l'angle.** *ah-reh-tay voo zee-ssee ah lahngl*
Stop at the next block.	**Arrêtez-vous à la prochaine rue.** *ah-reh-tay voo ah lah proh-shehn rew*
Wait for me. I'll be right back.	**Attendez-moi, s'il vous plaît. Je reviens tout de suite.** *ah-tahn-day mwah seel voo pleh zhuh ruh-vyan toot sweet*
How much do I owe you?	**Je vous dois combien?** *zhuh voo dwah kohn-byan*
This is for you.	**Voilà pour vous.** *vwah-lah poor voo*

PLACES TO GO/SIGHTSEEING

Where is the Tourist Office?	**Où est le Syndicat d'Initiative?** *oo eh luh san-dee-kah dee-nee-ssyah-teev*
I need an (English speaking) guide.	**J'ai besoin d'un guide (qui parle anglais).** *zhay buh-zwan duhn geed (kee pahrl ahn-gleh)*
How much does he charge _____?	**C'est combien _____?** *seh kohn-byan*
■ per hour	**à l'heure** *ah luhr*
■ per day	**à la journée** *ah lah zhoor-nay*
There are two (four, six) of us.	**Nous sommes deux (quatre, six).** *noo sohm duh (kah-truh, seess)*
Where can I buy a guidebook? (a map?) (a street map?)	**Où puis-je acheter un guide touristique? (une carte?) (un plan de la ville?)** *oo pweezh ahsh-tay uhn geed too-reess-teek (ewn kahrt) (uhn plahn duh lah veel)*

What are the main attractions?	**Qu'est-ce qu'il y a de plus intéressant à voir?** *kehss keel yah duh plew zan-tay-reh-ssahn ah vwahr*
Are there trips through the city?	**Il y a des visites guidées à travers la ville?** *eel yah day vee-zeet gee-day ah trah-vehr lah veel*
Where do they leave from?	**D'où partent-elles?** *doo pahr tehl*
We want to see _____.	**Nous voudrions voir _____.** *noo vood-ree-yohn vwahr*

- the botanical garden **le jardin botanique** *luh zhahr-dan boh-tah-neek*
- the castle **le château** *luh shah-toh*
- the cathedral **la cathédrale** *lah kah-tay-drahl*
- the church **l'église** *lay-gleez*
- the concert hall **la salle de concert** *lah sahl duh kohn-ssehr*
- the downtown area **le centre de la ville** *luh sahn-truh duh la veel*
- the fountains **les fontaines** *lay fohn-tehn*
- the library **la bibliothèque** *lah bee-blee-oh-tehk*
- the main square **la place principale** *lah plahss pran-ssee-pahl*
- the market **le marché** *luh mahr-shay*
- the mosque **la mosquée** *lah mohss-kay*
- the museum (of fine arts) **le musée (des beaux arts)** *luh mew-zay (day boh zahr)*
- a nightclub **une boîte de nuit** *ewn bwaht duh nwee*
- the old part of town **la vieille ville** *lah vyehy veel*
- the opera **l'opéra** *loh-pay-rah*
- the palace **le palais** *luh pah-leh*

- the park **le parc** *luh pahrk*
- the stadium **le stade** *luh stahd*
- the synagogue **la synagogue** *lah see-nah-gohg*
- the university **l'université** *lew-nee-vehr-ssee-tay*
- the zoo **le zoo** *luh zoh*

Is it open?	**C'est ouvert?** *seh too-vehr*	
Is it closed?	**C'est fermé?** *seh fehr-may*	
At what time does it open?	**Ça ouvre à quelle heure?** *sah oo-vruh ah kehl uhr*	
At what time does it close?	**Ça ferme à quelle heure?** *sah fehrm ah kehl uhr*	
What's the admission price?	**Combien coûte un billet d'entrée?** *kohn-byan koot uhn-bee-yeh dahn-tray*	
How much do children pay?	**C'est combien pour les enfants?** *seh kohn-byan poor lay zahn-fahn*	
Can they go in free?	**Est-ce gratuit pour les enfants?** *ehss grah-twee poor lay zahn-fahn.*	
Until what age?	**Jusqu'à quel âge?** *zhewss-kah kehl ahzh*	
Is it all right to take pictures?	**Peut-on prendre des photos?** *puh tohn prahn-druh day foh-toh*	

A SIGHTSEEING ITINERARY

France is a country overwhelmingly rich in places and things to be seen. Its cities and countryside overflow with sites and institutions filled with historic, intellectual, and artistic tradition. Few indeed are the areas not commemorated by a general's triumph, a king's passage, an artist's inspiration, or a philosopher's thoughts. To attempt an exhaustive tour in the usual short vacation span would be foolhardy. We try here simply to suggest, in broad outline, some of the highlights, the best-known and most popular attractions to which visitors are drawn. Modern France has an extensive and sophisticated system of public transportation, enabling the traveler to get quickly to whatever area most interests him.

PARIS

Paris is the cultural, economic, political, and social center of France. Among its museums are: The *Louvre,* which contains the Venus de Milo and the Mona Lisa, with Leoh Ming Pei's controversial Pyramid in front, as well as art and antiquities from all over Europe; the *Army Museum* at the Invalides in which stands the tomb of Napoleon; the *Musée d'Orsay* (located in the old Gare d'Orsay, one of Paris's first railroad stations), which, in addition to housing some of the vast collection of Impressionist paintings formerly displayed in the Jeu de Paume Museum, traces the development of contrasting artistic styles at the end of the nineteenth and beginning of the twentieth centuries; the *Jeu de Paume Museum,* which now exhibits contemporary art, sculpture, and photography; the *Panthéon,* commemorating illustrious French men and women; the *Cluny Museum* with beautiful medieval art and a superb tapestry collection; the *Musée Grévin,* which displays delightful wax replicas of the rich and famous; the *Orangerie,* which contains modern art and early twentieth-century Impressionist paintings by, among others, Monet and Renoir; the *Picasso Museum,* which traces the development of the artist's work and where each room depicts a certain stage in his career; the *Rodin Museum,* in which sculptures are displayed in a lovely house and magnificent garden, the perfect setting for a typical French picnic; the *Musée National d'Art Moderne,* located within the Pompidou Center, which contains a large selection of very avant-garde paintings and sculptures; the *Maison de Victor Hugo,* located at 6 Place des Vosges, which displays memorabilia from the artist's life; and the *Cité des Sciences et d'Industrie,* located in a lovely park with gardens in northern Paris, with its geodesic dome and giant-screen science movies, which is a masterwork of modern architecture.

Those with an interest in church sculpture and architecture will be particularly interested in the Cathedral of *Notre-Dame*. Its spires, portals, stained glass windows, and flying buttresses make it an outstanding example of Gothic architecture. Vividly colored stained glass windows dating back to the thirteenth century and portraying over 1,000 biblical scenes make the *Sainte-Chapelle* church unique. *Sacré-Coeur*, the domed white church dominating Montmartre, resembles a mosque and is decorated on the interior with mosaics. The eighteenth–nineteenth-century church of the *Madeleine* with its colonnade is also of interest. The *Église St-Germain*, Paris's oldest church and one of the few remaining examples of the Romanesque style, certainly warrants a visit.

Noted public squares frequented by tourists include: the *Place de la Concorde*, where many historical figures, including Louis XVI and Marie Antoinette, were guillotined during the French Revolution. The obelisk in the middle of the square comes from the ruins of the Temple of Luxor in Egypt and is covered with hieroglyphics. The *Place Vendôme* is the site of the Vendôme column, which has scenes depicting Napoleon's military campaigns at its center. On top of the column is a statue of the emperor. *The Place de l'Opéra*, dominated by the Opéra (renovated in 1995), is the home of the national opera and ballet companies and is renowned for its architecture and décor. Its Gobelin tapestries, gilded mosaics, 1964 Chagall ceiling, and 6-ton chandelier attract many tourists. The *Place de la Bastille* is the site of the once famous prison, since destroyed, where the first shots of the French Revolution are commemorated every July 14. The *Place Charles de Gaulle*, upon which stands the Arc de Triomphe, is one of France's best known landmarks. Under the arch is the Tomb of the Unknown Soldier. Twelve avenues fan out from the arch, creating the pattern of a star. Leading to the arch, the Champs-Elysées is lined with trees, cafés, and luxurious shops. The *Place des Vosges*, an example of seventeenth-century secular architecture, is noted for its grassy enclosure containing a children's playground.

The *Centre National d'Art et de Culture Georges Pompidou*, on the site of the old Les Halles market, is a national museum with frequent expositions and a voluminous research library. From the observation deck on the roof you can see all of Paris.

Since almost one-half of the area of the site is open, spontaneous public spectacles and unprogrammed outdoor events hosted by jugglers, artists, acrobats, mimes, musicians, and fire-eaters are not uncommon, and attract large crowds.

The center is easily recognizable because of its network of boldly colored pipes and tubes of all sizes adorning the outside walls. The exterior, glass-enclosed tubular escalators also give a panoramic view of Paris.

With a focus on contemporary art, the center offers numerous exhibits and activities, a huge library, a museum of modern art, a movie library (**la cinémathèque**), and an institute for acoustic and musical research and coordination.

The *Eiffel Tower* stands over 1,000 feet tall and acts as a radio and television transmitter. From any of its three different levels one gets a panoramic view of Paris. At its base there is a popular restaurant. Walking along the *quais* of the *Seine* you will find the parapets lined with quaint bookshops. *Montmartre*, or the "Butte," as it is commonly known, is a center of artistic life where bohemianism may be said to have its roots. The *Latin Quarter* is the home of the Sorbonne University and an intellectual hub.

At the *Palais de Justice*, the seat of the courts and all the judicial system, you will see the *Conciergerie*, which served as a prison during the Revolution. A guillotine remains in the chapel where prisoners were led before their executions. Also not to be missed are *La Bourse* or Stock Exchange, *Le Marché aux puces*, the Paris flea market, and the *Comédie Française*, the theater that houses France's leading dramatic groups.

When your feet hurt and you want to take a break, relax in the *Tuileries* gardens, beside the Seine. Statues, figures, and decorative vases line these formal French gardens. The *Bois de Boulogne* is a vast park containing ornamental lakes, flower gardens, cafés, restaurants, two racetracks, and a children's amusement park. Best, however, not to frequent it at night. The *Bois de Vincennes* contains museums and a zoo. The *Luxembourg* gardens, on the left bank, are often used by students.

The *Cimetière Père-Lachaise* (Père-Lachaise Cemetery) would interest those who want to see the graves of renowned French personages such as Balzac, Colette, Delacroix, Molière, Édith Piaf, and Seurat, as well as foreigners Chopin, Oscar Wilde, Gertrude Stein, and James Douglas "Jim" Morrison.

Two areas of particular interest within Paris are *La Défense*, where modern sculpture created by celebrated artists from around the world adorns the streets and buildings, and *Le Marais*, where small streets, gothic churches, and old-fashioned houses lend a flavor of the Middle Ages to the neighborhood.

Just outside Paris is *Versailles*, the luxurious palace known for its architecture, style, and gardens. Not to be missed is the fabulous *Galerie des Glaces* (Hall of Mirrors), where the Treaty of Versailles was signed in 1919. A bus tour from Paris to Versailles might also include side trips to *Fontainebleau* and *Chantilly* castles. The *Basilica de Saint Denis*, and the small city of Sèvres, known for its multicolored porcelain, are also not far from the capital. Many tourists are attracted to Monet's house at *Giverny*, where the rooms have been restored according to the artist's original designs, and one can enjoy the luxurious garden and a water garden with lilies and bridges.

Travel Tips A one-, three-, or five-day museum pass may be purchased from your travel agent within the United States or at various locations throughout Paris. For a very reasonable fee, the pass entitles the bearer to free admission to most of the museums throughout the city and to certain other monuments and places of interest. A major plus is that one does not have to wait to enter and immediately passes to the front of the line. The only drawback to the pass is that it must be used on consecutive days.

FARTHER AFIELD

A bus tour of the Loire Valley allows you to visit many splendid castles:

Amboise—a castle that offers a beautiful view across the river.

Angers—a castle and two museums, one famous for medieval tapestry and the other for its nineteenth-century sculpture.

Azay-le-Rideau—a castle with romantic appeal and charm.

Blois—a castle whose architecture represents many styles.

Chambord—the largest of all the châteaux, surrounded by a vast forest.

Chaumont—a castle offering a fantastic view across the river.

Chenonceau—a castle in a truly magnificent setting.

Cheverny—one of the last castles to be built.

Chinon—a truly authentic castle.

Villandry—a castle with formal, Renaissance gardens.

A tour of medieval French Gothic churches would certainly prove worthwhile. Among the most popular are:

Amiens—the largest completed Gothic cathedral.

Beauvais—the highest cathedral in France; its nave was never built.

Chartres—a cathedral containing sculptures representing biblical personages. The stained glass windows of the cathedral are exquisite and unique.

Reims—the cathedral where the kings of France were crowned.

Rouen—a cathedral that incorporates almost all intermediate styles of Gothic architecture.

The beaches of *Normandy*, where the Allies landed in 1944, will be of special interest to history buffs.

Mont-Saint-Michel, a monastery surrounded by a medieval fortress, is situated on a small island in the English Channel, between Normandy and Brittany. Tourists must beware of the surrounding quicksand that reaches the island only during high tide.

Carcassonne, in southern France, is one of the finest examples of a medieval, fortified European city.

Every year Catholics make a pilgrimage to *Lourdes*, a city at the foot of the Pyrénées, the mountains that separate France from Spain. It is believed that here, in 1858, the Virgin Mary appeared to the peasant girl, Bernadette. For this reason, many people bathe in the sacred waters of the grotto where the vision appeared, hoping to find a miracle that will restore their health.

The seaside resort of *Deauville*, in Normandy, comes alive in the summer when casinos, horse racing, and an exciting nightlife attract the rich and famous.

Biarritz, in the Pays Basque, near Spain, is a popular summer resort city. Here you can enjoy watching pelote, the regional sport known as jai alai in the United States.

Strasbourg, an industrial city, has a cathedral famous for its astronomical clock. It also contains the offices of the EEC, the European Economic Community, previously known as the European Common Market.

The cities of *Chamonix* and *Grenoble*, and the *French Alps*, are extremely popular and offer a wide variety of winter activities.

Nice, capital of the *Côte d'Azur (Riviera)*, vacation spot of the jet set and refuge from the ravages of winter, has pebble beaches and a casino. If you prefer a sand beach, *Cannes*, also on the *Côte d'Azur*, is a pleasant alternative.

A visit to the *wine country*, the regions of Bordeaux, Champagne, and Languedoc, will be interesting and informative.

Corsica, birthplace of Napoleon, is a French island in the Mediterranean Sea, 200 kilometers from Nice. This island boasts beautiful scenery and tiny villages that maintain their medieval charm.

On a side trip to *Monaco*, a visit to Prince Rainier's palace provides a view of the harbor and the yachts moored there. The casino at *Monte Carlo* is its principal attraction.

In *Avignon* there is the *Palace of the Popes* and the *Bridge of St. Bénezet*. Nîmes and Arles, quaint cities noted for their Roman ruins, have amphitheaters still in their original form.

OUTSIDE FRANCE

For a glimpse of France closer to the United States, visit *Québec* with its magnificent beaches, parks, mountains, forests, and lakes. Participate in your favorite summer or winter sport. See the old and the new cities and visit the charming castles.

If you prefer a tranquil vacation, visit a tropical island. Rest in the shade of the palm and coconut trees of *Martinique* or *Guadeloupe* in the Lesser Antilles. Enjoy the beaches, the languorous lifestyle, and the fruit-flavored daiquiris. In Martinique, tour the capital, *Fort-de-France*, see the ruins of *Saint-Pierre* and *Mt. Pelée*, and the luxuriant rain forest. In Guadeloupe, the town of *Gosier* is the heart of vacation life. At *Le Moule*, the horseshoe beach is one of the island's most popular attractions. Or visit *Haiti*, on the island of Hispaniola, in the Greater Antilles. Horseback ride to the famed *Citadelle*, tour *Port-au-Prince*, the capital, relax by the *waterfalls of Cayes*, and lie on the beautiful beaches of *Port Salut*.

A trip to the French side of *Saint-Martin*, and to its quaint village of *Grand Case*, famous for its beautiful beaches, exquisite restaurants, and fabulous duty-free French stores, is a must.

A most exotic vacation might lead you to Western Africa, where French is spoken in *Senegal*, *Mali*, *Guinea*, *Niger*, and *the Ivory Coast*.

AMUSEMENT PARKS

Two amusement parks not far from Paris will delight children and adults as well.

Just 20 miles east of Paris at Marne-La-Vallée is *Euro-Disney*'s new $4 billion theme park, complete with Mickey Mouse, Donald Duck, and their friends. Its 29 attractions in five different "lands" and the six hotels, artificial lakes, and entertainment grounds cover an area one-fifth the size of Paris. The park is serviced by the **R.E.R. (Réseau Express Régional)**, the suburban railroad line that makes Paris a mere 45 minutes away. The **TGV (train à grande vitesse)**, the high-speed French train, also includes a stop on its lines to accommodate tourists. Although the Disney Company remains adamant in its decision not to serve traditional French wine, it boasts that the quality of food in Euro-Disney surpasses that of its other theme parks.

But if it's typical French amusement that you seek, try *Parc Astérix*, 20 miles north of Paris. A giant roller coaster, a dolphin lake, and a replica of a Romano-Gallic village dominate this park, based on the exploits of Astérix le Gaulois, the famous and much-loved comic-book character, whose fictional exploits took place 2,000 years ago during the Roman invasion of France. North of *Metz*, in the region of Alsace-Lorraine, children can enjoy the *Nouveau Monde des Schtroumpfs*, a theme park featuring the Smurfs.

PLANNING A TRIP

During your stay, you may want to plan some longer excursions. In France you can get around by moped (**mobylette**), bicycle, or even hiking. For more extensive trips, boats, planes, and trains are all readily available, as are rental cars (see Driving a Car). You may even rent a barge to travel through France on an elaborate canal system.

Travel Tips Most airlines allow passengers to select a seat location and the type of meal preferred at the time reservations are made.Especially on overseas flights, good choices mean the difference between a pleasant or a miserable trip. To get some sleep, choose a window seat well away from the galley (kitchen area). If you like to walk around, request an aisle seat. To watch the movie, avoid the row facing the bulkhead. If you don't smoke, ask to be placed well away from the smokers. The reservations agent will know the aircraft being used and can help you pick the best location. Among the meal options are vegetarian, kosher, and low-fat menus. If you have other special dietary needs, ask the reservations agent if those can be met. Be sure to confirm your seat assignment and meal choice when checking in for the flight.

AIR SERVICE

The two major airlines that service France are Air France (mainly for international flights) and Air Inter (for domestic flights). Although very time-efficient, air travel is an expensive option.

The Concorde, which flies at approximately 800 mph, can fly from New York to Paris in approximately 3 hours and 45 minutes, about half the time required by a regular airline flight. The cost of a round-trip ticket is generally prohibitive for most (several thousand dollars) unless there are special fares available.

When is there a flight to _____?	**Il y a un vol pour _____ quand?** *eel yah uhn vohl poor _____ kahn*
I would like a round-trip (one-way) ticket in tourist class (first class).	**Je voudrais un aller et retour (un aller simple) en seconde classe (première classe).** *zhuh voo-dreh zuhn ah-lay ay ruh-toor (uhn nah-lay san-pluh) ahn suh-gohnd klahss (pruh-myehr klahss)*
A seat _____.	**Une place _____.** *ewn plahss*
■ in the smoking section	**dans la section fumeurs.** *dahn lah sehk-ssyohn few-muhr*
■ in the nonsmoking section	**dans la section non-fumeurs.** *dahn lah sehk ssyohn nohn few-muhr*
■ next to the window	**à côté de la fenêtre** *ah koh-tay duh lah fuh-neh-truh*
■ on the aisle	**côté couloir** *koh-tay koo-lwahr*
What is the fare?	**Quel est le tarif?** *kehl eh luh tah-reef*
Are meals served?	**Sert-on des repas?** *sehr tohn day ruh-pah*
At what time does the plane leave?	**L'avion part à quelle heure?** *lah-vyohn pahr tah kehl uhr*
At what time do we arrive?	**À quelle heure arrivons-nous?** *ah kehl uhr ah-reev-ohn noo*
What is my flight number?	**Quel est le numéro de mon vol?** *kehl eh luh new-may-roh duh mohn vohl*
What gate do we leave from?	**De quelle porte partons-nous?** *duh kehl pohrt pahr-tohn noo*
I want to confirm (cancel) my reservation for flight _____.	**Je voudrais confirmer (annuler) ma réservation pour le vol numéro _____.** *zhuh voo-dreh kohn-feer-may (ah-new-lay) mah ray-zehr-vah-ssyohn poor luh vohl new-may-roh*

I'd like to check my bags.	**Je voudrais enregistrer mes bagages.** *zhuh voo-dreh zah<u>n</u>-ruh-zheess-tray may bah-gahzh*
I have only carry-on baggage.	**J'ai seulement des bagages à main.** *zhay suhl-mah<u>n</u> day bah-gazh ah ma<u>n</u>*
Please pass my film (camera) through by hand.*	**Passez mon film (appareil) à la main, s'il vous plaît.** *pah-ssay moh<u>n</u> film (ah-pah-rehy) ah lah ma<u>n</u> seel voo pleh*

NOTE: Some high-speed film can be damaged by airport security X rays. It is best to pack film in your suitcase, protected in a lead insulated bag. If you have film in your camera or carry-on baggage, avoid problems and ask the guard to pass it through by hand instead. If the guard refuses, bow to his wishes.

SHIPBOARD TRAVEL

If you plan to travel by boat, a **Tourisme Fluvial** brochure may be obtained from a travel agent or tourist office.

Where is the dock?	**Où est le dock?** *oo eh luh dohk*
When does the next boat leave for _____?	**Quand part le prochain bateau pour _____?** *kah<u>n</u> pahr luh proh-sha<u>n</u> bah-toh poor*
How long does the crossing take?	**La traversée dure combien de temps?** *lah trah-vehr-ssay dewr koh<u>n</u>-bya<u>n</u> duh tah<u>n</u>*
At what ports do we stop?	**Dans quels ports est-ce qu'on fait escale?** *dah<u>n</u> kehl pohr ehss koh<u>n</u> feh ehss-kahl*

How long is the stopover?	**L'escale dure combien de temps?** *lehss-kahl dewr koh<u>n</u>-bya<u>n</u> duh tah<u>n</u>*
When do we dock?	**Quand est-ce qu'on y arrive?** *kah<u>n</u> tehss koh<u>n</u> nee ah-reev*
At what time do we have to be back on board?	**À quelle heure faut-il retourner au bateau?** *ah kehl uhr foh teel ruh-toor-nay oh bah-toh*
I'd like a ____ ticket.	**Je voudrais un billet ____.** *zhuh voo dreh zuh<u>n</u> bee-yeh*
■ first-class	**de première classe** *duh pruh-myehr klahss*
■ tourist-class	**de deuxième classe** *duh duh-zyehm klahss*
■ cabin	**de cabine** *duh kah-been*
Can you give me something for seasickness?	**Pouvez-vous me donner quelque chose contre le mal de mer?** *poo-vay voo muh doh-nay kehl-kuh shohz koh<u>n</u>-truh luh mahl duh mehr*

TRAIN SERVICE

The French railway system is extensive, serving small as well as large cities. Known to be fast, punctual, and comfortable, the **S.N.C.F.** (Société Nationale des Chemins de fer Français) is considered Europe's most efficient train service.

Train schedules may be obtained in every major railroad station and a complete S.N.C.F. timetable may be purchased at newsstands in the stations. Seat reservations are rarely necessary, except when traveling on a **TGV** (**train à grande vitesse**) or on longer international trips. Tickets must be validated before boarding the train. Due to the efficiency of the French train service, long-distance buses are rare.

The T.G.V. makes the regions of Rhône-Alps, Savoy, Rhône Valley, Provence, Languedoc, and even western Switzerland only a few hours' journey from Paris. There are also special tourist trains (**CEVENOL**) running from Paris to Marseilles.

TYPES OF TRAINS

TEE (Trans-Europe-Express)	Has only first-class seating, plus supplementary charge.
TGV (train à grande vitesse)	High-speed train with first- and second-class seating.
Rapide	Express that stops only at major stations. Luxury accommodations are available.
Express	Long-distance train.
Omnibus	Local train.

If you have to sleep on a train you will find the following expressions useful:

Wagon-lit	A first-class private sleeping compartment for one or two (with sink and mirror).
Couchette	A second-class sleeping compartment with six bunks. If you are not a party of six, you may have to share it with

strangers. You sleep in your clothes.

Coach You sleep, if possible, fully dressed, sitting in your first- or second-class seat.

EATING ON A TRAIN

You can get anything from a light snack and drinks to a full meal on the train. Use the **wagon-restaurant** (dining car). Also, when the train pulls into a large station, call out the window to the vendors of sandwiches, cheese, and drinks. You may, if you prefer, carry on your own meals and refreshments, as the dining car can be very expensive.

STATION

Where is the train station? (the ticket office)	**Où est la gare? (le guichet)** *oo eh lah gahr (luh gee-sheh)*
I'd like to see the schedule.	**Je voudrais voir l'horaire.** *zhuh voo-dreh vwahr loh-rehr*
A first-class (second-class) ticket to _____, please.	**Un billet de première classe (seconde classe) pour _____, s'il vous plaît.** *uhn bee yeh duh pruh-myehr klahss (suh-gohnd klahss) poor _____ seel voo pleh*
■ a one-way (round-trip) ticket	**un aller simple (un aller et retour)** *uhn nah-lay san-pluh (uhn nah-lay ay ruh-toor)*
I would like a (no) smoking compartment.	**Je voudrais un compartiment (non-) fumeurs.** *zhuh voo-dreh zuhn kohn-pahr-tee-mahn (nohn) few-muhr*
At what time does the train arrive (leave)?	**Le train arrive (part) à quelle heure?** *luh tran ah-reev (pahr) ah kehl uhr*

From what platform does it leave?	**Il part de quel quai (de quelle voie)?**	*eel pahr duh kehl kay (duh kehl vwah)*
At what platform does it arrive?	**Il arrive à quel quai (à quelle voie)?**	*eel ah-reev ah kehl kay (ah kehl vwah)*
Does this train stop at _____?	**Est-ce que ce train s'arrête à _____?**	*ehss kuh suh tran sah-reht ah*
Is the train on time?	**Le train est à l'heure?**	*luh tran eh tah luhr*
How long does it stop?	**Il s'arrête pendant combien de temps?**	*eel sah-reht pan-dan kohn-byan duh tahn*
Is there time to get a bite?	**On a le temps de prendre quelque chose?**	*ohn ah luh tahn duh prahn-druh kehl-kuh shohz*
Is there a dining car (sleeping car)?	**Il y a un wagon restaurant (un wagon-lit)?**	*eel yah uhn vah-gohn rehss-toh-rahn (uhn vah-gohn lee)*
Is it _____?	**Est-ce _____?**	*ehss*
■ a through train	**un rapide**	*uhn rah-peed*
■ a local	**un omnibus**	*uhn nohm-nee-bewss*
■ an express	**un express**	*uhn nehkss-prehss*
Do I have to change trains?	**Dois-je changer de train?**	*dwahzh shahn-zhay duh tran*
Is this seat taken?	**Est-ce que cette place est occupée?**	*ehss kuh seht plahss eh toh-kew-pay*
Where are we now?	**Où sommes-nous maintenant?**	*oo sohm noo mant-nahn*
Will we arrive on time? (late?)	**On arrive à l'heure? (en retard?)**	*ohn ah-reev ah luhr (ahn ruh-tahr)*

DRIVING A CAR

ROAD SYSTEM

You may choose to drive on one of the following kinds of roads:

Autoroute	a high-speed superfreeway for long-distance trips. These are toll roads.
Route nationale	a main highway used by cars going from one small town to another
Route départementale	a minor highway
Chemin communal	a local road
Chemin rural	a scenic country road

In order to escape the horrendous traffic jams, the fearless European drivers, and the impossibility of finding a legal parking spot, avoid driving in Paris at all costs.

To rent a car, a passport and major credit card are generally required. It is not necessary to obtain an international license, since U.S. and Canadian drivers' licenses are valid in France.

A good idea would be to purchase a French **Code de la Route,** which explains driving rules and regulations. The French Government Tourist Office issues free road maps. Speed limits are high and it will take some time getting used to the French way of driving. Remember to buckle up.

PARKING

During the day, you may park at parking meters located in metropolitan areas, or you may find a spot in a "Blue Zone." To park there you must use a special parking disk (**disque**), which can be obtained free of charge at auto clubs, garages, gas stations, hotels, police stations, or tourist offices. You must set the time of your arrival, and departure time will show automatically on the disk. The disk should be displayed on your windshield. Be careful: If you are caught cheating, you risk a fine. Parking at night is usually free.

SIGNS
Familiarize yourself with the traffic signs listed below:

Accotement non stabilisé	Soft shoulder
Allumez vos phares	Put on headlights
Arrêt interdit	No stopping
Attention	Caution
Céder le passage	Yield
Chaussée déformée	Poor roadway
Chute de pierres	Falling rocks
Circulation interdite	No thoroughfare
Descente (Pente) dangereuse	Steep slope (hill)
Déviation	Detour
Douane	Customs
École	School
Entrée interdite	No entrance
Fin d'interdiction de _____	End of _____ zone
Interdiction de doubler	No Passing
Interdiction de stationner	No Parking
Interdit aux piétons	No Pedestrians
Piste réservée aux transports publics	Lane for Public Transportation
Ralentir (Ralentissez)	Slow

Réservé aux piétons	Pedestrians only
Sens interdit	Wrong way
Sens unique	One Way
Serrez à gauche (à droite)	Keep left (right)
Sortie d'autoroute	Freeway (throughway) Exit
Sortie de véhicules	Vehicle Exit
Stationnement autorisé	Parking Permitted
Stationnement interdit	No Parking
Tenez la droite (gauche)	Keep to the right (left)
Verglas	Icy Road
Virage dangereux	Dangerous Curve
Voie de dégagement	Private Entrance
Zone Bleue	Blue Zone (parking)

Guarded railroad crossing   Yield   Stop

Right of way   Dangerous intersection ahead   Gasoline (petrol) ahead

Parking   No vehicles allowed   Dangerous curve

Pedestrian crossing   Oncoming traffic has right of way   No bicycles allowed

No parking allowed   No entry   No left turn

No U-turn

No passing

Border crossing

Traffic signal ahead

Speed limit

Traffic circle (roundabout) ahead

Minimum speed limit

All traffic turns left

End of no passing zone

One-way street

Detour

Danger ahead

Entrance to expressway

Expressway ends

CAR RENTALS

You may use your driver's license to drive in France. Cars may be rented or leased at airports or major railroad stations. This can be quite costly since the price of gasoline abroad is prohibitive. The most economical method of renting a car is to reserve it with one of the rental agencies before you leave home.

Where can I rent _____?	**Où puis-je louer _____.**	*oo pweezh loo-ay*
■ a car	**une voiture**	*ewn vwah-tewr*
■ a motorcycle	**une motocyclette**	*ewn moh-toh-see-kleht*
■ a bicycle	**une bicyclette**	*ewn bee-ssee-kleht*
■ a scooter	**un scooter**	*uhn skoo-tehr*
■ a moped	**une mobylette**	*ewn moh-bee-leht*
I want _____.	**Je voudrais _____.**	*zhuh voo-dreh*
■ a small car	**une petite voiture**	*zewn puh-teet vwah-tewr*
■ a large car	**une grande voiture**	*zewn grahnd vwah-tewr*
■ a sports car	**une voiture de sport**	*zewn vwah-tewr duh spohr*
I prefer automatic transmission.	**Je préfère la transmission automatique.**	*zhuh pray-fehr lah trah<u>n</u>z-mee-ssyoh<u>n</u> oh-toh-mah-teek*
How much does it cost _____?	**Quel est le tarif _____?**	*kehl eh luh tah-reef*
■ per day	**à la journée**	*ah lah zhoor-nay*
■ per week	**à la semaine**	*ah lah suh-mehn*
■ per kilometer	**au kilomètre**	*oh kee-loh-meh-truh*
How much is the insurance?	**Quel est le montant de l'assurance?**	*kehl eh luh mohn-tahn duh lah-ssew-rah<u>n</u>ss*

Is the gas included?	**Est-ce que l'essence est comprise?** *ehss kuh leh-ssah<u>n</u>ss eh koh<u>n</u>-preez*
What kind of gas does it take?	**Quelle essence emploie-t-elle?** *kehl eh-ssah<u>n</u>ss ah<u>n</u>-plwah-tehl*
Do you accept credit cards?	**Acceptez vous des cartes de crédit?** *ahk-ssehp-tay voo day kahrt duh kray-dee*
Which ones?	**Lesquelles?** *lay-kehl*
Here's my driver's license.	**Voici mon permis de conduire.** *vwah-ssee moh<u>n</u> pehr-mee duh koh<u>n</u>-dweer*
Do I have to leave a deposit?	**Dois-je verser des arrhes?** *dwah<u>zh</u> vehr ssay day <u>z</u>ahr*
I want to rent the car here and leave it in _____ (name of city).	**Je veux louer la voiture ici et la laisser à _____.** *zhuh vuh loo-ay lah vwah tewr ee ssee ay lah leh-ssay ah*
Is there a drop-off charge?	**Faut-il payer plus en cas de non-retour ici?** *foh-teel peh-yay plews ah<u>n</u> kah duh noh<u>n</u>-ruh-toor ee-ssee*

ON THE ROAD

Excuse me.	**Excusez-moi.** *ehkss-kew-zay mwah* **Pardon** *pahr-doh<u>n</u>*
Can you tell me _____?	**Pouvez-vous me dire _____?** *poo-vay voo muh deer*
How do I get to _____?	**Comment va-t-on à _____?** *koh-mah<u>n</u> vah-toh<u>n</u> ah*
I think we're lost.	**Nous sommes sur la mauvaise route.** *noo sohm sewr lah moh-vehz root*

Is this the road (way) to _____?	**Est-ce la route de _____?** *ehss lah root duh*
Do I go straight?	**Est-ce que je vais tout droit?** *ehss kuh zhuh veh too drwah*
Do I turn to the right (to the left)?	**Est-ce que je tourne à droite (à gauche)?** *ehss kuh zhuh toorn ah drwaht (ah gohsh)*
Where does this road go?	**Où mène cette route?** *oo mehn seht root*
How far is it from here to the next town?	**À quelle distance sommes-nous de la prochaine ville?** *ah kehl deess-tahnss sohm noo duh lah proh-shehn veel*
How far away is _____?	**À quelle distance est _____?** *ah kehl deess-tahnss eh*
Is the next town far?	**La prochaine ville, est-elle loin?** *lah proh-shehn veel eh-tehl lwan*
What's the next town called?	**Comment s'appelle la prochaine ville?** *koh-mahn sah-pehl lah proh-shehn veel*
Do you have a road map?	**Avez-vous une carte routière?** *ah-vay voo zewn kahrt roo-tyehr*
Can you show it to me on the map?	**Pourriez-vous me l'indiquer sur la carte?** *poo-ree-yay voo muh lan-dee-kay sewr lah kahrt*
Is the road in good condition?	**Est-ce que la route est en bon état?** *ehss kuh lah root eh tahn bohn nay-tah*
Is this the most direct way?	**Est-ce le chemin le plus direct?** *ehss luh shuh-man luh plew dee-rehkt*
Is it a toll road?	**Est-ce une autoroute à péage?** *ehss ewn oh-toh-root ah pay-ahzh*

AT THE SERVICE STATION

Gasoline is sold by the liter in Europe; for the traveler accustomed to gallons, it may seem confusing, especially if you want to calculate your mileage per gallon (kilometer per liter). Here are some tips on making those conversions.

LIQUID MEASURES			
LITERS	GALLONS	LITERS	GALLONS
1	0.26	50	13.0
5	1.3	60	15.6
10	2.6	70	18.2
20	5.2	80	20.8
30	7.8	90	23.4
40	10.4	100	26.0

DISTANCE MEASURES			
KILOMETERS	MILES	KILOMETERS	MILES
1	0.62	30	18.6
5	3.1	35	21.7
10	6.2	40	24.8
15	9.3	45	27.9
20	12.4	50	31.1
25	15.5	100	62.1

Where is a gas station?
Où se trouve une station-service? *oo suh troov ewn stah-ssyohn sehr-veess*

Fill'er up with _____ please.
Faites-le plein, s'il vous plaît _____. *feht-luh plan seel-voo pleh*
- diesel **du gas-oil** *dew gahz-wahl*
- regular **de l'ordinaire** *duh lohr-dee-nehr*
- super **du super** *dew sew-pehr*

Give me _____ liters please.
Donnez m'en _____ litres, s'il vous plaît. *doh-nay mahn _____ lee-truh seel voo pleh*

Please check _____.	**Veuillez vérifier _____.** *vuh-yay vay-ree-fyay*
■ the battery	**la batterie** *lah bah-tree*
■ the brakes	**les freins** *lay fran*
■ the carburetor	**le carburateur** *luh kahr-bew-rah-tuhr*
■ the oil	**le niveau de l'huile** *luh nee-voh duh lweel*
■ the spark plugs	**les bougies (f.)** *lay boo-zhee*
■ the tires	**les pneus** *lay pnuh*
■ the water	**le niveau de l'eau** *luh nee-voh duh loh*

I think there's something wrong with _____.	**Je crois que _____ ne fonctionne pas.** *zhuh krwah kuh _____ nuh fohnk-ssyohn pas*
■ the brakes	**les freins** *lay fran*
■ the bumper	**le pare-choc** *luh pahr-shohk*
■ the directional signal	**le clignotant** *luh klee-nyoh-tahn*
■ the door handle	**la poignée** *lah pwah-nyay*
■ the electrical system	**l'installation électrique** *lan-stah-lah-ssyohn ay-lehk-treek*
■ the exhaust	**l'échappement (m.)** *lay-shahp-mahn*
■ the fan	**le ventilateur** *luh vahn-tee-lah-tuhr*
■ the fan belt	**la courroie de ventilateur** *lah koor-wah duh vahn-tee-lah-tuhr*
■ the fender	**l'aile (f.)** *lehl*
■ the fuel pump	**la pompe à essence** *lah pohnp ah eh-ssahnss*
■ the gas tank	**le réservoir à essence** *luh ray-zehr-vwahr ah eh-ssahnss*
■ the gears	**l'engrenage (m.)** *lahn-gruh-nahzh*
■ the gearshift	**le changement de vitesses** *luh shahnzh-mahn duh vee-tehss*

■ the headlight **le phare** *luh fahr*

■ the hood **le capot** *luh kah-poh*

■ the horn **le klaxon** *luh klahk-ssohn*

■ the ignition **l'allumage (m.)** *lah-lew-mahzh*

■ the radio **la radio** *lah rah-dyoh*

■ the starter **le démarreur** *luh day-mah-ruhr*

■ the steering wheel **le volant** *luh voh-lahn*

■ the taillight **le feu arrière** *luh fuh ah-ryehr*

■ the transmission **la transmission** *lah trahnz-mee-ssyohn*

■ the trunk **le coffre** *luh koh-fruh*

■ the water pump **la pompe à eau** *lah pohnp ah oh*

■ the windshield wipers **les essuie-glaces** *lay zeh-sswee glahss*

What's the matter? **Qu'est-ce qui ne va pas?** *kehss kee nuh vah pah*

Is it possible to (Can you) fix it today? **Pouvez-vous la réparer aujourd'hui?** *poo-vay voo lah ray-pah-ray oh-zhoor-dwee*

Can you repair it temporarily? **Pouvez-vous la réparer provisoirement?** *poo-vay voo lah ray-pah-ray proh-vee-zwahr-mahn*

Do you have the part? **Avez-vous la pièce de rechange?** *ah-vay voo lah pyehss duh ruh-shahnzh*

How long will it take? **Combien de temps faudra-t-il?** *kohn-byan duh tahn foh-drah-teel*

Is everything O.K. now? **Tout est arrangé (réparé) maintenant?** *too teh tah-rahn-zhay (ray-pah-ray) mant-nahn*

How much do I owe you? **Combien vous dois-je?** *kohn-byan voo dwahzh*

Change the oil.	**Changez l'huile, s'il vous plaît.** *shahn-zhay lweel seel voo pleh*
Grease the car.	**Faites un graissage complet de la voiture, s'il vous plaît.** *feht zuhn greh-ssahzh kohn-pleh duh lah vwah-tewr seel voo pleh*
Charge the battery.	**Rechargez la batterie, s'il vous plaît.** *ruh-shahr-zhay lah bah-tree seel voo pleh*
Change this tire.	**Changez ce pneu.** *shahn-zhay suh pnuh*
Do you have rest-rooms?	**Avez-vous des toilettes?** *ah-vay voo day twah-leht*
Where are they?	**Où sont-elles?** *oo sohn-tehl*

TIRE PRESSURES			
Kg/Sq.Cm	Lb/Sq.In	Kg/Sq.Cm	Lb/Sq.In
1.2	17	2.1	30
1.3	18	2.2	31
1.4	20	2.3	33
1.5	21	2.4	34
1.6	23	2.5	36
1.7	24	2.6	37
1.8	26	2.7	38
1.9	27	2.8	40
2.0	28	2.9	41

ACCIDENTS, REPAIRS

The car overheats.	**La voiture chauffe.**	*lah vwah-tewr shohf*
It doesn't start.	**Elle ne démarre pas.**	*ehl nuh day-mahr pah*
I have a flat tire.	**J'ai un pneu crevé.**	*zhay-uhn pnuh kruh-vay*
My car has broken down.	**Ma voiture est en panne.**	*mah vwah-tewr eh tahn pahn*
The radiator is leaking.	**Le radiateur coule.**	*luh rah-dee-ah-tuhr kool*
The battery is dead.	**La batterie ne fonctionne plus.**	*lah bah-tree nuh fohnk-ssyohn plew*
The keys are locked inside the car.	**Les clés sont enfermées à l'intérieur de la voiture.**	*lay klay sohn tahn-fehr-may ah lan-tay-ree-yuhr duh lah vwah-tewr*
I need a mechanic (tow truck).	**Il me faut un mécanicien (une dépanneuse).**	*eel muh foh tuhn may-kah-nee ssyan (ewn day-pah-nuhz)*

Can you _____?	**Pouvez-vous _____?**	*poo-vay voo*
■ give me a hand	**me donner un coup de main**	*muh doh-nay uhn koo duh man*
■ help me	**m'aider**	*meh-day*
■ push me	**me pousser**	*muh poo-ssay*
■ tow me	**me remorquer**	*muh ruh-mohr-kay*

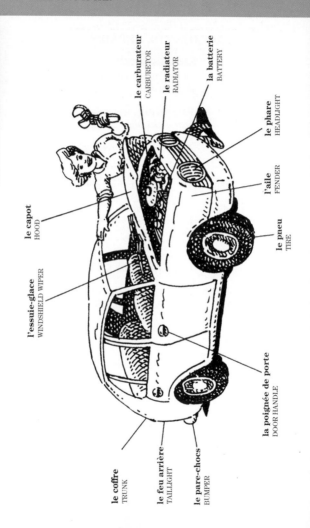

le carburateur
CARBURETOR

le radiateur
RADIATOR

la batterie
BATTERY

le phare
HEADLIGHT

l'aile
FENDER

le pneu
TIRE

le capot
HOOD

l'essuie-glace
WINDSHIELD WIPER

la poignée de porte
DOOR HANDLE

le coffre
TRUNK

le feu arrière
TAILLIGHT

le pare-chocs
BUMPER

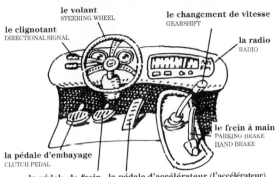

le volant
STEERING WHEEL

le changement de vitesse
GEARSHIFT

le clignotant
DIRECTIONAL SIGNAL

la radio
RADIO

le frein à main
PARKING BRAKE
HAND BRAKE

la pédale d'embayage
CLUTCH PEDAL

la pédale de frein
BRAKE PEDAL

la pédale d'accélérateur (l'accélérateur)
GAS PEDAL

I don't have any tools.	**Je n'ai pas d'outils.**	*zhuh nay pas doo-tee*
I need ___.	**Il me faut ___.**	*eel muh foh*
■ a flashlight	**une lampe de poche**	*ewn lahnp duh pohsh*
■ a hammer	**un marteau**	*uhn mahr-toh*
■ a jack	**un cric**	*uhn kreek*
■ a monkey wrench	**une clé anglaise**	*ewn klay ahn glehz*
■ pliers	**des pinces**	*day panss*
■ a screwdriver	**un tournevis**	*uhn toorn-veess*
I need ___.	**J'ai besoin ___.**	*zhay buh zwan*
■ a bolt	**d'un boulon**	*duhn boo-lohn*
■ a bulb	**d'une ampoule**	*dewn ahn-pool*
■ a filter	**d'un filtre**	*duhn feel-truh*
■ a nut	**d'un écrou**	*duhn nay-kroo*
Can you fix the car?	**Pouvez-vous réparer la voiture?**	*poo-vay voo ray-pah-ray lah vwah-tewr*

ENTERTAINMENT AND DIVERSION

MOVIES

Movies are generally shown from 2:00 P.M. to 10:00 P.M., with late night schedules on Saturday. *Pariscope* and *L'Officiel des Spectacles* are two guides to the movies in Paris, indicating the time and place of the film showing. The abbreviation **V.O. (version originale)** means that the original version of the movie in the language in which it was made is being shown. **V.F. (version française)** means that the movie is dubbed in French. In the movies or theater it is customary to tip the usher or usherette. Movies generally change on Wednesday. The bigger, more expensive, more comfortable movie houses are on the Champs-Elysées in Paris.

Let's go to the _____.	**Allons au _____.** *ah-lohn zoh*
■ movies	**cinéma** *see-nay-mah*
■ museum	**musée** *mew-zay*
■ theater	**théâtre** *tay-ah-truh*

What are they showing today?	**Qu'est-ce qu'on joue aujourd'hui?** *kehss kohn zhoo oh-zhoor-dwee*

It's _____.	**C'est _____.** *seh*
■ a mystery	**un mystère** *tuhn mee-sstehr*
■ a comedy	**une comédie** *tewn koh-may-dee*
■ a drama	**un drame** *tuhn drahm*
■ a musical	**une comédie musicale** *tewn koh-may-dee mew-zee-kahl*
■ a romance	**une histoire d'amour** *tewn eess-twahr dah-moor*
■ a Western	**un western** *tuhn wehss-tehrn*
■ a war film	**un film de guerre** *tuhn feelm duh gehr*

■ a science fiction film	**un film de science fiction** *tuhn feelm duh see-yahnss feek-ssyohn*
Is it in English?	**Est-ce en anglais?** *ehss ahn nahn-gleh*
Are there English subtitles?	**Il y a des sous-titres en anglais?** *eel yah day soo-tee-truh ahn nahn-gleh*
Where is the box office (time schedule)?	**Où est le bureau de location (l'horaire)?** *oo eh luh bew-roh duh loh-kah-ssyohn (loh-rehr)*
What time does the (first) show begin?	**À quelle heure commence le (premier) spectacle?** *ah kehl uhr koh-mahnss luh (pruh-myay) spehk-tah-kluh*
What time does the (last) show end?	**À quelle heure se termine le (dernier) spectacle?** *ah kehl uhr suh tehr-meen luh (dehr-nyay) spehk-tah-kluh*
I'd like to speak to an usherette.	**Je voudrais parler à une ouvreuse.** *zhuh voo-dreh pahr-lay ah ewn oo-vruhz*

THEATER

France has several national theaters such as the **Comédie Française** and the **Théâtre National de l'Odéon.** There are also about 50 private playhouses. Theaters are closed one day a week. The day is listed in the newspapers. Box offices are generally open from 11:00 A.M. to 6:00 P.M. Most of the theaters are closed one month in the summer, usually August.

For entertainment information in Paris consult *Pariscope*, the weekly entertainment magazine that is widely distributed free of charge.

I need tickets for tonight.	**Il me faut des billets pour ce soir.** *eel muh foh day bee-yeh poor suh swahr*

Two _____ seats.	**Deux places _____.**	*duh plahss*
■ orchestra	**à l'orchestre**	*ah lohr-kehss-truh*
■ balcony	**au balcon**	*oh bahl-koh<u>n</u>*
■ first balcony	**au premier balcon**	*oh pruh-myay bahl-koh<u>n</u>*
■ mezzanine	**au parterre**	*oh pahr-tehr*

OPERA-BALLET-CONCERTS

We would like to go to _____.	**Nous voudrions aller à _____.**	*noo voo-dree-yoh<u>n</u> zah-lay ah*
■ a ballet	**un ballet**	*uh<u>n</u> bah-leh*
■ a concert	**un concert**	*uh<u>n</u> koh<u>n</u>-ssehr*
■ an opera	**un opéra**	*uh<u>n</u> noh-pay-rah*
Is there a _____ nearby?	**Il y a par ici _____?**	*eel yah pahr ee-ssee*
■ concert hall	**une salle de concert**	*ewn sahl duh koh<u>n</u>-ssehr*
■ opera house	**un opéra**	*uh<u>n</u> noh-pay-rah*
What are they playing?	**Qu'est-ce qu'on joue?**	*kehss koh<u>n</u> zhoo*
Who is the conductor?	**Qui est le chef d'orchestre?**	*kee eh luh shehf dohr-kehss-truh*
I prefer _____.	**Je préfère _____.**	*zhuh pray-fehr*
■ classical music	**la musique classique**	*lah mew-zeek klah-sseek*
■ modern music	**la musique moderne**	*lah mew-zeek moh-dehrn*
■ folk dances	**les danses folkloriques**	*lay dahnss fohl-kloh-reek*

Are there any seats for tonight's performance?	**Il y a des places pour ce soir?** *eel yah day plahss poor suh swahr*
When does the season end?	**Quand se termine la saison théâtrale?** *kahn suh tehr-meen lah seh-zohn tay-ah-trahl*
Should I get the tickets in advance?	**Faut-il acheter les billets d'avance?** *foh teel ahsh-tay lay bee ych dah-vahnss*
Do I have to dress formally?	**La tenue de soirée est de rigueur?** *lah tuh-new duh swah-ray eh duh ree-guhr*
How much are the front row seats?	**Combien coûtent les places au premier rang?** *kohn-byan koot lay plahss oh pruh-myay rahn*
What are the least expensive seats?	**Quelles sont les places les moins chères?** *kehl sohn lay plahss lay mwan shehr*
How much are the tickets?	**Combien coûtent les billets?** *kohn-byan koot lay bee-yeh*
May I have a program?	**Un programme, s'il vous plaît.** *uhn proh-grahm seel voo pleh*
What opera are they putting on?	**Quel opéra jouent-ils?** *kehl oh-pay-rah zhoo teel*
Who's singing?	**Qui chante?** *kee shahnt*
Who's playing the lead?	**Qui joue le rôle principal?** *kee zhoo luh rohl pran-ssee-pahl*
Who are the members of the cast?	**Qui sont les membres de la troupe?** *kee sohn lay mahn-bruh duh lah troop*

Who is _____?	**Qui est _____?** *kee eh*
■ the tenor	**le ténor** *luh tay-nohr*
■ the baritone	**le baryton** *luh bah-ree-toh<u>n</u>*
■ the soprano	**le soprano** *luh soh-prah-noh*
■ the bass	**la basse** *lah bahss*

NIGHTCLUBS

If it's lively entertainment you want, try the bars, nightclubs, and discos in the major cities. Paris, of course, offers the widest selection of things to do. Nightclubs, providing dinner and a show, are very expensive. A late night drink at a jazz spot or bar might interest you. Discos abound with the latest in music and special lighting effects.

Let's go to a nightclub!	**Allons dans une boîte de nuit!** *ah-loh<u>n</u> dah<u>n</u> zewn bwaht duh nwee*
Is a reservation necessary?	**Faut-il réserver?** *foh teel ray-zehr-vay*
I feel like dancing.	**J'ai envie de danser.** *zhay ah<u>n</u>-vee du<u>h</u> dah<u>n</u>-ssay*

Is there a discotheque here?	**Il y a une discothèque par ici?** *eel yah ewn deess-koh-tehk pahr ee-ssee*
I'd like a table near the dance floor.	**Je voudrais avoir une table près de la piste (de danse).** *zhuh voo-dreh zuh-vwahr ewn tah-bluh preh duh lah peesst (duh dahnss)*
Is there a minimum (cover charge)?	**Il y a un prix d'entrée?** *eel yah uhn pree dahn-tray*
Where is the checkroom?	**Où est le vestiaire?** *oo eh luh vehss-tyehr*
At what time does the show begin?	**À quelle heure commence le spectacle?** *ah kehl uhr koh-mahnss luh spehk-tah-kluh*

CASINOS

While on the Côte d'Azur you must visit the world-famous Casino of Monte Carlo in Monaco. Unlike many other casinos, admission is free. There are other casinos throughout France, all of which are licensed, regulated, and monitored by the French government. A passport is needed to enter. Admission is restricted to adults (over 21 years of age).

QUIET RELAXATION

I would like to play cards.	**Je voudrais jouer aux cartes.** *zhuh voo-dreh zhoo-ay oh kahrt*
■ bridge	**au bridge** *oh breedzh*
■ black jack	**au black-jack** *oh blahk-zhahk*
■ poker	**au poker** *oh poh-kehr*
Where can I get a deck of cards?	**Où puis-je obtenir des cartes à jouer?** *oo pweezh ohp-tuh-neer day kahrt ah zhoo-ay*

Do you want to play ____?	**Voulez-vous jouer ____?** *voo-lay voo zhoo-ay*
■ checkers	**aux dames** *oh dahm*
■ dominoes	**aux dominos** *oh doh-mee-noh*
■ chess	**aux échecs** *oh zay-shehk*

____ is missing.	____ **manque.** *mah<u>n</u>k*
■ the king	**le roi** *luh rwah*
■ the queen	**la reine** *lah rehn*
■ the rook	**la tour** *lah toor*
■ the bishop	**le fou** *luh foo*
■ the knight	**le cavalier** *luh kah-vah-lyay*
■ the pawn	**le pion** *luh pee-yoh<u>n</u>*

SPORTS

Golf, tennis, swimming, cycling, skiing, basketball, ice-skating, fishing, hiking, and sailing are recreational activities in which you can participate throughout the country.

Boxing and wrestling matches, soccer, rugby, and pelote (jai alai) matches draw large crowds of spectators.

Two special events that attract natives and tourists alike are **Le Tour de France,** a three-week bicycle race across France (held each June) and **Le Mans,** a 24-hour Formula One auto race (also in June).

I like to play (do) ____.	**J'aime faire ____.** *zhehm fehr*
■ aerobics	**de l'aérobic (m.)** *duh lahy-roh-beek*
■ baseball	**du base-ball** *dew bayss-bohl*
■ basketball	**du basket-ball** *dew bahss-keht-bohl*
■ bicycling	**du vélo** *dew vay-loh*
■ boating	**du canotage** *dew kah-noh-tahzh*
■ bodybuilding	**de la musculation** *duh lah mew-skew-lah-syoh<u>n</u>*
■ canoeing	**du canoë** *dew kah-noh-ay*

- cycling **du cyclisme** *dew see-kleez-muh*
- diving **du plongeon** *dew plohn-zhohn*
- fishing **de la pêche** *duh lah pehsh*
- deep-sea fishing **de la pêche sous-marine** *duh lah pehsh soo mah-reen*
- football **du football américain** *dew foot-bohl ah-may-ree-kan*
- golf **du golf** *dew gohlf*
- hockey **du hockey** *dew oh-kee*
- horseback riding **de l'équitation (f.)** *duh lay-kee-tah-syohn*
- hunting **de la chasse** *duh lah shahss*
- ice skating **du patin à glace** *dew pah-tan ah glahss*
- jai alai **de la pelote (basque)** *duh luh puh-loht (bahsk)*
- jogging **du jogging** *dew zhoh-geeng*
- mountain climbing **de l'alpinisme (m.)** *duh lahl pee neez-muh*
- parasailing **du parachutisme** *dew pah-rah-shew-teez-muh*
- ping-pong **du ping-pong** *dew peeng-pohng*
- roller skating **du patin à roulettes** *dew pah-tan ah roo-leht*
- rugby **du rugby** *dew rewg-bee*
- sailing **du bateau à voiles** *dew bah-toh ah vwahl*
- scuba diving **de la plongée sous-marine** *duh lah plohn-zhay soo-mah-reen*
- skating **du patin** *dew pah-tan*
- skiing **du ski** *dew skee*
- soccer **du football** *dew foot-bohl*
- surfing **du surf** *dew sewrf*
- swimming **de la natation** *duh lah nah-tah-syohn*

- tennis **du tennis** *dew teh-nees*
- track and field **de l'athlétisme** *duh laht-lay-teez-muh*
- volleyball **du volley-ball** *dew voh-lee-bohl*
- waterskiing **du ski nautique** *dew skee noh-teek*
- windsurfing **de la planche à voiles** *duh lah plah<u>n</u>sh ah vwahl*

How about a game of golf?	**On fait une partie de golf?** *oh<u>n</u> feh tewn parh-tee duh gohlf*
How about a game of tennis?	**On fait un match de tennis?** *oh<u>n</u> feh tuh<u>n</u> mahtch duh teh-neess*

PLAYING FIELDS

Shall we go (to the) _____?	**On va _____?** *oh<u>n</u> vah*
Let's go (to the) _____.	**Allons _____.** *ah-loh<u>n</u>z*

- beach **à la plage** *ah lah plahzh*
- course (golf) **au parcours** *oh pahr-koor*
- court **au court** *oh koohr*
- court (jai alai) **au fronton** *oh froh<u>n</u>-toh<u>n</u>*
- field **au terrain** *oh teh-ra<u>n</u>*
- gymnasium **au gymnase** *oh zheem-nahz*
- mountain **à la montagne** *ah lah moh<u>n</u>-tah-nyuh*
- ocean **à l'océan (m.)** *ah loh-say-ah<u>n</u>*
- park **au parc** *oh pahrk*
- path **au sentier** *oh sah<u>n</u>-tyay*
- pool **à la piscine** *ah lah pee-sseen*
- rink **à la patinoire** *ah lah pah-tee-nwahr*
- sea **à la mer** *ah lah mehr*
- slope **à la piste** *ah lah peesst*
- stadium **au stade** *oh stahd*
- track **à la piste** *ah lah peesst*

SPORTS EQUIPMENT

I need _____.   **Il me faut _____.** *eel muh foh*

Could you lend   **Pourriez-vous me prêter (louer)**
(rent) me _____?   **_____?** *poor-yay voo muh preh-tay*
                         (loo-ay)

■ ball (football,   **un ballon** *uhn bah-lohn*
  soccer)

■ ball (jai alai)   **une pelote** *ewn puh-loht*

■ ball (baseball,   **une balle** *ewn bahl*
  tennis)

■ bat   **une batte** *ewn baht*

■ bicycle   **un vélo** *uhn vay-loh*
                       une bicyclette *ewn bee-ssee-kleht*

■ boat   **un bateau** *uhn bah-toh*

■ boots (ski)   **des chaussures de ski (f.)** *day*
                       shoh-sewr duh skee

■ canoe   **un canoë** *uhn kah-noh-ay*

■ diving suit   **un scaphandre** *uhn skah-fahn-*
                       druh

■ fishing rod   **une canne à pêche** *ewn kahn ah*
                       pehsh

■ flippers   **des nageoires (f.)** *day nahzh-wahr*

■ goggles   **des lunettes protectrices (f.)**
                       day lew-neht proh-tehk-treess

■ golf clubs   **des club de golf (m.)** *day klewb*
                       duh gohlf

■ helmet (diver's)   **un casque de scaphandre** *uhn*
                       kahsk duh skah-fahn-druh

■ jogging shoes   **des joggers** *day zhohg-gehr*

■ jogging suit   **un survêt** *uhn sewr-veh*

■ kneepads   **des genouillères (f.)** *day zhuh-*
                       noo-yehr

■ mitt   **un gant** *uhn gahn*

- net **un filet** *uhn fee-leh*
- poles (ski) **des bâtons (m.)** *day bah-tohn*
- puck (hockey) **une rondelle** *ewn rohn-dehl* (Canada)
  un palet *uhn pah-leh (France)*
- racquet **une raquette** *ewn rah-keht*
- sailboard **une planche à voile** *ewn plahnsh ah vwahl*
- skateboard **une planche à roulettes** *ewn plahnsh ah roo-leht*
- skates **des patins (m.)** *day pah-tan*
  - roller **à roulettes** *ah roo-leht*
  - ice **à glace** *ah glahss*
- ski bindings **des fixations de ski** *day feek-sah-syohn duh skee*
- skis **des skis (m.)** *day skee*
- stick (hockey) **une crosse** *ewn krohss*
- surfboard **une planche de surf** *ewn plahnsh duh sewrf*
- water skis **des skis nautiques (m.)** *day skee noh-teek*
- weights **des haltères (m.)** *day zahl-tehr*
- wet suit **une combinaison de plongée** *ewn kohn-bee-neh-zohn duh plohn-zhay*

SPECTATOR SPORTS

SOCCER

I'd like to see a soccer match.	**Je voudrais voir un match de football.** *zhuh voo-dreh vwahr uhn mahtch duh foot-bohl*
Where's the stadium?	**Où est le stade?** *oo eh luh stahd*

At what time does the match begin?	**Le match commence à quelle heure?** *luh mahtch koh-mah<u>n</u>ss ah kehl uhr*
When are they going to kick off?	**Quand vont-ils donner le coup d'envoi?** *kah<u>n</u> voh<u>n</u> teel doh nay luh koo dah<u>n</u>-vwah*
What teams are playing?	**Quelles équipes jouent?** *kehl zay-keep zhoo*
What is the score?	**Quel est le score?** *kehl eh luh skohr*

JAI ALAI

I'd like to see a jai alai match.	**Je voudrais voir un match de pelote.** *zhuh voo-dreh vwahr uh<u>n</u> mahtch duh puh-loht*
Where can I get tickets?	**Où puis-je me procurer des billets?** *oo pweezh muh proh-kew-ray day bee-yeh*
Where is the jai alai court?	**Où est le fronton?** *oo eh luh froh<u>n</u>-toh<u>n</u>*
Where do I place my bet?	**Où fait-on les paris?** *oo feh-toh<u>n</u> lay pah-ree*
Where is the window?	**Où est le guichet?** *oo eh luh gee-sheh*

HORSE RACING

Is there a racetrack here?	**Il y a un champ de courses par ici?** *eel yah uh<u>n</u> shah<u>n</u> duh koorss pahr ee-ssee*
I want to see the horse races.	**Je voudrais voir les courses de chevaux.** *zhuh voo-dreh vwahr lay koorss duh shuh-voh*

ACTIVE SPORTS

TENNIS

Do you play tennis?	**Jouez-vous au tennis?** *zhoo-ay voo oh teh-neess*
I'd like to play tennis.	**Je voudrais jouer au tennis.** *zhuh voo-dreh-zhoo-ay oh teh-neess*
I (don't) play very well.	**Je (ne) joue (pas) bien.** *zhuh (nuh) zhoo (pah) byan*
Do you know where there is a (good) court?	**Savez-vous où se trouve un bon court de tennis?** *sah-vay voo oo suh troov uhn bohn koohr duh teh-neess*
Can I rent racquets and balls?	**Puis-je louer des raquettes et des balles?** *pweezh loo-ay day rah-keht ay day bahl*
How much do they charge per hour (per day)?	**Quel est le tarif à l'heure/à la journée?** *kehl eh luh tah-reef ah luhr/ah lah zhoor-nay*
I serve (You serve) first.	**C'est à moi (à vous) le premier service.** *seh tah mwah (tah voo) luh pruh-myay sehr-veess*
You play very well.	**Vous jouez très bien.** *voo zhoo-ay treh byan*
You've won.	**Vous avez gagné.** *voo zah-vay gah-nyay*
I've won.	**J'ai gagné.** *zhay gah-nyay*
It's a tie.	**Match nul.** *mahtch newl*

BEACH/POOL

Oh! It's hot.	**Oh là là! Quelle chaleur!** *oh lah lah kehl shah-luhr*
I'd like to go to the beach (to the pool).	**J'ai envie d'aller a la plage (à la piscine).** *zhay ahn-vee dah-lay ah lah plahzh (ah lah pee-sseen)*
Is there a beach nearby?	**Il y a une plage tout près?** *eel yah ewn plahzh too preh*
How do you get there?	**On y va comment?** *ohn nee vah koh-mahn*
Which bus will take us to the beach?	**Quel bus faut-il prendre pour aller à la plage?** *kehl bewss foh teel prahn-druh poor ah-lay ah lah plahzh*
Is there a pool in the hotel?	**Il y a une piscine à l'hôtel?** *eel yah ewn pee-sseen ah loh-tehl*
Is it an indoor (outdoor) pool?	**Est-ce une piscine couverte (en plein air)?** *ehss ewn pee-sseen koo-vehrt (ahn pleh nehr)*
I (don't) know how to swim well.	**Je (ne) sais (pas) bien nager.** *zhuh (nuh) seh (pah) byan nah-zhay*
Is it safe to swim here?	**Peut-on nager ici sans danger?** *puh-tohn nah-zhay ee-ssee sahn dahn-zhay*
Are the waves big?	**Il y a de grandes vagues?** *eel yah duh grahnd vahg*
Are there sharks?	**Il y a des requins?** *eel yah day ruh-kan*
Is there any danger for children?	**Il y a du danger pour les enfants?** *eel yah dew dahn-zhay poor lay zahn-fahn*

Is there a lifeguard? **Il y a un maître-nageur?** *eel yah uhn meh-truh nah-zhuhr*

Where can I get _____? **Où puis-je obtenir _____?** *oo pweezh ohp-tuh-neer*

■ an air mattress **un matelas pneumatique** *uhn maht-lah pnuh-mah-teek*

■ a bathing suit **un maillot de bain** *uhn mah-yoh duh ban*

■ a beach ball **un ballon de plage** *uhn bah-lohn duh plahzh*

■ a beach chair **une chaise longue pour la plage** *ewn shehz lohng poor lah plahzh*

■ a beach towel **une serviette de plage** *ewn sehr-vyeht duh plahzh*

■ a chaise lounge **une chaise longue** *ewn shehz lohng*

■ sunglasses **des lunettes de soleil** *day lew-neht duh soh-leh*

■ suntan lotion **la lotion pour bronzer** *lah loh-ssyohn poor brohn-zay*

■ a surfboard **une planche de surf** *ewn plahnsh duh sewrf*

■ water skis **des skis nautiques** *day skee noh-teek*

ON THE SLOPES

Which ski area do you recommend? **Quelle station de ski recommandez-vous?** *kehl stah-ssyohn duh skee ruh-koh-mahn-day voo*

I am a novice (intermediate, expert) skier. **Je suis un(e) débutant(e) (un skieur moyen; un expert).** *zhuh swee zuhn (zewn) day bew-tahn(t) (zuhn skee-uhr mwah-yan/uhn ehks-pehr)*

What kind of lifts are there?	**Il y a quel type de téléski?** *eel yah kehl teep duh tay-lay-sskee*
How much does the lift cost?	**Combien coûte le trajet?** *kohn-byan koot luh trah-zheh*
Do they give lessons?	**On donne des leçons?** *ohn dohn day luh-ssohn*
Is there any cross-country skiing?	**On fait du ski de fond?** *ohn feh dew skee duh fohn*

Is there enough snow this time of year?	**Il y a assez de neige en ce moment?** *eel yah ah-ssay duh nehzh ahn suh moh-mahn*
How do I get there?	**On va comment à cet endroit-là?** *ohn vah koh-mahn ah seht ahn-drwah lah*
Can I rent ____ there?	**Peut-on y louer ____?** *puh-tohn nee loo-ay*

■ equipment	**un équipement de ski** *uhn nay-keep-mahn duh skee*
■ poles	**des bâtons** *day bah-tohn*
■ skis	**des skis** *day skee*
■ ski bindings	**des fixations de ski** *day feek-ssah-syohn duh skee*
■ ski boots	**des chaussures de ski** *day shoh-ssewr duh skee*

ON THE LINKS

Is there a golf course here?	**Il y a un terrain de golf par ici?** *eel yah uhn teh-ran duh gohlf pahr ee-ssee*
Can one rent clubs?	**Peut-on louer des clubs?** *puh tohn loo-ay day kluhb*

CAMPING

Campgrounds are located all over France. They are often crowded, especially in the month of August when most French families are on vacation. Arrive early to be sure of getting a spot. Campsites are rated by stars; the fewer the stars, the less desirable the site. Most sites have adequate facilities. Students are sometimes offered discounts. A camping permit is sometimes required. You may camp unofficially in a suitable place as long as you have permission from the landowner. Be sure to leave the property in the same condition as you found it.

Is there a camping site near here?	**Il y a un terrain de camping par ici?** *eel yah uhn teh-ran duh kahn-peeng pahr ee-ssee*
Can you show me how to get there?	**Pouvez-vous m'indiquer comment y aller?** *poo-vay voo man-dee-kay koh-mahn tee ah-lay*

Where is it on the map?	**Où se trouve-t-il sur la carte?** *oo suh troov teel sewr lah kahrt*
Where can we park our trailer?	**Où pouvons-nous garer notre caravane?** *oo poo-vohn noo gah-ray noh-truh kah-rah-vahn*
Where can we spend the night?	**Où pouvons-nous passer la nuit?** *oo poo-vohn noo pah-ssay lah nwee*
Can we camp for the night?	**Pouvons-nous camper cette nuit?** *poo-vohn noo kahn-pay seht nwee*
Is there _____?	**Il y a _____?** *eel yah*
■ drinking water	**de l'eau potable** *duh loh poh-tah-bluh*
■ running water	**de l'eau courante** *duh loh koo-rahnt*
■ gas	**du gaz** *dew gahz*
■ electricity	**de l'électricité** *duh lay-lehk-tree-ssee-tay*
■ a children's playground	**un terrain de jeu pour enfants** *uhn teh-ran duh zhuh poor ahn-fahn*
■ a grocery store	**une épicerie** *ewn ay-peess-ree*
■ toilets	**des toilettes** *day twah-leht*
■ showers	**des douches** *day doosh*
■ washrooms	**des lavabos** *day lah-vah-boh*
■ tents	**des tentes** *day tahnt*
■ cooking facilities	**des installations pour faire la cuisine** *day zan-stah-lah-ssyohn poor fehr lah kwee-zeen*
How much do they charge per person? (per trailer)?	**Quel est le tarif par personne (pour une caravane)?** *kehl eh luh tah-reef pahr pehr-ssohn (poor ewn kah-rah-vahn)*

| We intend staying _____ days/weeks. | **Nous comptons rester _____ jours/semaines.** *noo kohn-tohn rehss-tay _____ zhoor/suh-mehn* |

IN THE COUNTRYSIDE

I'd like to drive through the countryside.	**Je voudrais conduire dans la campagne.** *zhuh voo-dreh kohn-dweer dahn lah kahn-pah-nyuh*
Where can I rent a car for the day?	**Où puis-je louer une voiture à la journée?** *oo pweezh loo-ay ewn vwah-tewr ah lah zhoor-nay*
Are there tours to the country?	**Il y a des excursions à la campagne?** *eel yah day zehkss-kewr-zyohn ah lah kahn-pah-nyuh*
When do they leave?	**Quand sont les départs?** *kahn ssohn lay day-pahr*
From where do they leave?	**D'où partent-elles?** *doo pahrt-ehl*
Is there anyone who can drive me?	**Il y a quelqu'un qui puisse me conduire?** *eel yah kehl-kuhn kee pweess muh kohn-dweer*

Look at _____. **Regardez _____.** *ruh-gahr-day*
- the barn **la grange** *lah grahnzh*
- the bridge **le pont** *luh pohn*
- the farm **la ferme** *lah fehrm*
- the fields **les champs** *lay shahn*
- the flowers **les fleurs** *lay fluhr*
- the forest **la forêt** *lah foh-reh*
- the hill **la colline** *lah koh-leen*

- the lake **le lac** *luh lahk*
- the mountains **les montagnes** *lay mohn-tah-nyuh*
- the ocean **l'océan (m.)** *loh-ssay-ahn*
- the plants **les plantes** *lay plahnt*
- the pond **l'étang (m.)** *lay-tahn*
- the river **la rivière** *lah ree-vyehr*
- the stream **le ruisseau** *luh rwee-ssoh*
- the trees **les arbres** *lay zahr-bruh*
- the valley **la vallée** *lah vah-lay*
- the village **le village** *luh vee-lahzh*
- the waterfall **la cascade** *lah kahss-kahd*

Where does this _____ lead to?   **Où mène _____?** *oo mehn*

- path **ce sentier** *suh sahn-tyay*
- road **ce chemin** *suh shuh-man*
- highway **cette grande route** *seht grahnd root*

How far away is _____?   **À quelle distance est _____?** *ah kehl deess-tahnss eh*

- the city **la ville** *lah veel*
- the inn **l'auberge (f.)** *loh-behrzh*

How long does it take to get to _____?   **Combien de temps faut-il pour aller à _____?** *kohn-byan duh tahn foh teel poor ah-lay ah*

I'm lost.   **J'ai perdu mon chemin.** *zhay pehr-dew mohn shuh-man*

Can you show me the way to _____?   **Pouvez-vous m'indiquer le chemin pour _____?** *poo-vay voo man-dee-kay luh shuh-man poor*

FOOD AND DRINK

The world has only a few truly great cuisines, and French is one of them. Respected for its extensive selection of dishes, its inventive uses of ingredients, and its exactness in preparation, French food is always reliably appetizing. French people are inherently great cooks, for they have been developing the elements of good taste since childhood. Wherever you eat in France, whether in Paris or Lyons, in the country or in the city, the food you will be offered will be carefully and lovingly prepared.

The past masters—notably Carême and Escoffier—defined and codified French food, so that you will not find the variations in ingredients or preparations that you notice in most other foods; a hollandaise sauce, for example, will always be made with egg yolks, into which are whisked butter and a dash of vinegar or lemon juice. It will be the same sauce, whether you are enjoying it in a Paris bistro or a country inn. What will vary will be the particularly regional dishes—dishes from the provinces of France that are made chiefly by the cooks in small restaurants and inns.

France's restaurants are famous, and they alone are worth a trip to that country. The most famous ones are those graded with one, two, three, four, or five (best) crossed forks in the *Michelin Guide*. There are other ratings, too, especially from Gault & Millau, that tend to favor restaurants whose chefs prepare the **nouvelle cuisine** dishes. The five-fork restaurants are also among the most expensive and the most formal; these are the towers of **haute cuisine,** and all other restaurants strive to be in that category some day.

Eating in France is a somewhat structured affair. To make your stay enjoyable and to gather a bit of the French flavor, we suggest you follow the French manner of eating. First, here are the types of restaurants you are likely to encounter.

Auberge, Relais, Hostellerie	a country inn.
Bistro	a small neighborhood restaurant in town, similar to a pub or tavern and usually very informal.

Brasserie	a large café that serves quick meals throughout the day or evening; most meals involve only the entrée, such as a steak or chop.
Cabaret	a nightclub where you may also eat a meal.
Café	a neighborhood spot to socialize, either indoors or out, where you can linger over coffee or a glass of wine or beer and perhaps have a little snack. Cafés also serve breakfast (usually a **croissant** and **café au lait**) and later in the day serve soft drinks and ice cream.
Casse-croûte	a restaurant specializing in sandwiches.
Crêperie	a small stand specializing in the preparation of crêpes—thin pancakes dusted with sugar or covered with jam and rolled up.
Fast-food	a small place to eat an American-style snack, mostly hamburgers and French fries; most are in Paris along the Champs-Elysée, and many are American chains such as McDonald's and Burger King.
Restaurant	an establishment that can range from a small, family-owned inn, where mom seats you, dad cooks the meal, and the children serve you, to a formal, three-star palace where you receive the most elegant service and most beautifully garnished foods.
Self	a cafeteria, popular with students and usually located near a university.
Troquet	a wine shop where you can also have a snack.

By law, all establishments serving food must post a menu showing the prices. Most often, you will see two menus posted, one that lists the *à la carte* offerings, and the other that has one, two, or three different *prix fixe* meals. You can, of course, order the dishes you wish following the *à la carte* menu, but the resulting cost will be higher than if you choose one of the menus. The menus are a good choice since they always feature a freshly prepared entrée and usually reflect the specialty of the chef. When there is more than one menu from which to choose, they will differ depending upon the number of courses or the relative value of the entrée; lower-priced menus usually include a grilled steak or chicken dish as entrée, while the higher-priced one might feature an additional cheese course or perhaps both fish and meat courses. In some regions, especially those that receive a number of tourists, you'll often see a special "tourist" menu, which will feature a specialty of the region—cassoulet in Languedoc or truffles in Perigord, for example. Wherever you eat, look for the **plat du jour** (day's specialty) or the **spécialités de la maison** (chef's specialties).

Most menus include a line at the bottom stating that the service charge is included in the price of the meal; it is usually about 15%. It is also customary to leave some small change on the table for the waiter, usually what would round off your bill. If you order a wine other than the house wine, you should also tip the steward, although the service for wine is sometimes also included in the bill. Often, especially in very casual restaurants, the wine is included in the menu (**boisson comprise**). If you want a simple, inexpensive wine, select the house wine, which will usually be a regional wine; if you want advice in a casual restaurant, ask the waiter—as a Frenchman, he will have been brought up to know wines and will recommend one that you will enjoy drinking with what you are eating (see also pages on wine, 131–135).

MEALS OF THE DAY

Most tourists will have their breakfast in the hotel, so much of the information that follows applies to lunch and dinner. Breakfast, **le petit déjeuner,** is usually small, consisting of a croissant or part of a loaf of day-old French bread, with butter and jam. It is usually served with **café au lait**—a large cup or bowl of hot coffee mixed half-and-half with steamed milk; this breakfast is called **café complet** and it is what you will most often be served, especially if breakfast is included in the cost of your room. You may also order hot tea or hot chocolate for breakfast.

Lunch and dinner in France are about the same in character and courses. Lunch, referred to as **le déjeuner,** is usually served between 12:30 and 3:00 P.M. Especially in smaller towns or on the road, be sure to stop early—by 12:15 to secure a table for lunch; many local spots have reserved tables for residents; you'll even see their napkins saved from the previous day.

In warm weather, do what many French people do for lunch—picnic. Especially if you are sightseeing and don't want to take the time for a lengthy lunch, buy some French bread in a **boulangerie**, then go next door to the **charcuterie** for 100 grams of **pâté de campagne**, stop in an **épicerie** for salads or sliced tomatoes and some cheese, and also pick up a bottle of wine or mineral water. Take the food to a park or stop along the road in a field and enjoy your lunch. In France, you'll find the roads are vacated by 12:30, and everyone has pulled over, set up tables, and begun to eat. In Paris, they will go to the **Jardin des Plantes** or **Bois de Boulogne.**

Dinner (**le dîner**) is a bit more formal than lunch and usually served more graciously. In Paris, people eat late—8:00 P.M. is the earliest—while in the country, you can properly begin by 7:30. It is a time for the enjoyment of food and wine, and a meal can carry on for at least two hours. Most French people do not begin their meal with a cocktail, but sometimes will have an apéritif. The meal consists of the following courses, in this order: cold or hot hors d'oeuvres, soup, fish, meat or poultry with accompanying vegetables, cheese, dessert. In recent years, lighter eating patterns have cut down on the number of courses, and you can of course decline a particular course.

In the specialty restaurants—those particularly noted for their food—you will often see a **menu dégustation** or a **menu gastronomique.** The former is a dinner in which you receive a sampling of a large number of items on the menu, so as to try many of the chef's dishes—this is most popular in

nouvelle cuisine restaurants. The latter is a special menu for food lovers that features rare items or dishes that are difficult to prepare.

TYPES OF FRENCH COOKING

The basics of French food were established centuries ago, but there have been developments in recent years that have released this food from its straitjacket. The following is a breakdown of the types of food you are likely to encounter.

Haute Cuisine — This is classic French cooking, offered in the top restaurants. The food is refined and exquisitely presented.

Cuisine Bourgeoise — This is the country food of France, made for centuries in everyday kitchens; it is from this cuisine that **haute cuisine** was developed. This is the food you'll have in most bistros and small restaurants.

Nouvelle Cuisine — Developed in the 1970s and now less popular, this food represented a break from traditional flour-based sauces and rigid rules. Fruits were combined with meats and fish, sauces were reduced until thickened, and salads with elaborate arrangements were developed. This cuisine was promoted by such leaders as Paul Bocuse, Roger Vergé, and the Troisgros brothers; its influences are still apparent in most restaurants.

Cuisine Minceur — A special diet-conscious cuisine developed by Michel Guérard.

Nowadays, you'll find that menus will include a mixture of dishes—some considered **nouvelle cuisine** and others more along the line of traditional provincial food.

EATING OUT

Do you know a good restaurant?	**Connaissez-vous un bon restaurant?** *koh-neh-ssay voo uhn bohn rehss-toh-rahn*
It is very expensive?	**C'est très cher?** *seh treh shehr*
Do you know a restaurant that serves regional dishes?	**Connaissez-vous un restaurant de de cuisine régionale?** *koh neh ssay voo uhn rehss-toh-rahn duh kwee-zeen ray-zhyoh-nahl*
I'd like to make a reservation _____.	**Je voudrais retenir une table _____.** *zhuh voo-dreh ruh-tuh-neer ewn tah-bluh*
▦ for tonight	**pour ce soir** *poor suh swahr*
▦ for tomorrow evening	**pour demain soir** *poor duh-man swahr*
▦ for two (four) persons	**pour deux (quatre) personnes** *poor duh (kah-truh) pehr-ssohn*
▦ at 8 (8:30 P.M.)	**à vingt heures (vingt heures trente)** *ah van-tuhr (van-tuhr truhnt)*
Waiter!	**Monsieur! (Garçon!)** *muh-ssyuh (gahr-son)*
Miss!	**Mademoiselle!** *mahd-mwah-zehl*
A table for two in the corner (near the window).	**Une table pour deux dans un coin (près de la fenêtre).** *ewn tah-bluh poor duh dahn zuhn kwan (preh duh lah fuh-neh-truh)*
We'd like to have lunch (dinner) now.	**Nous voudrions déjeuner (dîner) maintenant.** *noo voo-dree-yohn day-zhuh-nay (dee-nay) mant-nahn*

The menu, please.

La carte (Le menu), s'il vous plaît.
lah kahrt (luh muh-new) seel voo pleh

I'd like the price-fixed menu.

Je voudrais le menu prix-fixe.
zhuh voo-dreh luh muh-new pree feekss

What's today's special?

Quel est le plat du jour? *kehl eh luh plah dew zhoor*

What's the house specialty?

Quelle est la spécialité de la maison? *kehl eh lah spay-ssyah-lee-tay duh lah meh-zohn*

What do you recommend?

Qu'est-ce que vous me recommandez? *kehss kuh voo muh ruh-koh-mahn-day*

Do you serve children's portions?

Servez-vous des demi-portions pour les enfants? *sehr-vay voo day duh-mee pohr-ssyohn poor lay zahn-fahn*

I'm (not) very hungry.

J'ai (Je n'ai pas) très faim.
zhay (zhuh nay pah) treh fan

We're in a hurry.

Nous sommes pressés. *noo sohm preh-ssay*

Will it take long?

Il faudra longtemps? *eel foh-drah lohn-tahn*

To begin with, bring _____.

Pour commencer, apportez _____.
poor koh-mahn-ssay, ah-pohr-tay

■ an apéritif

un apéritif *uhn nah-pay-ree-teef*

■ a cocktail

un cocktail *uhn kohk-tehl*

■ some white (red, rosé) wine

du vin blanc (rouge, rosé) *dew van blahn (roozh, roh-zay)*

■ some water

de l'eau *duh loh*

■ a bottle of mineral water, with (without) carbonation	**une bouteille d'eau minérale gazeuse (plate)** *ewn boo-tehy doh mee-nay-rahl gah-zuhz (plaht)*
■ a beer	**une bière** *ewn byehr*

I'd like to order now.	**Je voudrais commander maintenant.** *zhuh voo-dreh koh-mahn-day mant-nahn*
I'd like ____.	**Je voudrais ____.** *zhuh voo-dreh*

(See the listings that follow for individual dishes, and also the regional specialties noted on pages 130–131.)

Do you have a house wine?	**Avez-vous du vin ordinaire?** *ah-vay voo dew van ohr-dee-nehr*
Is it dry (mellow, sweet)?	**Est-ce sec (moelleux, doux)?** *ehss sehk (mwah-luh, doo)*
Please bring us ____.	**Apportez-nous s'il vous plaît ____.** *ah-pohr-tay noo seel voo pleh*
■ rolls	**des petits pains** *day puh-tee pan*
■ bread	**du pain** *dew pan*
■ butter	**du beurre** *dew buhr*
Waiter, we need ____.	**Monsieur (Garçon), apportez-nous ____, s'il vous plaît.** *muh-ssyuh (gahr-son) ah-pohr-tay noo ____ seel voo pleh*
■ a bowl	**un bol** *uhn bohl*
■ a carafe	**un carafe** *uhn kah-rahf*
■ a cup	**une tasse** *ewn tahss*
■ a dinner plate	**une assiette** *ewn-nah-syeht*
■ a fork	**une fourchette** *ewn foor-sheht*
■ a glass	**un verre** *uhn vehr*

■ a knife	**un couteau**	*uhn koo-to*
■ a menu	**un menu, une carte**	*uhn muh-new, ewn kahrt*
■ a napkin	**une serviette**	*ewn sehr-vyeht*
■ a place setting	**un couvert**	*uhn koo-vehr*
■ a saucer	**une soucoupe**	*ewn soo-koop*
■ a soup dish	**une assiette à soupe**	*ewn-nah-syeht ah soop*
■ a tablecloth	**une nappe**	*ewn nahp*
■ a teaspoon	**une cuiller**	*ewn kwee-yehr*
■ a toothpick	**un cure-dent**	*uhn kewr-dahn*
■ a wineglass	**un verre à vin**	*uhn vehr ah van*

APPETIZERS (STARTERS)

Appetizers can be either hot or cold; if you order both, have the cold one first. The following are among the most common items you'll see on a menu.

- **Artichauts à la vinaigrette:** Artichokes in a vinaigrette dressing.

- **Crudités variées:** Assorted vegetables—sliced tomatoes, shredded carrots, sliced cooked beets—in a vinaigrette dressing.

- **Escargots à la bourguignonne:** Snails cooked and served in the shell, seasoned with a garlic, shallot, and parsley butter.

- **Foie gras:** Fresh, often uncooked liver of a force-fed goose; sliced and served with toasted French bread slices.

- **Pâté:** Any of a number of meat loaves, made from puréed liver and usually also with meat—pork, veal, or chicken. **Pâté de foie gras** is made with goose liver; **pâté de campagne** is "of the country" and is a coarser mixed meat pâté; **pâté en croute** is a liver pâté encased in pastry.

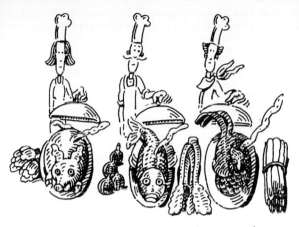

- **Quiche lorraine:** An egg custard tart, sometimes with bacon strips or bits; some versions now also made with Gruyère cheese.

- **Quenelles:** Light dumplings, usually made from **brochet** (pike) but also from shellfish; served in a white sauce.

- **Rillettes:** A pork mixture that has been potted, then served as a spread, usually with French bread.

- **Terrine:** A type of pâté, usually served from a deep pot rather than sliced as pâté would be. Terrines can be made from pork, poultry, game, or fish.

SOUPS

Some of those that appear on menus are the following.

- **Bisque d'écrevisses:** A creamy soup made with crawfish; other bisques are made with lobster, shrimp, or oysters.

- **Bouillabaisse:** A seafood stew, made with a variety of fish and shellfish depending on the region, seasoned with saffron and fennel or pernod.

- **Consommé:** A clear broth, made usually from chicken or beef and flavored with herbs; **en gelée** is consommé that has been jelled and sliced; **madrilène** is with tomatoes; **printanier** has a variety of vegetables.

- **Crème:** A creamy soup, made from any of a number of vegetables and usually enriched with egg yolks. **D'Argenteuil** is cream of asparagus soup; **de volaille** is a creamy chicken soup.

- **Petite marmite:** A rich consommé served with meat and vegetables.

- **Potage:** A coarser soup, usually made with a purée of vegetables; some varieties of potage are **parmentier** (leeks and potatoes), **au cresson** (watercress), and **julienne** (shredded vegetables).

- **Soupe à l'oignon:** Famous French onion soup, served over French bread and covered with cheese.

- **Velouté:** A creamy soup, most common of which are **de volaille** (cream of chicken) and **de tomate** (tomato).

EGG DISHES

As is true for most of the continent, eggs are not eaten for breakfast but rather are served as a beginning course in a variety of preparations.

- **Oeufs bercy:** Eggs baked with sausages in a tomato sauce.

- **Oeufs en cocotte:** Eggs gently baked in individual cups until softly cooked, sometimes with cream, then eaten with a spoon.

- **Oeufs en gelée:** Poached eggs that are set into jelled consommé and served chilled as a salad.

- **Omelette:** A French omelette is puffy and contains a variety of fillings—**aux fines herbes** is with a mixture of parsley, chives, and tarragon.

● **Piperade:** Scrambled eggs mixed with tomatoes, onions, and sweet peppers.

● **Soufflé:** Soufflés can be made with almost any ingredients—vegetables, chicken livers, cheese, ham, and so on; they are always light and puffy.

FISH COURSE

The French often eat a fish course preceding meat or poultry. You can also order the fish course as your main selection. Here are some of the names for fish and shellfish you'll find on menus; for the names of preparations, see pages 117–120. When there is no price on the menu, the abbreviation s.g. (*selon grosseur*) refers to a dish that is sold by weight.

les anchois	*lay zahn-shwah*	anchovies
les anguilles	*lay zahn-yee*	eel
le bar	*luh bahr*	bass (hake)
la barbue	*lah bahr-bew*	brill
la baudroie	*lah boh-drwah*	anglerfish, monkfish
le brochet	*luh broh-sheh*	pike
le cabillaud	*luh kah-bee-yoh*	cod
le calmar	*luh kahl-mahr*	squid
la carpe	*lah kahrp*	carp
le carrelet	*luh kahr-leh*	flounder
le congre	*luh kohn-gruh*	conger eel
les crevettes	*lay kruh-veht*	shrimp
la daurade	*lah doh-rahd*	porgy
les écrevisses	*lay zay-kruh-veess*	crawfish
les escargots	*lay zehss-kahr-goh*	snails

les harengs (fumés)	*lay ah-rah<u>n</u> (few-may)*	herring (smoked)
le homard	*luh oh-mahr*	lobster
les huîtres	*lay zwee-truh*	oysters
la lamproie	*lah lah<u>n</u>-prwah*	lamprey
la langouste	*lah lah<u>n</u>-goosst*	spiny lobster
les langoustines	*lay lah<u>n</u>-goo-ssteen*	large shrimp
la lotte	*lah loht*	monkfish
le loup de mer	*luh loo duh mehr*	sea bass
le maquereau	*luh mah-kroh*	mackerel
le merlan	*luh mehr-lah<u>n</u>*	whiting
la morue	*lah moh-rew*	cod
les moules	*lay mool*	mussels
les palourdes	*lay pah-loord*	clams
la perche	*lah pehrsh*	perch
les poulpes	*lay poolp*	octopus
la rascasse	*lah rahss-kahss*	scorpionfish
les sardines	*lay sahr-deen*	sardines
le saumon	*luh soh-moh<u>n</u>*	salmon
les scampi	*lay skah<u>n</u>-pee*	large shrimp
le thon	*luh toh<u>n</u>*	tuna
la truite	*lah trweet*	trout
le turbot	*luh tewr-boh*	European turbot

POULTRY AND GAME

The French have several names for chicken, depending on its size or age. They also have varying names for duck and some game. Below are some of the more common terms you'll see on menus:

la caille	*lah kahy*	quail
le cerf	*luh sehr*	venison
le canard, caneton	*luh kah-nahr, kahn-tohn*	duckling
le chapon	*luh shah-pohn*	capon
le chevreuil	*luh shuh-vruhy*	venison
le cochon de lait	*luh koh-shohn duh leh*	suckling pig
la dinde	*lah dand*	turkey
le faisan	*luh feh-zahn*	pheasant
le lapin	*luh lah-pan*	rabbit
le lièvre	*luh lyeh-vruh*	hare
l'oie (f.)	*lwah*	goose
le perdreau, la perdrix	*luh pehr-droh, lah pehr-dree*	partridge
le pigeon, le pigeonneau	*luh pee-zhohn, luh pee-zhoh-noh*	squab
la pintade, le pintadeau	*lah pan-tahd, luh pan-tah-doh*	guinea fowl
la poule	*lah pool*	stewing fowl
le poulet, poussin, la volaille	*luh poo-leh, poo-ssan, lah voh-lahy*	chicken

Suprême de volaille is the fillet from a young chicken breast, usually served with a sauce or garnish.

MEATS

Here are some basic terms for different kinds of meat, followed by a listing of some common cuts of meat and other terms you'll find on a menu.

l'agneau (m.)	*lah-nyoh*	lamb
le boeuf	*luh buhf*	beef
la chèvre	*lah sheh-vruh*	goat
le jambon	*luh zhah<u>n</u>-boh<u>n</u>*	ham
le mouton	*luh moo-toh<u>n</u>*	mutton
le porc	*luh pohr*	pork
le veau	*luh voh*	veal
les andouilles	*lay zah<u>n</u>-dooy*	pork sausages
le bifteck	*luh beef-tehk*	steak
le boudin	*luh boo-da<u>n</u>*	blood sausage
le carré d'agneau	*luh kah-ray dah-nyoh*	rack of lamb
le cervelas	*luh sehr-vuh-lah*	garlicky pork sausage
la cervelle	*lah sehr-vehl*	brains
la charcuterie	*lah shahr-kew-tree*	assorted sausages, pâtés, and terrines
le chateaubriand	*luh shah-toh-bree-ah<u>n</u>*	porterhouse steak
la côte de boeuf	*lah koht duh buhf*	ribs of beef
les côtelettes	*lay koht-leht*	cutlets

les côtes de porc, de veau	*lay koht duh pohr, duh voh*	chops, pork or veal
les crépinettes	*lay kray-pee-neht*	small sausages
l'entrecôte (f.)	*lahn-truh-koht*	sirloin steak
l'escalope (f.)	*lehss-kah-lohp*	cutlet
le filet de boeuf	*luh fee-leh duh buhf*	fillet of beef
le foie	*luh fwah*	liver
le gigot d'agneau	*luh zhee-goh dah-nyoh*	leg of lamb
la langue	*lah luh<u>ng</u>*	tongue
le lard	*luh lahr*	bacon
les médaillons de veau	*lay may-dah-yoh<u>n</u> duh voh*	medallions of veal
les noisettes	*lay nwah-zeht*	small fillets
les pieds de porc	*lay pyay duh pohr*	pig's feet
le ris de veau	*luh ree duh voh*	veal sweetbreads
les rognons d'agneau	*lay roh-nyoh<u>n</u> dah-nyoh*	lamb kidneys
le rosbif	*luh rohss-beef*	roast beef
les saucisses	*lay soh-sseess*	sausages
la selle d'agneau	*lah sehl dah-nyoh*	saddle of lamb
le steak	*luh stehk*	steak
le tournedos	*luh toor-nuh-doh*	small fillets of beef
les tripes	*lay treep*	tripe

I like it _____.	**Je le (la) prefère _____.**	*zhuh luh (lah) pray-fehr*
baked	**cuit au four**	*kwee(t) o foor*
boiled	**bouilli**	*boo-yee*
braised (stewed)	**braisé(e)**	*breh-zay*
breaded	**au gratin, gratiné**	*o grah-ta<u>n</u>, grah-tee-nay*
broiled	**rôti**	*ro-tee*
browned	**gratiné**	*grah-tee-nay*
chopped	**hâché**	*ah-shay*
fried	**frit(e)**	*free(t)*
grilled	**grillé**	*gree-yay*
in its natural juices	**au jus**	*o zhew*
mashed, pureed	**en purée**	*ah<u>n</u> pew-ray*
poached	**poché**	*poh-shay*
roasted	**rôti**	*ro-tee*
with sauce	**en sauce**	*ah<u>n</u> sos*
sautéed	**sauté**	*so-tay*
steamed	**à la vapeur**	*ah lah vah-puhr*
stewed	**en cocotte**	*ah<u>n</u> koh-koht*
well-done	**très cuit**	*treh kwee*
medium well	**bien cuit**	*bya<u>n</u> kwee*
medium	**à point**	*ah pwa<u>n</u>*
medium rare	**mi-saignant**	*mee seh-nyah<u>n</u>*
rare	**saignant**	*seh-nyah<u>n</u>*
very rare	**bleu**	*bluh*
I prefer my eggs _____.	**Je préfère mes oeufs _____.**	*zhuh pray-fehr may zuh*
fried	**au plat**	*o plah*
hard-boiled	**durs**	*dewr*

■ medium-boiled	**mollets**	*moh-leh*
■ poached	**pochés**	*poh-shay*
■ scrambled	**brouillés**	*broo-yay*
■ soft-boiled	**à la coque**	*ah lah kohk*

PROBLEMS

It's cold.	**C'est froid(e).**	*seh frwah(d)*
It's too rare.	**Ce n'est pas assez cuit(e).**	*suh neh pah zah-say kwee(t)*
It's overcooked.	**C'est trop cuit(e).**	*seh tro kwee(t)*
It's tough.	**C'est dur(e).**	*seh dewr*
It's burned.	**C'est brûlé(e).**	*seh brew-lay*
It's too salty.	**C'est trop salé(e).**	*seh tro sah-lay*
It's too sweet.	**C'est trop sucré(e).**	*seh tro sew-kray*
It's too spicy.	**C'est trop épicé(e).**	*seh tro ay-pee-say*
It doesn't smell good.	**Ça ne sent pas bon.**	*sah nuh sahn pah bohn*
It smells bad.	**Ça sent mauvais.**	*sah sahn moh-veh*
It's spoiled.	**C'est tourné(e).**	*seh toor-nay*
It's bitter.	**C'est aigre.**	*seh tehgr*
It tastes like ____.	**Ça a le goût de ____.**	*sah ah luh goo duh*

PREPARATIONS AND SAUCES

Of necessity, these descriptions are very brief and generalized, but they should give you an impression of what to expect.

● **Aioli:** Mayonnaise heavily flavored with garlic.

● **Allemande:** A light (blond) sauce.

- **À la bonne femme:** White wine sauce with vegetables.

- **Alsacienne:** With sauerkraut.

- **Béarnaise:** A butter-egg sauce flavored with shallots, wine, and tarragon.

- **Bercy:** Basic meat or fish sauce.

- **Beurre blanc:** Butter sauce flavored with shallots and wine.

- **Beurre noir:** Browned butter sauce.

- **Blanquette:** An egg-enriched cream sauce, usually part of a stewed dish.

- **Bordelaise:** A dish prepared with Bordeaux wine.

- **Bourguignonne:** A dish prepared with Burgundy red wine.

- **Bretonne:** A dish that includes beans.

- **Caen:** A dish made with Calvados (apple brandy).

- **Chantilly:** A sauce of whipped cream and hollandaise; as a dessert, made with sweetened whipped cream.

- **Chasseur:** A sauce made with mushrooms, white wine, shallots, and parsley.

- **Choron:** A béarnaise sauce with tomatoes.

- **Coquilles:** A preparation served in a scallop shell.

- **Coulibiac:** A preparation served in a pastry shell.

- **Crécy:** A dish made with carrots.

- **Daube:** A stew, usually beef, made with red wine, onions, and garlic.

- **Demi-deuil:** When slices of truffles are inserted beneath the skin of a chicken.

- **Diable:** A spicy sauce, usually with chili or cayenne pepper.

- **Duxelles:** A mushroom mixture, usually as a stuffing or sauce base.

- **Estragon:** A dish made with tarragon.
- **Farce:** A stuffing, or forcemeat filling.
- **Fenouil:** A sauce made with fennel.
- **Financière:** Madeira sauce with truffles.
- **Fines herbes:** A dish made with a variety of chopped fresh herbs.
- **Florentine:** A dish that includes spinach.
- **Forestière:** A dish made with wild mushrooms.
- **Fricassée:** A stewed or potted dish, usually chicken.
- **Gratin:** A crusty baked dish, named for the dish in which it is cooked.
- **Hollandaise:** An egg yolk and butter sauce, with vinegar or lemon juice.
- **Jardinière:** A dish with fresh vegetables.
- **Lyonnaise:** A preparation made with onions.
- **Madère:** A dish made with madeira wine.
- **Maître d'hôtel:** A butter sauce with parsley and lemon juice.
- **Marchand de vin:** A sauce with a meat stock and red wine.
- **Meunière:** A simple dish lightly dusted with flour and sautéed, served in a lemon-butter sauce.
- **Mornay:** A simple white sauce with grated cheese, usually gruyère.
- **Mousseline:** A hollandaise sauce with whipped cream.
- **Moutarde:** With mustard.
- **Nantua:** A basic white sauce with cream and shellfish.
- **Normande:** Either a fish sauce with oysters or shrimp, or a sauce with apples.

- **Parmentier:** A dish with potatoes.
- **Périgourdine:** With truffles.
- **Poivrade:** A dark sauce, seasoned with pepper.
- **Provençale:** A vegetable garnish, usually with tomatoes, olives, anchovies, and garlic.
- **Quenelles:** Light-as-air dumplings made from fish or shellfish.
- **Ragoût:** A thick stew.
- **Rémoulade:** A mayonnaise flavored with mustard and sometimes capers.
- **Véronique:** A dish with grapes.
- **Verte:** A green mayonnaise, flavored with parsley and other herbs.
- **Vinaigrette:** An oil and vinegar dressing for salads.
- **Vol-au-vent:** A puff-pastry shell in which a creamed meat dish is usually served.

VEGETABLES

l'artichaut (m.)	*lahr-tee-shoh*	artichoke
les asperges	*lay zahss-pehrzh*	asparagus
l'aubergine (f.)	*loh-behr-zheen*	eggplant
la betterave	*lah beh-trahv*	beet
les carottes	*lay kah-roht*	carrots
le céleri	*luh sayl-ree*	celery
le mäis	*luh mah-yeess*	corn
le céleri rave	*luh sayl-ree rahv*	knob celery
les champignons	*lay shah<u>n</u>-pee-nyoh<u>n</u>*	mushrooms
le chou	*luh shoo*	cabbage (green)
le chou-fleur	*luh shoo-fluhr*	cauliflower
la courgette	*lah koor-zheht*	zucchini

le cresson	*luh kreh-ssoh<u>n</u>*	watercress
les épinards	*lay zay-pee-nahr*	spinach
les flageolets	*lay flah-zhoh-leh*	green shell beans
les haricots verts	*lay ah-ree-koh vehr*	green beans
les oignons	*lay zoh-nyoh<u>n</u>*	onions
l'oseille (f.)	*loh-zehy*	sorrel
le piment	*luh pee-mah<u>n</u>*	green pepper
les pois	*lay pwah*	peas
le poireau	*luh pwah-roh*	leek
les pommes de terre	*lay pohm duh tehr*	potatoes
la tomate	*lah toh-maht*	tomato

SEASONINGS

Although French food is usually perfectly seasoned, personal preferences sometimes intercede. Here's how to ask for what you want.

I'd like _____.	**Je voudrais _____.**	*zhuh voo-dreh*
■ artificial sweetener	**du sucre artificiel**	*dew sew-kruh ahr-tee-fee-syehl*
■ butter	**du beurre**	*dew buhr*
■ horseradish	**du raifort**	*dew reh-fohr*
■ ketchup	**du ketchup**	*dew keht-chuhp*
■ margarine	**de la margarine**	*duh lah mahr-gah-reen*
■ mayonnaise	**de la mayonnaise**	*duh lah mah yoh-nehz*
■ mustard	**de la moutarde**	*duh lah moo-tahrd*
■ olive oil	**de l'huile d'olive**	*duh lweel doh-leev*

■ pepper (black)	**du poivre (noir)**	*dew pwah-vruh (nwahr)*
■ pepper (red)	**du poivre (rouge)**	*dew pwah-vruh (roozh)*
■ salt	**du sel**	*dew sehl*
■ sugar	**du sucre**	*dew sew-kruh*
■ vinegar	**du vinaigre**	*dew vee-neh-gruh*
■ Worcestershire sauce	**de la sauce anglaise**	*du lah sohss ahn-glehz*

CHEESE COURSE

The cheese course is offered after the meat course and before the dessert. Most often, the restaurant will offer a tray of cheeses, from which you select two or three that balance one another. The cheese course is an opportunity to sample some cheeses that never get exported.

What is that cheese?	**Quel est ce fromage?**	*kehl eh suh froh-mahzh*
Is it _____?	**Est-il _____?**	*eh-teel*
■ mild	**maigre**	*meh-gruh*
■ sharp	**piquant**	*pee-kahn*
■ hard	**fermenté**	*fehr-mahn-tay*
■ soft	**à pâte molle**	*ah paht mohl*

Among the more popular cheeses are the following.

● **Banon:** Made from sheep's or goat's milk, a soft cheese with a natural rind; a mild cheese with a nutty flavor.

● **Bleu d'auvergne:** Made from cow's milk, this soft cheese has an internal mold and when cut, the veins are visible. Has a very sharp flavor.

● **Boursin:** A soft cow's milk cheese, with a mild flavor, sometimes enhanced with herbs.

- **Brie:** A variety of cheeses made from cow's milk and with a bloomy rind. Varieties range in flavor from mild to very pronounced, some with a fruity flavor.

- **Camembert:** Less delicate than brie, but also a cow's milk cheese with a thin white rind. Should be eaten firm.

- **Cantal:** A cow's milk cheese that varies with length of aging. Some varieties are softer and milder, while more aged ones are hard and with a more pronounced flavor.

- **Chèvre:** Any of an almost infinite variety of goat's milk cheeses, which vary from very soft to quite firm, and from mild and creamy to tart and crumbly. There will always be a few chèvres on the cheese tray.

- **Colombière:** This cow's milk cheese is soft and supple, with a mild flavor.

- **Munster:** A cow's milk cheese that is soft and spicy, with a tangy flavor. In Alsace, where the cheese comes from, it is eaten young.

- **Pont-l'evêque:** A cow's milk cheese that is very smooth and supple, with a pronounced flavor.

- **Port-salut:** The brand name for the Saint-Paulin from the monastery of Port-du-Salut.

- **Reblochon:** A soft cow's milk cheese with a mild and creamy flavor.

- **Roquefort:** A sheep's milk cheese that is soft and pungent. The cheese is cured in caves, an ancient process with rigid standards for production. Texture is very buttery.

- **Saint-Paulin:** Made from cow's milk, this is a velvety smooth cheese with a mild flavor.

- **Tomme de savoie:** A mild cow's milk cheese with a nutty flavor.

Petit Suisse is a fresh, unsalted cheese made from cow's milk and enriched with cream, then molded into heart shapes and sprinkled with sugar; it is a common dessert.

Fromage à la crème is *fromage blanc*, a rich, creamy white cheese made from unskimmed cow's milk. It is eaten topped with cream and sugar for breakfast.

Fondue is a specialty of Switzerland and parts of France that border on Switzerland. It is a large pot of bubbling melted cheese (usually Gruyère or Emmenthal), into which are dipped cubes of French bread. Fondue is served as a warming lunch or dinner course.

Raclette is a specialty of French-speaking Switzerland. It involves the slow melting of a hard cheese, usually alongside a roaring fire, during which the diners scrape off the cheese, as it melts, onto slices of French bread.

FRUITS AND NUTS

Here are the names of some common fruits, followed by nuts.

l'abricot	*lah-bree-koh*	apricot
l'ananas	*lah-nah-nah*	pineapple
la banane	*lah bah-nahn*	banana
les cassis	*lay kah-sseess*	black currants
la cerise	*lah suh-reez*	cherry
le citron	*luh see-trohn*	lemon
la datte	*lah daht*	date
la figue	*lah feeg*	fig
les fraises	*lay frehz*	strawberries
les fraises des bois	*lay frehz day bwah*	wild strawberries
les framboises	*lay frahn-bwahz*	raspberries
les groseilles	*lay groh-sehy*	red currants
la limette	*lah lee-meht*	lime
la mandarine	*lah mahn-dah-reen*	tangerine
le melon	*luh muh-lohn*	melon
les mûres	*lay mewr*	mulberries

les myrtilles	*lay meer-tee*	blueberries
l'orange	*loh-rah<u>n</u>zh*	orange
la noix de coco	*lah nwah duh koh-koh*	coconut
le pamplemousse	*luh pah<u>n</u>-pluh-mooss*	grapefruit
la pêche	*lah pehsh*	peach
la poire	*lah pwahr*	pear
la pomme	*lah pohm*	apple
la prune	*lah prewn*	plum
le pruneau	*luh prew-noh*	prune
le raisin	*luh reh-za<u>n</u>*	grape
le raisin sec	*luh reh-za<u>n</u> sehk*	raisin
l'amande (f.)	*lah-mah<u>n</u>d*	almond
le marron	*luh mah-roh<u>n</u>*	chestnut
la noisette	*lah nwah-zeht*	hazelnut
les noix	*lay nwah*	nuts

DESSERTS—SWEETS

Often, a restaurant will display its desserts on a table in the dining room or the waiter will roll the cart to your table so you can make a selection. On the cart will be a variety of tarts, fruits in light syrup, and pastries. Here are some common items you might consider for dessert.

- **Bavaroise:** A bavarian cream; mont-blanc is a bavarian cream made with chestnuts.

- **Beignets:** Fritters, often made from fruit such as apple.

- **Bombe:** An ice cream construction, often with different flavors and sometimes also with sherbet.

- **Charlotte:** An assemblage of sponge fingers and pudding; usually the sponge cake is used to line the dish and the pudding is in the center.

- **Crème caramel:** An egg custard served with a caramel sauce.

- **Crêpes:** Dessert crêpes, the most famous of which are **Crêpes Suzette**, made with orange flavoring and served flaming with Grand Marnier.

- **Gâteau:** An elaborate layer cake, made with thin layers of sponge cake and pastry cream, and decorated.

- **Mousse au chocolat:** An airy pudding made with chocolate, cream, eggs, and brandy, garnished with whipped cream.

- **Macédoine de fruits:** A fresh fruit salad.

- **Oeufs à la neige:** Soft meringue ovals served floating on a custard sauce.

- **Omelette norvégienne:** Baked Alaska.

- **Pâtisserie:** Pastry selection of any variety, including éclairs, millefeuilles, savarin, Saint-Honoré (creampuff cake).

- **Poires Belle-Hélène:** Poached pears, served with vanilla ice cream and chocolate sauce.

- **Profiteroles:** Cream puffs, served with chocolate sauce.

- **Soufflé:** There are an endless variety of sweet soufflés, the most famous one being the Grand Marnier soufflé.

- **Tarte:** An open-faced fruit pie, often made with apples or plums.

In addition, ice cream is a French favorite, as is sherbet and *granité* (fruit ice).

ice cream	**une glace**	*ewn glahss*
■ chocolate	**au chocolat**	*oh shoh-koh-lah*
■ vanilla	**à la vanille**	*ah lah vah-nee*
■ strawberry	**à la fraise**	*ah lah frehz*
sundae	**une coupe**	*ewn koop*

| sherbet | **un sorbet** | *uhn sohr-beh* |
| fruit ice | **un granité** | *uhn grah-nee-tay* |

SPECIAL CIRCUMSTANCES

Many travelers have special dietary requirements, so here are a few phrases that might help you get what you need or avoid what doesn't agree with you.

I am on a diet.	**Je suis au régime.**	*zhuh swee zo ray-zheem*
I'm a vegetarian.	**Je suis végétarien(ne).**	*zhuh swee vay-zhay-tah-ryan (ryen)*
I can't eat anything made with ____.	**Je ne peux rien manger de cuisiné au (à la) ____.**	*zhuh nuh puh ryan mahn shay duh kwee-zee-nay o (ah lah)*
I can't have ____.	**Je ne tolère ____.**	*zhuh nuh toh-lehr*

■ any dairy products **aucun produit laitier** *o-kuhn proh-dwee leh-tyay*

■ any alcohol **aucun produit alcoolique** *o-kuhn proh-dwee ahl-koh-leek*

■ any saturated fats **aucune matière grasse animale** *o-kewn mah-tyehr grahs ah-nee-mahl*

■ any seafood **aucun fruit de mer** *o-kuhn frweed mehr*

| I'm looking for a dish ____. | **Je cherche un plat ____.** | *zhuh shehrsh uhn plah* |

■ high in fiber **riche en fibre** *reesh ahn feebr*

■ low in cholesterol **léger en cholestérol** *lay-zhay ahn koh-lehs-tay-rohl*

■ low in fat **léger en matières grasses** *lay-zhay ahn mah-tyehr grahs*

- low in sodium **léger en sodium** *lay-zhay ahn sohd-yuhm*

- nondairy **non-laitier** *nohn-leh-tyay*

- salt-free **sans sel** *sahn sehl*

- sugar-free **sans sucre** *sahn sewkr*

- without artificial coloring **sans colorant** *sahn koh-loh-rahn*

- without preservatives **sans conservateurs** *sahn kohn-sehr-vah-tuhr*

BEVERAGES

See pages 131–135 for information on French apéritifs, wines, and brandies. As for other beverages, we give you the following phrases to help you ask for exactly what you wish.

Waiter, please bring me _____.	**Monsieur (Garçon), apportez-moi** _____. *muh-ssyuh (gahr-son) ah-pohr-tay mwah*
coffee	**du café** *dew kah-fay*
■ (decaffeinated)	**décaféiné** *day-kah-fay-ee-nay*
■ with milk (morning only)	**du café au lait** *dew kah-fay oh leh*
■ espresso	**du café-express** *dew kah-fay ehkss-prehss*
■ with cream	**du café-crème** *dew kah-fay krehm*
■ black coffee	**du café noir** *dew kah-fay nwahr*
■ decaffeinated coffee	**du café decaféiné** *dew kah-fay day-kah-fay-ee-nay*
■ iced coffee	**du café glacé** *dew kah-fay glah-ssay*
cider (alcoholic)	**du cidre** *dew see-druh*
juice	**du jus de fruits** *dew zhew duh frwee*
lemonade	**de la citronnade** *duh lah see-troh-nahd*

milk	**du lait**	*dew leh*
■ cold	**froid**	*frwah*
■ hot	**chaud**	*shoh*
■ milk shake	**un frappé**	*uhn frah-pay*
orangeade	**une orangeade**	*ewn oh-rahn-zhahd*
punch	**un punch**	*uhn puhnsh*
soda	**un soda**	*uhn soh-dah*
tea	**un thé**	*uhn tay*
■ with milk	**au lait**	*oh leh*
■ with lemon	**au citron**	*oh see-trohn*
■ with sugar	**sucré**	*sew-kray*
■ iced	**glacé**	*gluh-ssay*
water	**de l'eau (f.)**	*duh loh*
■ cold	**de l'eau fraîche**	*duh loh frehsh*
■ ice	**de l'eau glacée**	*duh loh glah-ssay*
■ mineral	**de l'eau minérale**	*duh loh mee-nay-rahl*
■ with carbonation	**gazeuse**	*gah-zuhz*
■ without carbonation	**plate**	*plaht*

SETTLING UP

The bill normally includes a surcharge for service. In addition, most people leave the small change from the bill as a token of appreciation.

The check, please.	**L'addition, s'il vous plaît.**	*lah-dee-ssyohn seel voo pleh*
Separate checks.	**Des additions séparées.**	*day zah-dee-ssoyhn say-pah-ray*
Is the service (tip) included?	**Le service est compris?**	*luh sehr-veess eh kohn-pree*

I didn't order this.	**Je n'ai pas commandé ceci.** *zhuh nay pah koh-mahn-day suh-ssee*
I think there's a a mistake.	**Je crois qu'il y a une erreur.** *zhuh krwah keel yah ewn ehr-ruhr*
This is for you.	**Ceci est pour vous.** *suh-ssee eh poor voo*

REGIONAL FRENCH SPECIALTIES

French food is noted for its ingredients: wild mushrooms such as **chanterelles, cèpes,** and **morels;** truffles; fresh **foie gras;** chickens from Bresse; butter and cream from Normandy; cheese from all parts of France. Below we give you some of the notable dishes from some of the provinces of France, most of which are famous for their regional ingredients.

- **Alsace-Lorraine:** This region has a strong German influence in its food and the most famous dish is **choucroute garnie,** a sauerkraut, pork, and sausage mixture; also **pâté de foie gras, quiche lorraine,** and **chicken in Riesling wine**. The food is hearty, with much emphasis on fish, fruit, and pork.

- **Bordeaux:** Food from here is prepared simply, with Bordeaux wine, **cèpes,** and **confit d'oie,** a potted goose, preserved in its own fat. This is a noted wine-producing area.

- **Brittany: Crêpes** are the best-known food from here, with a variety of sweet and savory fillings. There is also much seafood and sausages. Cider is the popular beverage.

- **Burgundy:** With Lyons in the gastronomic center, this region has some of the best food in France. The chickens from Bresse are world famous, as is the beef; from Burgundy we also get the savory mustards, spiced gingerbread, and black-currant liqueur— cassis. This is also a major wine-producing region.

- **Normandy:** Foods from here are marked by a use of apples or apple **eau de vie** (brandy). The fish dishes in this region are noteworthy.

- **Provence:** This is a southern region that uses a lot of olive oil and garlic in its dishes. Fish and seafood predominate, with a generous use of vegetables and fruits. The most famous dish is **bouillabaisse**, a fish stew. **Salade niçoise**, with lettuce, tuna, hard-cooked eggs, olives, and anchovies, and **pissaladière**, a pizza made with anchovies, are also popular.

- **Paris:** Food from all parts of France influences the dishes that are served in Paris. Those especially Parisian are **boeuf à la mode** (boiled beef with vegetables) and brie cheese.

APÉRITIFS, WINES, AND AFTER-DINNER DRINKS

APÉRITIFS

Most French people prefer to drink an apéritif before a meal rather than a cocktail. An apéritif is an appetite stimulant, and can be a variety of drinks, ranging from a simple vermouth or vermouth mixed with a liqueur (such as cassis), to a distilled drink such as Cynar, made from artichoke hearts. Among the most popular are:

Byrrh **Dubonnet** **Saint-Raphaël**	wine- and brandy-based, flavored with herbs and bitters
Pernod **Ricard**	anise-based, licorice-flavored
Vermouth	fortified wine made from red or white grapes
Cynar	bitter tasting, distilled from artichoke hearts

WINE

The high quality of the soil and the moderate climate have given French vineyards their historically unique position among wine-producing countries. Wine served with meals follows a progression from the light white wines to richer, heartier reds. (One wouldn't drink a Mâcon after a Pommard, or a Bordeaux after a Burgundy.)

White wines and rosés are served very cold (52°F). Beaujolais, although red, should be lightly chilled. Bordeaux is served at room temperature (62°F), Burgundy just above room temperature. Sweet wines should be chilled, and Champagne iced. The chart below will help you select a wine to suit your tastes and your food.

wine	**le vin**	*luh va<u>n</u>*
■ red wine	**le vin rouge**	*luh va<u>n</u> roozh*
■ rosé	**le vin rosé**	*luh va<u>n</u> roh-zay*
■ sparkling wine	**le vin mousseux**	*luh va<u>n</u> moo-ssuh*
■ sherry	**un sherry**	*uh<u>n</u> sheh-ree*
■ white wine	**le vin blanc**	*luh va<u>n</u> blah<u>n</u>*

AFTER-DINNER DRINKS

Brandy is often enjoyed after a lengthy, especially fine meal. **Cognac,** the finest of brandies, is distilled from grapes grown in the Charente district, the principal city of which is Cognac. It is usually aged for 20 years in barrels made from Limousin oak trees. Four different types, which differ in character and taste, are Rémy-Martin, Martel, Courvoisier, and Hennessy. These cognacs are considerably less expensive in France than elsewhere.

Armagnac comes from the Basque region. It is often bottled straight, rather than blended as cognac is.

Eaux-de-vie are distilled fruit brandies. Unlike cognac and other brandies, they are aged in crockery, not wood, so their taste is harsher. Some eaux-de-vie are **kirsch** (black cherry), **framboise** (wild raspberries), **poire William** (Swiss William pears), **mirabelle** (yellow plum), **calvados** (apple), and **marc** (from stems, pits, and skins of certain grapes).

Some liqueurs to choose from are:

absinthe light drink with a pronounced anise aroma.

anisette clear, sweet aromatic liqueur made from aniseeds and herbs.

Bénédictine a blend of 150 different herbs and plants.

B & B a combination of Bénédictine and brandy.

Chambord raspberry-flavored, combined with honey.

Chartreuse a combination of 130 herbs, in green and yellow.

Cointreau made from sweet and bitter tropical orange peels blended with cognac.

Crème de Cassis made from black currants.

Grand Marnier an orange-flavored liqueur made from the peel of bitter Curaçao oranges and blended with cognac.

WINE	REGION	DESCRIPTION	ORDER WITH
Anjou	Loire	semisweet rosé	fish, meat, game, poultry, esp. ham
Beaujolais	Burgundy	light, young, fruity red wine	meat, poultry, fowl, cheese
Chablis	Burgundy	dry white, flinty bouquet, nutty taste	fish, seafood, esp. lobster
Champagne	Champagne	delicate, sparkling white wine	
		Extra Dry (fruity)—medium	aperitif
		dry	
		Brut—driest	aperitif
		Sec—least dry	dessert
Chardonnay	Burgundy	delicate, fruity, flinty wine	fish
Châteauneuf-du-Pape	Rhône	full-bodied red wine	game, poultry, meat
Côte de Beaune	Burgundy	very delicate light red wine	meat, esp. prime ribs, fowl, poultry
Côte de Bourg	Bordeaux	medium, full-bodied red wine	meat, poultry, fowl, cheese
Côtes du Rhône	Rhône	light fruity red wine full-bodied white wine	meat, poultry, fowl fish, poultry

Gewürztraminer	Alsace	light, crisp white wine	fish, poultry, some cheese
Graves (blanc)	Bordeaux	soft white wine	fish, poultry
Graves (rouge)	Bordeaux	robust red wine	meat, fowl, poultry, cheese
Mâconnais (Pouilly-Fuissé)	Burgundy	light, dry, white wine	fish, seafood, egg and cheese dishes
Médoc	Bordeaux	light red wine	meat, poultry, fowl, cheese
Merlot	Bordeaux	dry, fruity wine	roasted meat, poultry, cheese
Muscadet	Loire	light, dry white wine	fish, seafood, esp. scallops
Muscat	Alsace	sweet white wine (also sparkling)	fish, seafood, desserts
Pinot	Alsace	light, fruity, white wine	fish, shellfish, cold vegetable dishes, egg and cheese dishes
Pomerol	Bordeaux	mellow, full-bodied red wine	meat, fowl, poultry, cheese
Riesling	Alsace	light, fruity, white wine	fish, shellfish, cold vegetable dishes, egg and cheese dishes
Saumur	Loire	dry, white wine	fish, seafood, poultry
Sauternes (Barsac)	Bordeaux	honey-sweet white wine	desserts
St-Emilion	Bordeaux	full-bodied, dark red wine	meat, fowl, poultry, cheese, esp. ham
Vouvray	Loire	white or sparkling white	fish, seafood, meat

MEETING PEOPLE

Remember to shake hands when meeting people; a French person may feel offended if you do not. It is customary for the French to greet each other—men and women alike—by kissing on both cheeks.

In general, Europeans don't ask many personal questions at the beginning of an acquaintance. They make contact through a neutral topic such as the weather or the traffic.

The French café is the perfect neighborhood spot for young and old to go to socialize at any time of the day or evening. There one meets friends, watches passersby, reads a newspaper, or relaxes with a drink or a snack.

SMALL TALK

Where are you from?	**D'où êtes-vous?**	*doo eht voo*
Do you live here?	**Habitez-vous ici?**	*ah-bee-tay voo zee-ssee*
What is your name, address, and phone number?	**Quelles sont vos coordonnées?**	*kehl sohn voh koh-ohr-doh-nay*
I am ____.	**Je suis ____.**	*zhuh swee*
■ from the United States	**des États-Unis**	*day zay-tah zew-nee*
■ from England	**d'Angleterre**	*dahn-gluh-tehr*
■ from Canada	**du Canada**	*dew kah-nah-dah*
■ from Australia	**d' Australie**	*dohss-trah-lee*
I like France (Paris) very much.	**J'aime beaucoup la France (Paris).**	*zhehm boh-koo lah frahnss (pah-ree)*
How long will you be staying?	**Combien de temps resterez-vous ici?**	*kohn-byan duh than rehss-tray voo zee-ssee*

I'll stay for a few days (a week).	**Je resterai quelques jours (une semaine).** *zhuh rehss-tray kehl-kuh zhoor (ewn suh-mehn)*
Where are you staying?	**Où restez-vous?** *oo rehss-tay voo*
What do you think of _____?	**Que pensez-vous de _____?** *kuh pahn-ssay voo duh*
I (don't) like it very much.	**Je (ne) l'aime (pas) beaucoup.** *zhuh (nuh) lehm (pah) boh-koo*
I think it's very _____.	**Je pense qu'il (qu'elle) est _____.** *zhuh pahnss keel (kehl) eh*
■ beautiful	**beau ('belle')** *boh ('behl')*
■ interesting	**intéressant(e)** *an-tay-reh-ssahn(t)*
■ magnificent	**magnifique** *mah-nyee-feek*
■ wonderful	**formidable** *fohr-mee-dah-bluh*

GREETINGS AND INTRODUCTIONS

May I introduce _____?	**Je peux vous présenter _____?** *zhuh puh voo pray-zahn-tay*
■ my family	**ma famille** *mah fah-meey*
■ my brother	**mon frère** *mohn frehr*
■ my father	**mon père** *mohn pehr*
■ my friend	**mon ami(e)** *mohn nah-mee*
■ my boyfriend	**mon petit ami** *mohn puh-tee tah-mee*
■ my girlfriend	**ma petite amie** *mah puh-teet tah-mee*
■ my husband	**mon mari** *mohn mah-ree*
■ my mother	**ma mère** *mah mehr*
■ my sister	**ma soeur** *mah suhr*

■ my sweetheart	**mon(ma) fiancé(e)** *mohn (mah) fee-yahn-ssay*
■ my wife	**ma femme** *mah fahm*
Glad to meet you.	**Enchanté(e).** *ahn-shahn-tay*
The pleasure is mine.	**Moi de même.** *mwah duh mehm*
Allow me to introduce myself.	**Permettez-moi de me présenter.** *pehr-meh-tay mwah duh muh pray-zahn-tay*
My name is _____.	**Je m'appelle _____.** *zhuh mah-pehl*
I am a(an) _____.	**Je suis _____.** *zhuh sweez*
■ accountant	**comptable** *kohn-tah-bluh*
■ artist	**artiste** *ahr-teesst*

■ businessperson	**homme (femme) d'affaires**	*ohm (fahm) dah-fehr*
■ dentist	**dentiste**	*dahn-teesst*
■ doctor	**docteur**	*dohk-tuhr*
■ hairdresser	**coiffeur ('-euse')**	*kwah-fuhr (fuhz)*
■ jeweler	**bijoutier (-ière)**	*bee-zhoo-tyay (tyehr)*
■ lawyer	**avocat(e)**	*ah-voh-kaht*
■ merchant	**commerçant(e)**	*koh-mehr-sahn (sahnt)*
■ nurse	**infirmier (-ière)**	*an-feer-myay (myehr)*
■ police officer	**agent de police**	*uh-zhuhn duh puh-leess*
■ secretary	**secrétaire (m. or f.)**	*seh-kray-tehr*
■ student	**étudiant(e)**	*ay-tew-dyahn(t)*
■ teacher	**professeur**	*proh-feh-suhr*
I am retired.	**Je suis en retraite.**	*zhuh sweez ahn ruh-treht*

DATING AND SOCIALIZING

Would you like to dance?	**Vous voulez danser?** *voo voo-lay dahn-say*
Yes, all right. With pleasure.	**Oui, d'accord. Avec plaisir.** *wee dah-kohr ah-vehk pleh-zeer*
Would you like a cigarette (a drink)?	**Voudriez-vous une cigarette (une boisson)?** *voo-dree-yay voo zewn see-gah-reht (ewn bwah-ssohn)*

Do you have a light?	**Avez-vous du feu?** *ah-vay voo dew fuh*
Do you mind if I smoke?	**Ça vous dérange si je fume?** *sah voo day-rah<u>n</u>zh see zhuh fewm*
May I take you home?	**Puis-je vous raccompagner chez vous?** *pweezh voo rah-koh<u>n</u>-pay-nyah shay voo*
May I call you?	**Puis-je vous téléphoner?** *pweezh voo tay-lay-foh-nay*
What is your telephone number?	**Quel est votre numéro de téléphone?** *kehl eh voh-truh new-may-roh duh tay-lay fohn*
Here's my telephone number (address).	**Voici mon numéro de téléphone (mon adresse).** *vwah-ssee moh<u>n</u> new-may-roh duh tay-lay fohn (moh<u>n</u> nah-drehss)*
You must visit us.	**Vous devez nous rendre visite.** *voo duh-vay noo rah<u>n</u>-druh vee-zeet*
Are you free tomorrow?	**Etes-vous libre demain?** *eht voo lee-bruh duh-ma<u>n</u>*
Are you free this evening?	**Etes-vous libre ce soir?** *eht voo lee-bruh suh swahr*
Would you like to go out together?	**Voudriez-vous sortir ensemble?** *voo-dree-yay voo sohr-teer ah<u>n</u>-sah<u>n</u>-bluh*
I'll wait for you in front of the hotel.	**Je vous attendrai devant l'hôtel.** *zhuh voo zah-tahn-dray duh-vah<u>n</u> loh-tehl*
I'll pick you up at your house (hotel).	**Je viendrai vous prendre chez vous (à votre hôtel).** *zhuh vya<u>n</u>-dray voo prah<u>n</u>-druh shay voo (ah voh-truh oh-tehl)*

SAYING GOOD-BYE

Nice to have met you.	**(Je suis) enchanté(e) d'avoir fait votre connaissance.** *(zhuh sweez) ahn-shahn-tay dah-vwahr feh voh-truh koh-neh-ssahnss*
The pleasure is mine.	**Le plaisir est partagé.** *luh pleh-zeer eh pahr-tah-zhay*
Regards to ____.	**Mon meilleur souvenir à ____.** *mohn meh-yuhr soo-vuh-neer ah*

SHOPPING

SHOPS/STORES

It is best to start by shopping in the large department stores so that you can browse without feeling obligated to make a purchase. Most department stores are open Monday through Saturday, from 9:30 A.M. to 6:30 P.M. Many boutiques are open on Sunday, closed on Monday. In Switzerland, however, stores are open from 8:00 A.M. to 6:30 P.M. and on Saturday from 8:00 A.M. to 4:00 P.M. Smaller stores have similar hours and many close between noon and 2:00 P.M. Most of the hairdressers are closed on Monday, and the fashion boutiques on Monday morning. Sales are usually at the beginning of January and at the end of June and the beginning of July. Most of the stores (even the department stores) remain closed on public holidays. Food stores are open on Sunday morning from 8:00 A.M. to noon.

In Paris the main shopping centers are located in the Palais de Congrès de Paris, the Montparnasse area, and in the Forum des Halles. Sales usually take place the first week in January and the last week of June or July. Couturier sales are in March or July.

Large department stores line the boulevards of the Right Bank, especially around the Opéra and the Gare St-Lazare. The Galeries Lafayette, au Printemps, La Samaritaine, and Bazar de l'Hôtel de Ville offer a vast selection of items, cater to foreign visitors, employ multilingual sales personnel, and have **bureaux de change** on the premises.

Prisunic and Monoprix are two less elegant department stores, more comparable to five-and-dime stores. They may be found throughout Paris. Tati, one of the least expensive department stores in Paris, boasts a large selection of reasonably priced goods, many imported from Algeria and Morocco.

Not to be missed is the ultramodern, mostly subterranean Forum des Halles mall, with hundreds of stores, fast-food restaurants, **bureaux de change,** a holography museum, and much more.

The huge **centres commerciaux** (malls) outside of Paris are dominated by the Auchan and Carrefour chain of stores, which are surrounded by walkways containing smaller boutiques and shops that cater to every taste, as well as banks and restaurants.

GOING SHOPPING

I'd like to go shopping today.	**Je voudrais aller faire des courses aujourd'hui.** *zhuh voo-dreh zah-lay fehr day koorss oh-zhoor-dwee*
Where is _____?	**Où se trouve _____?** *oo suh troov*
■ a bakery	**une boulangerie** *ewn boo-lahnzh-ree*
■ a bookstore	**une librairie** *ewn lee-breh-ree*
■ a butcher	**une boucherie** *ewn boosh-ree*
■ a camera shop	**un magasin d'appareils-photo** *uhn mah-gah-zan dah-pah-rehy foh-toh*
■ a candy store	**une confiserie** *ewn kohn-feess-ree*
■ a clothing store	**un magasin de vêtements** *uhn mah-gah-zan duh veht-mahn*
for children's clothes	**pour enfants** *poor ahn-fahn*
men's store	**pour hommes** *poor ohm*
women's boutique	**pour femmes** *poor fahm*
■ a delicatessen	**une charcuterie** *ewn shahr-kew-tree*
■ a department store	**un grand magasin** *uhn grahn mah-gah-zan*
■ a drugstore	**une pharmacie** *ewn fahr-mah-ssee*
■ a florist	**un fleuriste** *uhn fluh-reesst*

- a gift (souvenir) shop — **un magasin de souvenirs** *uhn mah-gah-zan duh soov-neer*
- a grocery store — **une épicerie** *ewn ay-peess-ree*
- a hardware store — **une quincaillerie** *ewn kahn-kahy-ree*
- a jewelry store — **une bijouterie** *ewn bee-zhoo-tree*

Travel Tips A value-added tax (T.V.A.) of over 18% is levied on all goods except medicine, food, and books. A 33% luxury tax is added to such items as jewelry, video, and photography equipment. This money may, however, be refunded to you. A *détaxe* desk in most large department stores helps non-European foreigners receive a 13–23% discount on large purchases of luxury items. Spending 1200 francs or more in one store, within a six-month period, entitles the buyer to this rebate. Naturally, it is essential that you save all sales slips for the *détaxe*. They will be stamped by a French custom official upon departure from the country.

- a liquor store — **un magasin de vins et spiritueux** *uhn mah-gah-zan duh van ay spee-ree-tew-uh*
- a newsstand — **un kiosque à journaux** *uhn kee-ohsk ah zhoor-noh*
- an optician — **un opticien** *uhn nohp-tee-ssyan*
- a record store — **un magasin de disques** *uhn mah-gah-zan duh deessk*
- a shoemaker — **un cordonnier** *uhn kohr-doh-nyay*
- a shoe store — **un magasin de chaussures** *uhn mah-gah-zan duh shoh-ssewr*
- a supermarket — **un supermarché** *uhn sew-pehr-mahr-shay*
- a tobacco shop — **un bureau de tabac** *uhn bew-roh duh tah-bah*

■ a toy store   **un magasin de jouets**   *uhn mah-gah-zan duh zhoo-eh*

■ a watchmaker   **un horloger**   *uhn nohr-lohzh-yay*

■ a wine merchant   **un négociant en vins**   *uhn nay-gohss-yahn ahn van*

Sir.	**Monsieur.** *muh-ssyuh*
Young man.	**Jeune homme.** *zhuhn ohm*
Miss.	**Mademoiselle.** *mahd mwah-zehl*
Madam.	**Madame.** *mah-dahm*
Can you help me?	**Pouvez-vous m'aider?** *poo-vay voo meh-day*
I'm looking for ____.	**Je cherche ____.** *zhuh shehrsh*
Are there any sales?	**Il y a des soldes?** *eel yah day sohld*
I would like to buy in bulk.	**Je voudrais acheter en gros.** *zhuh voo-dreh zahsh-tay ahn groh*
Do you accept credit cards?	**Acceptez-vous les cartes de crédit?** *ahk-sehp-tay voo lay kahrt duh kray-dee*
Which ones?	**Lesquelles?** *lay-kehl*
Where is the Lost and Found?	**Où est le Bureau des Objets Trouvés?** *oo eh luh bew-roh day zohb-zheh troo vay*
I can't find what I'm looking for.	**Je ne trouve pas ce que je cherche.** *zhuh nuh troov pah suh kuh zhuh shersh*

BOOKS

Where is the best (biggest) bookstore here?	**Où se trouve la meilleure (la plus grande) librairie par ici?** *oo suh troov lah meh-yuhr (lah plew grah<u>nd</u>) lee-breh-ree pahr ee-ssee*
I'm looking for a copy of _____.	**Je cherche un exemplaire de _____.** *zhuh shehrsh uh<u>n</u> nehg-zah<u>n</u>-plehr duh*
The author of the book is _____.	**L'auteur du livre est _____.** *loh-tuhr dew lee-vruh eh*
I don't know the title (author).	**Je ne sais pas le titre (le nom de l'auteur).** *zhuh nuh seh pah luh tee-truh (le noh<u>n</u> duh loh-tuhr)*
I'm just looking.	**Je regarde tout simplement.** *zhuh ruh-gahrd too sa<u>n</u>-pluh-mah<u>n</u>*
Do you have books (novels) in English?	**Avez-vous des livres (des romans) en anglais?** *ah-vay voo day lee-vruh (day roh-mah<u>n</u>) ah<u>n</u> ah<u>n</u>-gleh*
I would like _____.	**Je voudrais _____.** *zhuh voo-dreh*
■ a guidebook	**un guide touristique** *uh<u>n</u> geed too-reess-teek*
■ a map of the city	**un plan de la ville** *uh<u>n</u> plah<u>n</u> duh lah veel*
■ a pocket dictionary	**un dictionnaire de poche** *uh<u>n</u> deek-ssyoh-nehr duh pohsh*
■ a French-English dictionary	**un dictionnaire français-anglais** *uh<u>n</u> deek-ssyoh-nehr frah<u>n</u>-sseh ah<u>n</u>-gleh*
Where can I find _____?	**Où puis-je trouver _____?** *oo pweezh troo-vay*
■ detective stories	**des romans policiers** *day roh-mah<u>n</u> poh-leess-yay*

- history books **des livres d'histoire** *day lee-vruh deess-twahr*
- novels **des romans** *day roh-mahn*
- science fiction books **des livres de science fiction** *day lee-vruh duh see-yahnss feek-syohn*
- short story books **des contes** *day kohnt*

I'll take these books. **Je vais prendre ces livres.** *zhuh veh prahn-druh say lee-vruh*

CLOTHING

Where is the _____ department? **Où est le rayon des _____.** *oo eh luh reh-yohn day*

Would you please show me _____? **Veuillez me montrer?** *vuh-yay muh mohn-tray*

- a bathing suit **un maillot de bain** *uhn mah-yoh duh ban*
- a belt **une ceinture** *ewn san-tewr*
- a blouse **un chemisier** *uhn shuh-mee-zyay*
- boots **des bottes (f.)** *day boht*
- a bra **un soutien-gorge** *uhn soo-tyan gohrzh*
- a dress **une robe** *ewn rohb*
- an evening gown **une robe du soir** *ewn rohb duh swahr*
- gloves **des gants (m.)** *day gahn*
- handkerchiefs **des mouchoirs** *day moo-shwahr*
- a hat **un chapeau** *uhn shah-poh*
- a jacket **un veston** *uhn vehss-tohn*
- jeans **un jean** *uhn zheen*
- a jogging suit **un survêt, un jogging** *uhn sewr-veh uhn zhoh-geeng*

■ an overcoat	**un manteau/pardessus** *uhn mahn-toh/pahr-duh-ssew*
■ pajamas	**un pyjama** *uhn pee-zhah-mah*
■ panties (women)	**un slip** *uhn sleep*
■ pants	**un pantalon** *uhn pahn-tah-lohn*
■ pantyhose	**des collants** *day koh-lahn*
■ a raincoat	**un imperméable** *uhn nan-pehr-may-ah-bluh*
■ a robe	**une robe de chambre** *ewn rohb duh shahn-bruh*
■ sandals	**des sandales (f.)** *day sahn-dahl*
■ scarf	**une écharpe** *ewn ay-shahrp*
■ a shirt	**une chemise** *ewn shuh-meez*
■ shoes	**des chaussures (f.)** *day shoh-ssewr*
■ shorts (briefs)	**un caleçon** *ewn kahl-ssohn*
■ a skirt	**une jupe** *ewn zhewp*
■ a slip	**un jupon** *uhn zhew-pohn*
■ slippers	**des pantoufles (f.)** *day pahn-too-fluh*

■ sneakers	**des baskets (f.)**	*day bahs-keht*
	des tennis (f.)	*day teh-nees*
■ socks	**des chaussettes**	*day shoh-sseht*
■ stockings	**des bas**	*day bah*
■ a suit	**un complet** (for men)/**un tailleur** (for women) *uhn kohn-pleh/uhn tah-yuhr*	
■ a sweater	**un chandail** *uhn shahn-dahy*	
	un pull *uhn pewl*	
■ a T-shirt	**un tee-shirt** *uhn tee-shehrt*	
■ a tie	**une cravate** *ewn krah-vaht*	
■ an umbrella	**un parapluie** *unn pah-rah-plwee*	
■ an undershirt (T-shirt)	**un sous-vêtement** *uhn soo veht-mahn*	
■ a vest	**un gilet** *uhn zhee-leh*	
■ a wallet	**un portefeuille** *uhn pohr-tuh-fuhy*	

I'd like short (long) sleeves.	**Je voudrais les manches courtes (longues).** *zhuh voo-dreh lay mahnsh koort (lohng)*
■ sleeveless	**sans manches** *sahn mahnsh*

Do you have anything _____?	**Avez-vous quelque chose _____?** *ah-vay voo kehl-kuh shohz*
■ else	**d'autre** *doh-truh*
■ larger	**de plus grand** *duh plew grahn*
■ smaller	**de plus petit** *duh plew puh-tee*
■ longer	**de plus long** *duh plew lohn*
■ shorter	**de plus court** *duh plew koor*
■ more (less) expensive	**de plus (moins) cher** *duh plew (mwan) shehr*
■ of better quality	**de meilleure qualité** *duh meh-yuhr kah-lee-tay*
■ cheaper	**de moins cher** *duh mwan shehr*

| I don't like the color. | **Je n'aime pas la couleur.** *zhuh nehm pah lah koo-luhr* |
| Do you have it in ____? | **L'avez-vous en ____?** *lah-vay voo zahn* |

- beige   **beige** *behzh*
- black   **noir** *nwahr*
- blue   **bleu** *bluh*
- brown   **brun/marron** *bruhn/mah-rohn*
- gray   **gris** *gree*
- green   **vert** *vehr*
- navy blue   **bleu marine** *bluh mah-reen*
- orange   **orange** *oh-rahnzh*
- pink   **rose** *rohze*
- purple   **mauve** *mohv*
- red   **rouge** *roozh*
- white   **blanc** *blahn*
- yellow   **jaune** *zhohn*

| I prefer a lighter (darker) color. | **Je préfère une couleur plus claire (foncée).** *zhuh pray-fehr ewn koo-luhr plew klehr (fohn-ssay)* |

CHART OF MATERIALS

- corduroy   **velours côtelé** *vuh-loor koht-lay*
- cotton   **coton** *koh-tohn*
- denim   **jean** *zheen*
- felt   **feutre** *fuh-truh*
- flannel   **flanelle** *flah-nehl*
- gabardine   **gabardine** *gah-bahr-deen*
- lace   **dentelle** *dahn-tehl*

■ leather	**cuir**	*kweer*
■ linen	**lin**	*la<u>n</u>*
■ nylon	**nylon**	*nee-loh<u>n</u>*
■ permanent press	**infroissable**	*an-frwah-ssah-bluh*
■ polyester	**polyester**	*poh-lee-ehss-tehr*
■ satin	**satin**	*sah-ta<u>n</u>*
■ silk	**soie**	*swah*
■ suede	**daim**	*da<u>n</u>*
■ terrycloth	**tissu-éponge**	*tee-ssew-ay-poh<u>n</u>zh*
■ velvet	**velours**	*vuh-loor*
■ wool	**laine**	*lehn*

Show me something ____.

Montrez-moi quelque chose _____.
moh<u>n</u>-tray mwah kehl-kuh-shohz

■ in a solid color	**d'uni**	*dew-nee*
■ with stripes	**à rayures**	*ah rah-yewr*
■ with polka dots	**à pois**	*ah pwah*
■ in plaid	**en tartan**	*ah<u>n</u> tahr-tah<u>n</u>*
■ in herringbone	**à chevrons**	*ah shuh-vroh<u>n</u>*
■ checked	**à carreaux**	*ah kah-roh*

Please take my measurements.

Veuillez prendre mes mesures.
vuh-yay prah<u>n</u>-druh may muh-zewr

I take size (My size is) ____.

Je porte du (Ma taille est) _____.
zhuh pohrt dew (mah tahy eh)

■ small	**petit (petite)**	*puh-tee (puh-teet)*
■ medium	**moyen (moyenne)**	*mwah-ya<u>n</u> (mwah-yehn)*
■ large	**grand (grande)**	*grah<u>n</u> (grah<u>n</u>d)*

Can I try it on?

Puis-je l'essayer? *pweezh leh-sseh-yay*

| Can you alter it? | **Pouvez-vous le/la retoucher?** |
| | *poo-vay voo luh-lah ruh-too-shay* |

| Can I return the article? | **Puis-je rendre cet article?**   *pweezh rahn-druh seht ahr-tee-kluh* |

| Is it handmade? | **C'est fait à la main?**   *seh feh tah lah man* |

| The zipper doesn't work. | **La fermeture-éclair ne marche pas.** *lah fehr-muh-tewr ay-klehr nuh mahrsh pah* |

| It doesn't fit me. | **Cela ne me va pas.**   *suh-lah nuh muh vah pah* |

| It fits very well. | **Ça va à la perfection.**   *Sah vah ah lah pehr-fehk-ssyohn* |

| I'll take it. | **Je le/la prends.**   *zhuh luh/lah prahn* |

| Will you wrap it? | **Voulez-vous l'emballer, s'il vous plaît?**   *voo-lay voo lahn-bah-lay seel voo pleh* |

| I'd like to see a pair of shoes (boots). | **Je voudrais voir une paire de chaussures (bottes).**   *zhuh voo-dreh vwahr ewn pehr duh shoh-ssewr (boht)* |

| Show me that pair. | **Montrez-moi cette paire.**   *mohn-tray mwah seht pehr* |

| I take size ____. | **Je chausse du ____.**   *zhuh shohss dew* |

| These shoes are too narrow (wide). | **Ces chaussures sont trop étroites (larges).**   *say shoh-ssewr sohn troh pay-trwaht (lahrzh)* |

| They fit fine. | **Elles me vont très bien.**   *ehl muh vohn treh byan* |

| I'll take them. | **Je vais les prendre.**   *zhuh veh lay prahn-druh* |

CONVERSION TABLES FOR CLOTHING SIZES

WOMEN

SHOES

American	4	4½	5	5½	6	6½	7	7½	8	8½	9	9½	10
Continental	35	35	36	36	37	37	38	38	39	39	40	40	41

DRESSES, SUITS

American	8	10	12	14	16	18
Continental	36	38	40	42	44	46

BLOUSES, SWEATERS

American	32	34	36	38	40	42
Continental	40	42	44	46	48	50

MEN

SHOES

American	7	7½	8	8½	9	9½	10	10½	11	11½
Continental	39	40	41	42	43	43	44	44	45	45

SUITS, COATS

American	34	36	38	40	42	44	46	48
Continental	44	46	48	50	52	54	56	58

SHIRTS

American	14	14½	15	15½	16	16½	17	17½
Continental	36	37	38	39	40	41	42	43

| I also need shoelaces. | **Il me faut aussi des lacets.** *eel muh foh toh-ssee day lah-sseh* |
| That's all I want for now. | **C'est tout pour le moment.** *seh too poor luh moh-mahn* |

ELECTRIC APPLIANCES

Electric current in the U.S. is 110V AC, whereas in France it is 220V AC. Unless your electric shaver or alarm clock is able to handle both currents, you will need to purchase an adaptor. When making a purchase, please be aware that *some* French products are engineered to work with either system whereas others will require an adaptor. When making a purchase, be careful to check the warranty to ensure that the product is covered internationally.

I want to buy _____.	**Je voudrais acheter_____.** *zhuh voo-dreh zahsh-tay*
■ an adaptor	**un adaptateur** *uhn nah-dahp-tah-tuhr*
■ a battery	**une pile** *ewn peel*
■ a blender	**un mixer** *uhn meek-sehr*
■ a CD player	**un lecteur de CD** *uhn lehk-tuhr duh say day*
■ an electric shaver	**un rasoir électrique** *uhn rah-zwahr ay-lehk-treek*
■ a food processor	**un robot ménager** *uhn roh-boh may-nah-zhay*
■ a hair dryer	**un sèche-cheveux** *uhn sehsh shuh-vuh*
■ a headset	**un casque** *uhn kahsk*
■ a plug	**une fiche** *ewn feesh*

■ a (portable) radio **une radio (portative)** *ewn rah-dyoh (pohr-tah-teev)*

■ a personal stereo player **un baladeur** *uhn bah-lah-duhr*

■ a microwave oven **un four à micro-ondes** *uhn foor ah mee-kroh ohnd*

■ a toaster **un grille-pain** *uhn gree pan*

■ a transformer **un transformateur** *uhn trahnz-fohr-mah-tuhr*

FOOD AND HOUSEHOLD ITEMS

Don't forget to bring your own basket when you go to the food market. Large paper bags are not given out. The cashier does not load the basket for you; you must do that yourself. The French are more inclined than we are to shop in specialty stores, so you may want to follow their lead, buying bread in the **boulangerie**, pastries in a **pâtisserie**, or candy in a **confiserie**.

I'd like _____. **Je voudrais _____.** *zhuh voo-dreh*

Could you give me _____. **Pourriez-vous me donner _____.** *poo-ree-yay voo muh doh-nay*

■ a bar of soap **une savonnette** *ewn sah-voh-neht*

■ a bottle of juice **une bouteille de jus de fruits** *ewn boo-tehy duh zhew duh frwee*

■ a box of cereal **une boîte de céréales** *ewn bwaht duh say-ray-ahl*

■ a can of tomato sauce **une boîte de sauce-tomate** *ewn bwaht duh sohss toh-maht*

■ a dozen eggs **une douzaine d'oeufs** *ewn doo-zehn duh*

- a jar of coffee

  un bocal de café *uhn boh-kal duh kah-fay*

- a kilo (2.2 lbs.) of potatoes

  un kilo de pommes de terre *uhn kee-loh duh pohm duh tehr*

- a half-kilo of butter

  un demi-kilo de beurre *uhn duh-mee kee-loh duh buhr*

- 200 grams (about $\frac{1}{2}$ pound) of cookies

  deux cents grammes de biscuits *duh sahn grahm duh beess-kwee*

- a hundred grams of bologna

  cent grammes de mortadelle *sahn grahm duh mohr-tah-dehl*

- a half-kilo (1.1 lbs.) of cherries

  un demi-kilo de cerises *uhn duh-mee kee-loh duh suh-reez*

- a liter (quart) of milk

  un litre de lait *uhn lee-truh duh leh*

- a package of candies

  un paquet de bonbons *uhn pah-keh duh bohn-bohn*

- a $\frac{1}{4}$ pound of cheese

  cent grammes de fromage *sahn grahm duh froh-mahzh*

- a quart of milk

  un litre de lait *uhn lee-truh duh leh*

- a roll of toilet paper

  un rouleau de papier hygiénique *uhn roo-loh duh pah-pyay ee-zhyay-neek*

- a kilo of oranges

  un kilo d'oranges *uhn kee-loh doh-rahnzh*

METRIC WEIGHTS AND MEASURES

Solid Measures
(approximate measurements only)

OUNCES	GRAMS (GRAMMES)	GRAMS	OUNCES
$\frac{1}{4}$	7	10	$\frac{1}{3}$
$\frac{1}{2}$	14	100	$3\frac{1}{2}$
$\frac{3}{4}$	21	300	$10\frac{1}{2}$
1	28	500	18

POUNDS	KILOGRAMS (KILO)	KILOGRAMS	POUNDS
1	$\frac{1}{2}$	1	$2\frac{1}{4}$
5	$2\frac{1}{4}$	3	$6\frac{1}{2}$
10	$4\frac{1}{2}$	5	11
20	9	10	22
50	23	50	110
100	45	100	220

Liquid Measures
(approximate measurements only)

OUNCES	MILLILITERS (MILLILITRES)	MILLILITERS	OUNCES
1	30	10	$\frac{1}{3}$
6	175	50	$1\frac{1}{2}$
12	350	100	$3\frac{1}{2}$
16	475	150	5

GALLONS	LITERS (LITRES)	LITERS	GALLONS
1	$3\frac{3}{4}$	1	$\frac{1}{4}$ (1 quart)
5	19	5	$1\frac{1}{3}$
10	38	10	$2\frac{1}{2}$

Note: Common measurements for purchasing food are a kilo or fractions thereof: 100 (cent), 200 (deux cents), and 500 (cinq cents) grams (grammes). See also Numbers, pages 14–17.

THE CHARCUTERIE

A **charcuterie** is a rather special type of French delicatessen where you can buy food to take out, including various sausages and smoked meats. You will often see ordinary butcher's meat being sold in the same case as the sausage. Besides smoked meats you can find simple items like salads or pâté. The **Rue de boucherie** in Paris is a street entirely filled with **charcuteries,** where you can go from one to another, selecting the items that appeal to you for your lunch or for a picnic.

JEWELRY

I'd like to see _____.	**Je voudrais voir _____.**	*zhuh voo-dreh vwahr*
▪ a bracelet	**un bracelet**	*uhn brahss-leh*
▪ a brooch, a pin	**une broche**	*ewn brohsh*
▪ a chain	**une chaînette**	*ewn sheh-neht*
▪ a charm	**un porte-bonheur**	*uhn pohrt boh-nuhr*
▪ some earrings	**des boucles d'oreille**	*day boo-kluh doh-rehy*
▪ a necklace	**un collier**	*uhn koh-lyay*
▪ a ring	**une bague**	*ewn bahg*
an engagement ring	**une bague de fiançailles**	*ewn bahg duh fee-ahn-ssahy*
a wedding ring	**une alliance**	*ewn ah-lee-ahnss*
▪ a watch (digital)	**une montre (digitale)**	*ewn mohn-truh (dee-zhee-tahl)*
Is this _____?	**Est-ce _____?**	*ehss*
▪ gold	**en or**	*ahn nohr*
▪ platinum	**en platine**	*ahn plah-teen*
▪ silver	**en argent**	*ahn nahr-zhahn*

■ stainless steel   **en acier inoxydable** *ahn nah-ssyay ee-nohk-ssee-dah-bluh*

■ solid gold   **en or massif** *ahn nohr mah-sseef*

■ gold plated?   **en plaqué or?** *ahn plah kay ohr*

How many carats   **Combien de carats y a-t-il?** *kohn*
is it?   *byan duh kah-rah ee ah teel*

What is that stone?   **Quelle est cette pierre?** *kehl eh seht pyehr*

I would like _____.   **Je voudrais _____.** *zhuh voo-dreh*

■ an amethyst   **une améthyste** *zewn ah-may-teesst*

■ an aquamarine   **une aigue-marine** *zewn ehy muh-reen*

■ a diamond   **un diamant** *zuhn dee-ah-mahn*

■ an emerald   **une émeraude** *zewn aym-rohd*

■ ivory   **un ivoire** *zuhn nee-vwahr*

■ jade   **un jade** *zuhn zhahd*

■ onyx   **un onyx** *zuhn oh-neeks*

■ pearls   **des perles** *day pehrl*

■ a ruby   **un rubis** *zuhn rew-bee*

■ a sapphire   **un saphir** *zuhn sah-feer*

■ a topaz   **une topaze** *zewn toh-pahz*

■ turquoise   **une turquoise** *zewn tewr-kwahz*

How much is it?   **Cela coûte combien?** *suh-lah koot kohn-byan*

I'll take it.   **Je le (la) prends.** *zhuh luh (lah) prahn*

AUDIOVISUAL EQUIPMENT

Please see the note under Electric Appliances on page 154. In addition, Europe uses broadcasting and recording systems that are often incompatible with those of the U.S. Unless expressly warranted, French TVs, VCRs, VCR tapes, computers, and telephone answering systems will not operate properly in the U.S.

Is there a record shop around here?	**Il y a un magasin de disques par ici?**	*eel yah uhn mah-gah-zan duh deessk pahr ee-ssee*
Do you sell _____?	**Vendez-vous _____?**	*vahn-day voo*
■ cassettes	**des cassettes**	*day kah-seht*
■ CDs	**des CDs**	*day say-day*
■ records	**des disques**	*day deessk*
Do you have the songs of _____?	**Avez-vous les chansons de _____?**	*ah-vay voo lay shahn-sohn duh*
Do you have the latest hits of _____?	**Avez-vous les derniers succès de _____?**	*ah-vay-voo lay dehr-nyah sewk-sseh duh*
Is it recorded digitally?	**Est-ce un enregistrement digital?**	*ehs uhn ahn-reh-zheess-truh-mahn dee-zhee-tahl*
Where is the _____ section?	**Où est le rayon de _____?**	*oo eh luh reh-yohn duh*
■ blues	**blues**	*blewz*
■ classical music	**la musique classique**	*lah mew-zeek klah-sseek*
■ folk music	**la musique folklorique**	*lah mew-zeek fohl-kloh-reek*
■ jazz	**du jazz**	*dew zhahz*

- French music **la musique française** *lah mew-zeek frah_n_-ssehz*

- opera **l'opéra (m.)** *loh-pay-rah*

- pop music **la musique pop** *lah mew-zeek pohp*

- rock music **la musique rock** *lah mew-zeek ruhk*

Where is the nearest electronics store? **Où est le magasin d'équipement électronique le plus proche?** *oo eh luh mah-gah-zan day-keep-mahn ay-lehk-troh-neek luh plew prohsh*

I am looking for _____. **Je cherche _____.** *zhuh shehrsh*

- an amplifier **un amplificateur** *uh_n_ nah_n_-plee-fee-kah-tuhr*

- cassettes
  analog
  digital
  des cassettes (f.) *day kah-seht*
  analogiques *ah-nah-loh-zheek*
  numériques (digitals) *new-may-reek (dee-zhee-tahl)*

- a (small) cassette player **un (petit) lecteur de cassettes** *uh_n_ (puh-tee) lehk-tuhr duh kah-seht*

- a (small) cassette recorder **un (petit) magnétophone à cassettes** *uh_n_ (puh-tee) mah-nyay-toh-fohn nah kah-seht*

- a CD **un CD** *uh_n_ say-day*

- a CD player **un lecteur de CD** *uh_n_ lehk-tuhr duh say-day*

- a CD recorder **un magnétophone à CD** *uh_n_ mah-nyay-toh-fohn ah say-day*

- headphones **un écouteur portatif** *uh_n_ nay-koo-tuhr pohr-tah-teef*
  un casque à écouteurs *uh_n_ kahsk ah ay-koo-tuhr*
  cordless **sans fil** *sah_n_ feel*

- a minidisk **un mini-disque** *uh_n_ mee-nee-deesk*

■ a minidisk player — **un lecteur de mini-disques** *uhn lehk-tuhr duh mee-nee-deesk*

■ a personal stereo — **un baladeur** *uhn bah-lah-duhr*

■ a receiver — **un récepteur** *uhn ray-sehp-tuhr*

■ recordable CDs — **des CD enregistrables** *day say-day ahn-reh-gees-trah-bluh*

■ speakers — **des haut-parleurs stéréo (m.)** *day zoh-pahr-luhr stay-ray-oh*

■ surround sound — **le son surround** *luh sohn sew-rond*

■ a tuner — **un syntoniseur** *uhn sahn-toh-nee-zuhr*

Whom should I contact if this device doesn't work? — **Qui dois-je contacter si cet appareil ne marche (fonctionne) pas?** *kee dwahzh kohn-tahk-tay see seh tah-pah-rehy nuh mahrsh (fohnk-syohn) pah*

I would like _____. — **Je voudrais _____.** *zhuh voo-dreh*

■ a camcorder — **un caméscope** *uhn kah-may-skohp*

  digital — **numérique (digital)** *new-may-reek (dee-zhee-tahl)*

■ a DVD — **un vidéodisque numérique (digital)** *uhn vee-day-oh deesk new-may-reek (dee-zhee-tahl)*

■ DVD movies — **des films DVD (m.)** *day feelm day-vay-day*

■ a DVD player — **un lecteur de DVD** *uhn lehk-tuhr duh day-vay-day*

  un lecteur de vidéo-disque numérique *uhn lehk-tuhr duh vee-day-oh-deesk new-may-reek*

■ a VCR — **un magnétoscope** *uhn mah-nyay-toh-skohp*

■ a VCR tape (blank) — **une bande magnétique** *ewn bahn mah-nyay-teek*

■ a videocassette (digital)

une vidéocassette numérique (digitale) *ewn vee-day-oh kah-seht new-may-reek (dee-zhee-tahl)*

Do you rent (sell) videotapes and (or) digital video disks with English subtitles?

Louez (Vendez)-vous des vidéocassettes et (ou) des vidéodisques numériques (digitaux) avec des soustitres en anglais? *loo-way (vahn-day) voo day vee-day-oh-kah-seht ay (oo) day vee-day-oh-deesk new-may-reek (dee-zhee-toh) ah-vehk day soo-truh ahn ahn-gleh*

NEWSSTAND

Do you carry newspapers (magazines) in English?

Avez-vous des journaux (magazines) en anglais? *ah-vay voo day zhoor-noh (mah-gah-zeen) ahn nahn-gleh*

How much is it?

C'est combien? *seh kohn-byan*

I'd like _____.

Je voudrais _____. *zhuh voo-dreh*

■ a daily

un quotidien *zuhn koh-tee-dyan*

■ a weekly

un hebdomadaire *zuhn ehb-doh-mah-dehr*

■ a monthly

un mensuel *zuhn mahn-ssew-ehl*

I'd like to buy some postcards.

Je voudrais acheter des cartes postales. *zhuh voo-dreh zahsh-tay day kahrt pohss-tahl*

Do you have stamps?

Avez-vous des timbres? *ah-vay voo day tan-bruh*

PHOTOGRAPHIC SUPPLIES

Where is there a camera shop?
Il y a un magasin de photos où? *eel yah uhn mah-gah-zan duh foh-toh oo*

Do you develop film here?
Développez-vous les films ici? *day-vloh-pay voo lay feelm ee-ssee*

How much does it cost for one roll?
Ça coûte combien le développement d'une pellicule? *sah koot kohn-byan luh day-vlohp-mahn dewn peh-lee-kewl*

I have two rolls.
J'ai deux pellicules. *zhay duh peh-lee-kewl*

I want _____.
Je voudrais _____. *zhuh voo-dreh*

■ a print of each with a glossy finish
une épreuve de chacune sur papier brillant *zewn ay-pruhv duh shah-kewn sewr pah-pyay bree-yahn*

with a matte finish
sur papier mat *sewr pah-pyay maht*

■ an enlargement
un agrandissement *zuhn nah-grahn-deess-mahn*

I want a roll of 24 (36) exposures of color (black and white) film.
Je voudrais une pellicule de vingt-quatre (trente-six) en couleur (noir et blanc). *zhuh voo-dreh zewn peh-lee-kewl duh van-kah-truh (trahn-seess) ahn koo-luhr (nwahr ay blahn)*

■ for slides
pour diapositives *poor dee-ah-poh-zee-teev*

■ a film pack, number . . .
une cartouche, numéro . . . *ewn kahr-toosh, new-may-roh*

When can I pick up the pictures?	**Quand puis-je venir chercher les photos?** *kahn pweezh vuh-neer shehr-shay lay foh-toh*
Do you sell cameras?	**Vendez-vous des appareils?** *vahn-day voo day zah pah rehy*
I want an expensive (inexpensive) (disposable) camera.	**Je cherche un appareil cher (pas très cher) (jetable)** *zhuh shehrsh uhn nah-pah-rehy shehr (pah treh shehr) (zheh-tah-bluh)*

SOUVENIRS

You may want to purchase specialties of certain cities or regions as gifts or as souvenirs.

FRANCE

Alençon	lace products
Aubusson, Beauvais	rugs
Baccarat	crystal
Besançon	watches and clocks
Grasse	perfume (Coty, Fragonard, Lanvin)
Grenoble	gloves
Limoges, Sèvres	fine porcelain
Nancy	crystal
Paris	haute couture, high-style fashions at stores like Rive Gauche, Galeries Lafayette, Au Printemps, La Samaritaine

If you are in Paris, you may be able to pick up real bargains at the Flea Market (Marché aux Puces) and, at the small book shops along the Seine, old books, magazines, or comic strips.

Don't forget the famous wines and cheeses, of course!

BELGIUM

Ghent and Kortrijk	linen
Brussels, Brugge	lace
Antwerp	diamonds and jewelry
Val-Saint-Lambert	crystal and glassware
Dinant and Brugge	copperware

Everywhere in the country you can find the renowned Belgian beers, candy, and chocolate.

SWITZERLAND

There are "Swiss-craft" shops throughout the country where you will find a large selection of handmade products from all parts of Switzerland. Typical items include: linen, embroideries, fine handkerchiefs, textiles, wood carvings, ceramics, music boxes, and multiblade knives. Switzerland is also known for its watches, cuckoo clocks, fondue forks and pots, and, of course, the large variety of chocolates and cheese.

Don't forget the high quality of Swiss-printed books.

GIFT SHOP

I'd like ____.	**Je voudrais ____.**	*zhuh voo-dreh*
■ a pretty gift	**un joli cadeau**	*zuhn zhoh-lee kah-doh*
■ a small gift	**un petit cadeau**	*zuhn puh-tee kah-doh*
■ a souvenir	**un souvenir**	*zuhn soov-neer*
It's for ____.	**C'est pour ____.**	*seh poor*
Could you suggest something?	**Pourriez-vous me suggérer quelque chose?**	*poo-ree-yay voo muh sewg-zhay-ray kehl-kuh shohz*

Would you show me your selection of _____?	**Voudriez-vous me montrer votre choix de _____?** *voo-dree-yay voo muh mohn-tray voh-truh shwah duh*
■ blown glass	**verre soufflé** *vehr soo-flay*
■ carved objects	**objets sculptés** *ohb-zheh skewl-tay*
■ cut crystal	**cristal taillé** *kreess-tahl tah-yay*
■ dolls	**poupées** *poo-pay*
■ earthenware (pottery)	**poterie** *poh-tree*
■ fans	**éventails** *ay-vahn tahy*
■ jewelry	**bijouterie** *bee-zhoo-tree*
■ lace	**dentelles** *dahn tehl*
■ leather goods	**objets en cuir** *ohb-zheh ahn kweer*
■ liqueurs	**liqueurs** *lee-kuhr*
■ musical instruments	**instruments de musique** *an-strew-mahn duh mew-zeek*
■ perfumes	**parfums** *pahr-fuhn*
■ pictures	**tableaux** *tah-bloh*
■ posters	**affiches** *ah-feesh*
■ religious articles	**articles religieux** *ahr-tee-kluh ruh-lee-zhuh*
I don't want to spend more than _____ euros.	**Je ne voudrais pas dépenser plus de _____ euros.** *zhuh nuh voo-dreh pah day-pahn-ssay plew duh _____ ew-roh*

Travel Tips A wonderful gift that is very reasonably priced is a hand-painted watercolor scene, sold and packaged in heavy-duty cardboard tubes by artists from their stalls along the Seine in Paris.

ANTIQUE SHOPPING

French-speaking Europe boasts a large number of antique shops where you can find old books, watches, toys, and antiquities.

Haggle as much as you can!

PRINCIPAL SHOPPING AREAS FOR ANTIQUES

FRANCE

Paris

Rue du Bac and Rue des Saints Pères	7ème arrondissement
Marché aux Puces	18ème arrondissement
Quai Voltaire	7ème arrondissement
Rue Jacob and Rue Bonaparte	6ème arrondissement

BELGIUM

Brussels	le Sablon (there is also an open-air market here on Saturday and on Sunday morning)
Antwerp	Near the House of Rubens

STATIONERY

I want to buy _____.	**Je voudrais acheter _____.** *zhuh voo-dreh zahsh-tay*
■ a ball-point pen	**un stylo à bille** *uhn stee-loh ah bee*
■ a deck of cards	**un paquet de cartes** *uhn pah-keh duh kahrt*

■ envelopes	**des enveloppes**	*day zahn-vlohp*
■ an eraser	**une gomme**	*ewn gohm*
■ glue	**de la colle**	*duh lah kohl*
■ a notebook	**un cahier**	*uhn kah-yay*
■ paper	**du papier**	*dew pah-pyay*
■ pencils	**des crayons**	*day kreh-yohn*
■ a pencil sharpener	**un taille-crayon**	*uhn tahy kreh-yohn*
■ a ruler	**une règle**	*ewn reh-gluh*
■ Scotch tape	**une bande adhésive (du scotch)**	*ewn bahnd ahd-ay-zeev (dew skohtsh)*
■ some string	**de la ficelle**	*duh lah fee-ssehl*
■ stationery	**du papier à lettres**	*dew pah-pyay ah leh-truh*
■ wrapping paper	**du papier d'emballage**	*dew pah-pyay dahn-bah-lahzh*
■ a writing pad	**un bloc**	*uhn blohk*

TOBACCO SHOP

Tobacco, cigarettes, and cigars may be purchased from a state-licensed tobacconist. Look for the signs with the red cones outside cafés and bars.

Newly promulgated laws have outlawed smoking in many public places and fines are imposed. Be careful to heed the no smoking signs: DÉFENSE DE FUMER.

A pack (carton) of cigarettes, please.	**Un paquet (une cartouche) de cigarettes, s'il vous plaît.**	*uhn pah-keh (ewn kahr-toosh) duh see-gah-reht seel voo pleh*
■ filtered	**avec filtre**	*ah-vehk feel-truh*
■ unfiltered	**sans filtre**	*sahn feel-truh*

■ menthol   **mentholées**   *mahn-toh-lay*

■ king-size   **long format**   *lohn fohr-mah*

Are these cigarettes (very) strong (mild)?	**Ces cigarettes sont elles (très) fortes (douces)?** *say see-gah-reht sohn tehl (treh) fohrt (dooss)*
Do you have American cigarettes?	**Avez-vous des cigarettes américaines?** *ah-vay voo day see-gah-reht ah-may-ree-kehn*
What brands?	**Quelles marques?** *kehl mahrk*
Please give me a pack of matches also.	**Donnez-moi aussi une boîte d'allumettes, s'il vous plaît.** *doh-nay mwah oh-ssee ewn bwaht dah-lew-meht seel voo pleh*
Do you sell _____?	**Vendez-vous _____?** *vahn-day voo*

■ chewing tobacco   **du tabac à chiquer**   *dew tah-bah ah shee-kay*

■ a cigarette holder   **un fume-cigarettes**   *uhn fewm see-gah-reht*

■ cigars   **des cigares**   *day see-gahr*

■ flints   **des pierres à briquet**   *day pyehr ah bree-keh*

■ lighter fluid   **de l'essence à briquet**   *duh leh-ssahnss ah bree-keh*

■ lighters   **des briquets**   *day bree-keh*

■ pipes   **des pipes**   *day peep*

■ pipe tobacco   **du tabac pour pipe**   *dew tah-bah poor peep*

TOILETRIES

There are pharmacies, **drogueries,** and drugstores in France

A green cross identifies a pharmacy, which sells over the counter and prescription drugs, personal hygiene items, and some cosmetics.

A **droguerie** sells chemical products, paints, household cleaners, detergents, and accessories such as mops, brooms, buckets, and some personal hygiene items and cosmetics.

The *drugstores* in France resemble small department stores. They sell newspapers, international magazines, books, maps, guides, small gifts, records, and have fast-food restaurants for items such as ice cream, sandwiches, or drinks. Many of these drugstores even have a counter where prescriptions can be filled. Perfumes and cosmetics may also be purchased at a *parfumerie*.

Do you have _____?	**Avez-vous _____?** *ah-vay voo*
■ a brush	**une brosse** *ewn brohss*
■ cleansing cream	**une crème démaquillante** *ewn krehm day-mah-kee-yah<u>n</u>t*
■ a comb	**un peigne** *uh<u>n</u> peh-nyuh*
■ condoms	**des préservatifs** *day pray-zehr-vuh-teef*
■ (disposable) diapers	**des couches (disponibles)** *day koosh (deess-poh-nee-bluh)*
■ emery boards	**des limes à ongles** *day leem ah oh<u>n</u>-gluh*
■ eyeliner	**du traceur à paupières** *dew trah-ssuhr ah poh-pyehr*
■ eyebrow pencil	**un crayon pour les yeux** *uh<u>n</u> kreh-yoh<u>n</u> poor lay zyuh*
■ eye shadow	**du fard à paupières** *dew fahr ah poh-pyehr*

■ gel   **du gel coiffant**   *dew zhehl kwah-fahn*

■ hairspray   **de la laque**   *duh lah lahk*

■ lipstick   **du rouge à lèvres**   *dew roozh ah leh-vruh*

■ makeup   **du maquillage**   *dew mah-kee-yahzh*

■ mascara   **du mascara**   *dew mahss-kah-rah*

■ a mirror   **un miroir**   *uhn meer-wahr*

■ mousse   **de la mousse coiffante**   *duh lah mooss kwah-fahnt*

■ mouthwash   **de l'eau dentifrice**   *deh-loh dahn-tee-freess*

■ nail clippers   **un coupe-ongles**   *uhn koop ohn-gluh*

■ a nail file   **une lime à ongles**   *ewn leem ah ohn-gluh*

■ nail polish   **du vernis à ongles**   *dew vehr-nee ah ohn-gluh*

■ nail polish remover   **du dissolvant**   *dew dee-ssohl-vahn*

■ a prophylactic   **un préservatif**   *uhn pray-sehr-vah-teef*

■ a razor   **un rasoir**   *uhn rah-zwahr*

■ razor blades   **une lame de rasoir**   *ewn lahm duh rah-zwahr*

■ rouge   **du fard**   *dew fahr*

■ sanitary napkins   **des serviettes hygiéniques**   *day sehr-vyeht ee-zhyay-neek*

■ (cuticle) scissors   **des ciseaux**   *day see-zoh*

■ shampoo   **du shampooing**   *dew shahn-pwan*

■ shaving lotion **la lotion à raser** *lah loh-ssyohn ah rah-zay*

■ soap **du savon** *dew sah-vohn*

■ a sponge **une éponge** *ewn ay-pohnzh*

■ talcum powder **du talc** *dew tahlk*

■ tampons **des tampons périodiques** *day tahn-pohn pay-ree-oh-deek*

■ tissues **des mouchoirs en papier** *day moo-shwahr ahn pah-pyay*

■ toilet paper **du papier hygiénique** *dew pah-pyay ee-zhyay-neek*

■ a toothbrush **une brosse à dents** *ewn brohss ah dahnt*

■ toothpaste **de la pâte dentifrice** *duh lah paht dahn-tee-freess*

■ tweezers **une pince à épiler** *ewn panss ah ay-pee-lay*

PERSONAL CARE AND SERVICES

If your hotel doesn't offer these amenities, ask the desk clerk to recommend someone nearby.

AT THE BARBER/BEAUTY SALON

Where is there a good _____?
Où y a-t-il un bon _____?
oo ee ah teel uhn bohn

■ barber shop
coiffeur? *kwah-fuhr*

■ beauty salon
salon de beauté *sah-lohn duh boh-tay*

I'd like an appointment for (day) at (hour).
Je voudrais prendre rendez-vous pour _____ à _____. *zhuh voo-dreh prahndr rahn-day-voo poor _____ ah*

Do I have to wait long?
Faut-il attendre long temps? *foh teel ah-tahn-druh lohn-tahn*

I would like _____.
Je voudrais _____. *zhuh voo-dreh*

■ a color rinse
un shampooing colorant *uhn shahn-pwan koh-loh-rahn*

■ a facial massage
un massage facial *uhn mah-ssahzh fah-ssyahl*

■ a haircut
une coupe de cheveux *ewn koop duh shuh-vuh*

blunt
en carré *ahn kah-ray*

layered
dégradée *day-grah-day*

■ highlights
des reflets *day ruh-fleh*

■ a manicure
une manucure *ewn mah-new-kewr*

■ a pedicure
une pédicurie *ewn pay-dee-kew-ree*

■ a permanent
une permanente *ewn pehr-mah-nahnt*

- a shampoo **un shampooing** *uhn shahn-pwan*
- a shave **me faire raser** *muh fehr rah-zay*
- a tint **des reflets** *day ruh-fleh*
- a touch-up **une retouche** *ewn ruh-toosh*
- a trim **une coupe** *ewn koop*
- a wash and set **un shampooing et une mise en plis** *uhn shahn-pwan ay ewn meez uhn plee*
- a waxing **une épilation** *ewn ay-pee-lah-syohn*

I want it (very) short (long).
Je les veux (très) courts (longs). *zhuh lay vuh (treh) koor (lohn)*

You can cut a little _____.
Vous pouvez dégager un peu _____. *voo poo-vay day-gah-zhay uhn puh*

- in back **derrière** *deh-rychr*
- in front **devant** *duh-vahn*
- off the top **dessus** *duh-ssew*
- on the sides **aux côtés** *oh koh-tay*

I part my hair _____.
Je fais la raie _____. *zhuh feh lah ray*

- on the left **à gauche** *ah gohsh*
- on the right **à droite** *ah drwaht*
- in the middle **au milieu** *oh meel-yuh*

I comb my hair straight back.
Je me peigne en arrière. *zhuh muh peh-nyuh ahn nah-ryehr*

Cut a little bit more here.
Coupez un peu plus ici. *koo-pay uhn puh plew ee-ssee*

That's enough.
Ça suffit. *sah sew-fee*

It's fine that way.
C'est parfait comme ça. *seh pahr-feh kohm sah*

I (don't) want _____.	**Je (ne) veux (pas de) _____.** *zhuh (nuh) vuh (pah duh)*
■ hairspray	**la laque** *lah lahk*
■ shampoo	**un shampooing** *uh<u>n</u> shan-pwa<u>n</u>*
■ lotion	**une lotion** *ewn loh-ssyoh<u>n</u>*
Trim my _____.	**Rafraîchissez-moi _____.** *rah-freh-sshee-ssay mwah*
■ beard	**la barbe** *lah bahrb*
■ moustache	**la moustache** *lah mooss-tahsh*
■ sideburns	**les favoris** *lay fah-voh-ree*
I'd like to look at myself in the mirror.	**Je voudrais me regarder dans le miroir.** *zhuh voo-dreh muh ruh-gahr-day dah<u>n</u> luh meer-wahr*
How much do I owe you?	**Je vous dois combien?** *zhuh voo dwah koh<u>n</u>-bya<u>n</u>*
I'd like to see a color chart.	**Je voudrais voir une échelle de teintes.** *zhuh voo-dreh vwahr ewn ay-shehl duh ta<u>n</u>t*

I want _____.	**Je voudrais _____.**	*zhuh voo-dreh*
■ auburn	**auburn**	*oh-buhrn*
■ black	**noir**	*nwahr*
■ (light) blond	**blond (clair)**	*blohn (klehr)*
■ brunette	**brun**	*bruhn*
■ a darker color	**une teinte plus foncée**	*ewn tant plew fohn-ssay*
■ a lighter color	**une teinte plus claire**	*ewn tant plew klehr*
■ the same color	**la même couleur**	*lah mehm koo-luhr*

ALL-OCCASION PROBLEM SOLVERS

Where is the nearest _____?	**Où est le (la) _____ plus proche?** *oo eh luh (lah) _____ plew prohsh*
At what time do you open?	**Vous êtes ouvert à quelle heure?** *voo zeh too-vehr ah kehl uhr*
At what time do you close?	**Vous fermez à quelle heure?** *voo fehr-may ah kehl uhr*
What days are you open? (closed?)	**Vous êtes ouvert (vous fermez) quels jours?** *voo zeht oo-vehr (voo fehr-may) kehl zhoor*
Can you fix _____?	**Pouvez-vous réparer _____?** *poo-vay voo ray-pah-ray*
■ these boots	**ces bottes** *say boht*
■ this button	**ce bouton** *suh boo-tohn*
■ this camera	**cet apareil** *seht tah-pah-rehy*
■ this jacket	**ce veston** *suh vehss-tohn*
■ this shirt	**cette chemise** *seht shuh-meez*
■ these shoes	**ces chaussures** *say shoh-sewr*
■ this watch	**cette montre** *seht mohn-truh*
■ this zipper	**cette fermeture-éclair** *seht fehr-muh-tewr ay-klehr*

There's a button missing.	**Il y a un bouton qui manque.** *eel yah uhn boo-tohn kee mahnk*
Can you sew it back on?	**Pouvez-vous le recoudre?** *poo-vay voo luh ruh-koo-druh*
Can you fix it (them) today?	**Pouvez-vous le (la, l', les) réparer aujourd'hui?** *poo-vay voo luh (lah, lay) ray-pah-ray oh-zhoor-dwee*
May I have a receipt?	**Puis-je avoir un reçu?** *pweezh ah-vwahr uhn ruh-sew*
Can you fix it (them) temporarily (while I wait)?	**Pouvez-vous le (la, l', les) réparer provisoirement (pendant que j'attends)?** *poo-vay voo luh (lah, lay) ray-pah-ray proh-vee-zwahr-mahn (pahn-dahn kuh zhah-tahn)*
When will it (they) be ready?	**Ça sera prêt quand?** *sah suh-rah preh kahn*
I need it (them) (for) _____ promptly.	**J'en ai besoin (pour) _____ sans délai.** *zhahn nay buh-zwan (poor) sahn day-leh*
■ today	**aujourd'hui** *oh-zhoord-wee*
■ tonight	**ce soir** *suh swahr*
■ tomorrow	**demain** *duh-man*
■ the day after tomorrow	**après-demain** *ah-preh duh-man*
■ next week	**la semaine prochaine** *lah suh-mehn proh-shehn*
■ as soon as possible	**aussitôt que possible** *oh-see-toh kuh poh-see-bluh*
How much will it cost?	**Ça coûtera combien?** *sah koot-rah kohn-byan*

LAUNDRY AND DRY CLEANING

Where is the nearest ___ ?	**Où est la _____ la plus proche?** *oo eh lah _____ lah plew prohsh*
■ laundry	**blanchisserie** *blahn-sheess-ree*
■ laundromat	**laverie automatique** *lah-vree oh-toh-mah-teek*
■ dry cleaner's	**teinturerie** *tahn-tew-ruh-ree*
I have a lot of clothes to be _____.	**J'ai beaucoup de vêtements à faire _____.** *zhay boh-koo duh veht-mahn ah fehr*
■ dry-cleaned	**nettoyer à sec** *neh-twah-yay ah sehk*
■ washed	**laver** *lah-vay*
■ mended	**réparer** *ray-pah-ray*
■ ironed	**repasser** *ruh-pah-ssay*
This isn't my laundry.	**Ce n'est pas ma lessive.** *suh neh pah mah lay-sseev*

Travel Tips Every traveler needs to carry a few small items for emergencies. Sealed, pre-wet washcloths, Band-Aids, a fold-up toothbrush, a small tube of toothpaste, a tiny sewing kit, notebook and pen, and aspirin are musts for the handbag or backpack. Skip Swiss army knives or any object that could be considered a weapon by airport security guards.

SHOE REPAIRS

Put on (half) soles and rubber heels.	**Mettez les (demi-) semelles et les talons en caoutchouc.** *meh-tay lay (duh-mee) suh-mehl ay lay tah-lohn ahn kah-oo-tshoo*
I'd like to have my shoes shined (too).	**Je voudrais un cirage (aussi).** *zhuh voo-dreh zuhn see-rahzh (oh-ssee)*

WATCH REPAIRS

I need ____.	**Il me faut ____.** *eel muh foh*
■ a battery	**une pile** *tewn peel*
■ a crystal, glass	**un verre** *tuhn vehr*
■ an hour hand	**une petite aiguille** *tewn puh-teet ay-gwee*
■ a minute hand	**une aiguille des minutes** *tewn ay-gwee day mee-newt*
■ a screw	**une vis** *tewn veess*
■ a second hand	**une aiguille des secondes** *tewn ay-gwee day suh-gohnd*
■ a watchband	**un bracelet de montre** *tuhn brahs-leh duh mohn-truh*
Can you look at it?	**Pouvez-vous l'examiner?** *poo-vay voo lehg-zah-mee-nay*
Can you clean it?	**Pouvez-vous la nettoyer?** *poo-vay voo lah neh-twah-yay*
I dropped it.	**Je l'ai laissé tomber.** *zhuh lay leh-ssay tohn-bay*
It's fast (slow).	**Cette montre avance (retarde).** *seht mohn-truh ah-vahnss (ruh-tahrd)*
It's stopped.	**Elle s'est arrêtée.** *ehl seh tah-reh-tay*

CAMERA REPAIRS

My camera doesn't work well.
Mon appareil ne fonctionne pas bien. *mohn nah-pah-rehy nuh fohnk-ssyohn pah byun*

It fell (into the water).
Il est tombé (dans l'eau). *eel eh tohn-bay (dahn loh)*

AT THE OPTICIAN

I've broken a lens (the frame).
J'ai cassé un verre (la monture). *zhay kah ssay uhn vehr (lah mohn-tewr)*

Can you put in a new lens?
Pouvez-vous mettre un nouveau verre? *poo-vay voo meh-truh uhn noo-voh vehr*

Do you sell progressive lenses?
Vendez-vous des verres progressifs? *vahn-day voo day vehr proh-greh-sseef*

Can you tighten the screw?
Pouvez-vous resserrer la vis? *poo-vay voo ruh-sseh-ray lah veess*

I don't have any others.
Je n'ai pas d'autre paire. *zhuh nay pah doh-truh pehr*

Do you sell contact lenses?
Vendez-vous des verres de contact? *vahn-day voo day vehr duh kohn-tahkt*

I've lost a contact lens.
J'ai perdu un verre de contact. *zhay pehr-dew uhn vehr duh kohn-tahkt*

Can you replace it right away?
Pouvez-vous le remplacer tout de suite? *poo-vay voo luh rahn-plah-ssay toot sweet*

Do you sell sunglasses?	**Vendez-vous des lunettes de soleil?** *vahn-day voo day lew-neht duh soh-lehy*

PHOTOCOPIES

Some drugstores and stationery stores will have photocopy machines.

Do you have a photocopier?	**Avez-vous un photo-copieur?** *ah-vay-voo uhn fot-toh-koh-pyuhr*
I would like to make a photocopy of this paper (this document).	**Je voudrais faire une photocopie de ce papier (ce document).** *zhuh voo-dreh fehr ewn foh-toh-koh-pee duh suh pah-pyay (suh doh-kew-mahn)*
What is the cost per page?	**Quel est le prix par page?** *kehl eh luh pree pahr pahzh*
Can you enlarge it (by 25 percent)?	**Pouvez-vous l'élargir (de vingt-cinq pour cent)?** *poo-vay voo lay-lahr-zheer (duh van-sank poor sahn)*
Can you reduce it (by 50 percent)?	**Pouvez-vous le réduire (de cinquante pour cent)?** *poo-vay voo luh ray-dweer (duh san-kahnt poor sahn)*
Can you make a color copy?	**Pouvez-vous en faire une copie en couleurs?** *poo-vay voo ahn fehr ewn koh-pee ahn koo-luhr*

MEDICAL CARE

AT THE PHARMACY

A green cross indicates a pharmacy, where you buy over-the-counter or prescription drugs. If the pharmacy is closed there will be a sign on the door to indicate which pharmacies are open in the neighborhood.

Where is the nearest (all-night) pharmacy?	**Où se trouve la pharmacie de garde (de nuit) la plus proche?** *oo suh troov lah fahr-mah-ssee duh gahrd (duh nwee) lah plew prohsh*
At what time does the pharmacy open (close)?	**À quelle heure ouvre (ferme) la pharmacie?** *ah kehl uhr oo-vruh (fehrm) lah fahr-mah-ssee*
I need something for ____.	**Il me faut quelque chose pour ____.** *eel muh foh kehl-kuh shohz poor*
■ a cold	**un rhume** *uhn rewm*
■ constipation	**la constipation** *lah kohn sstee-pah-ssyohn*
■ a cough	**une toux** *ewn too*
■ diarrhea	**la diarrhée** *lah dee-ah-ray*
■ a fever	**une fièvre** *ewn fyeh-vruh*
■ hay fever	**le rhume des foins** *luh rewm day fwan*
■ a headache	**un mal de tête** *uhn mahl duh teht*
■ insomnia	**l'insomnie** *lan-sohm-nee*
■ the flu	**la grippe** *lah greep*
■ nausea	**la nausée** *lah noh-zay*
■ sunburn	**les coups de soleil** *lay koo duh soh-lehy*

■ a toothache	**un mal de dents** *uhn mahl duh dahn*
■ an upset stomach	**les indigestions** *lay zan-dee-zhehss-tyohn*
Is a prescription needed for the medicine?	**Faut-il avoir une ordonnance pour ce médicament?** *foh-teel ah-vwahr ewn ohr-doh-nahnss poor suh may-dee-kah-mahn*
Can you fill this prescription for me now?	**Pourriez-vous me préparer cette ordonnance maintenant?** *poo-ree-yay voo muh pray-pah-ray seht ohr-doh-nahnss mant-nahn*
It's an emergency.	**C'est urgent.** *seh tewr-zhahn*
Can I wait for it?	**Puis-je l'attendre?** *pweezh lah-tahn-druh*
How long will it take?	**Ça prendra combien de temps?** *sah prahn-drah kohn-byan duh tahn*
When can I come for it?	**Quand puis-je venir la chercher?** *kahn pweezh vuh-neer lah shehr-shay*
I would like _____.	**Je voudrais _____.** *zhuh voo-dreh*
■ alcohol	**de l'alcool** *duh lahl-kohl*
■ an antacid	**un anti-acide** *zuhn nahn-tee ah-sseed*
■ an antiseptic	**un antiseptique** *zuhn nahn-tee-ssehp-teek*
■ aspirins	**des aspirines** *day zahss-pee-reen*
■ bandages	**des bandes** *day bahnd*
■ Band-Aids	**des bandages** *day bahn-dazh*
■ (absorbent) cotton	**du coton** *dew koh-tohn*

- cough drops **des pastilles contre la toux** *day pahss-tee kohn truh lah too*

- cough syrup **du sirop contre la toux** *dew see-roh kohn-truh lah too*

- eardrops **des gouttes pour les oreilles** *day goot poor lay zoh-rehy*

- eyedrops **des gouttes pour les yeux** *day goot poor lay zyuh*

- iodine **de la teinture d'iode** *duh lah tan-tewr dyohd*

- a (mild) laxative **un laxatif (léger)** *zuhn lahk-ssah-teef (lay-zhay)*

- milk of magnesia **le lait de magnésie** *luh leh duh muh-nyay zoo*

- suppositories **les suppositoires** *lay sew-poh-zee twahr*

- a thermometer **un thermomètre** *uhn tehr-moh-meh-truh*

- tranquilizers **des tranquillisants** *day trahn-kee-lee-zahn*

- vitamins **des vitamines** *day vee-tah-meen*

DOCTORS

You never know when you may need a doctor while on vacation. In Paris the U.S. Embassy (tel: (01) 43 12 23 47) has a list of English-speaking doctors. There is also an American Hospital where most of the doctors speak English (tel: (01) 46 41 25 25) and the Hertford British Hospital (tel: (01) 46 39 22 22). In other areas and situations, the following phrases will help you:

I don't feel well. I feel sick. **Je ne me sens pas bien.** *zhuh nuh muh sahn pah byan*

I need a doctor. **Il me faut un médecin.** *eel muh foh tuhn mayd-ssan*

Do you know a doctor who speaks English?	**Connaissez-vous un médecin qui parle anglais?**	*koh-neh-ssay voo uhn mayd-ssan kee pahrl ahn-gleh*
Where is his office?	**Où se trouve son cabinet?**	*oo suh troov sohn kah-bee-neh*

PARTS OF THE BODY

ankle	**la cheville**	*lah shuh-vee*
appendix	**l'appendice**	*lah-pan-deess*
arm	**le bras**	*luh brah*
back	**le dos**	*luh doh*
chest	**la poitrine**	*lah pwah-treen*
ear	**l'oreille**	*loh-rehy*
elbow	**le coude**	*luh kood*
eyes	**l'oeil**	*luhy*
face	**la figure**	*lah fee-gewr*
finger	**le doigt**	*luh dwah*
foot	**le pied**	*luh pyay*
hand	**la main**	*lah man*
head	**la tête**	*lah teht*
heart	**le coeur**	*luh kuhr*
hip	**la hanche**	*lah ahnsh*
knee	**le genou**	*luh zhuh-noo*
leg	**la jambe**	*lah zhahnb*
mouth	**la bouche**	*lah boosh*

neck	**le cou**	*luh koo*
nose	**le nez**	*luh nay*
shoulder	**l'épaule**	*lay-pohl*
skin	**la peau**	*lah poh*
throat	**la gorge**	*lah gohrzh*
tooth	**la dent**	*lah dahn*
wrist	**le poignet**	*luh pwah-nyeh*

TELLING THE DOCTOR

I have _____. **J'ai _____.** *zhay*

■ an abscess **un abcès** *uhn nahb-sseh*

■ a broken bone **une fracture** *ewn frahk-tewr*

■ a bruise **une contusion** *ewn kohn-tew-zyohn*

■ a burn **une brûlure** *ewn brew-lewr*

■ the chills **des frissons** *day free-ssohn*

■ a cold **un rhume** *uhn rewm*
  a chest cold **une bronchite** *ewn brohn-sheet*
  a head cold **un rhume de cerveau** *uhn rewm duh sehr-voh*

■ cramps **des crampes** *day krahnp*

■ a cut **une coupure** *ewn koo-pewr*

■ diarrhea **la diarrhée** *lah dee-ah-ray*

■ a fever **de la fièvre** *duh lah fyeh-vruh*

■ a fracture **une fracture** *ewn frahk-tewr*

■ a headache **mal à la tête** *mahl ah lah teht*

■ an infection **une infection** *ewn an-fehk-ssyohn*

■ a lump **une grosseur** *ewn groh-ssuhr*

■ something in my eye **quelque chose dans l'oeil** *kehl-kuh shohz dahn luhy*

■ a sore throat **mal à la gorge** *mahl ah lah gohrzh*

■ a stomachache	**mal à l'estomac**	_mahl ah lehss-toh-mah_
■ swelling	**une enflure**	_ewn ahn-flewr_
■ a wound	**une blessure**	_ewn bleh-ssewr_

I am constipated.	**Je suis constipé(e).** _zhuh swee kohn-sstee-pay_
It hurts me here.	**J'ai mal ici.** _zhay mahl ee-ssee_
My whole body hurts.	**Tout mon corps me fait mal.** _too mohn kohr muh feh mahl_
My _____ hurts since (yesterday, two days ago, last week).	**J'ai mal _____ depuis (hier, deux jours, la semaine passée).** _zhay mahl duh-pwee (yehr duh zhoor lah suh-mehn pah-ssay)_

■ ankle	**à la cheville**	_ah lah shuh-vee_
■ arm	**au bras**	_oh brah_
■ back	**au dos**	_oh doh_
■ chest	**à la poitrine**	_ah lah pwah-treen_
■ ear	**à l'oreille**	_ah loh-rehy_
■ elbow	**au coude**	_oh kood_
■ eyes	**aux yeux**	_oh zyuh_
■ face	**à la figure**	_ah lah fee-gewr_
■ finger	**au doigt**	_oh dwah_
■ foot	**au pied**	_oh pyay_
■ glands	**aux ganglions**	_oh gahn-glee-yohn_
■ hand	**à la main**	_ah lah man_
■ head	**à la tête**	_ah lah teht_
■ hip	**à la hanche**	_ah lah ahnsh_
■ knee	**au genou**	_oh zhuh-noo_
■ leg	**à la jambe**	_ah lah zhahnb_
■ lip	**à la lèvre**	_ah lah leh-vruh_
■ mouth	**à la bouche**	_ah lah boosh_

■ neck	**au cou**	*oh koo*
■ nose	**au nez**	*oh nay*
■ shoulder	**à l'épaule**	*ah lay-pohl*
■ throat	**à la gorge**	*ah lah gohrzh*
■ thumb	**au pouce**	*oh pooss*
■ toe	**à l'orteil**	*ah lohr-tehy*
■ tooth	**aux dents**	*oh dahn*
■ wrist	**au poignet**	*oh pwah-nyeh*

There is (no) _____ in my family.

Il y a (Il n'y a pas) _____ dans ma famille. *eel yah (eel nyah pah) _____ dahn mah fah-mee*

■ asthma **l'asthme (m.)** *lahs-muh*

■ diabetes **la diabète** *lah dee-yah-beht*

■ heart disease **la maladie cardiaque** *lah mah-lah-dee kahr dyahk*

I'm (not) allergic to antibiotics.

Je (ne) suis (pas) allergique aux antibiotiques. *zhuh (nuh) swee (pah) zah-lehr-zheek oh zahn tee bee-oh-teek*

I have a pain in my chest.

J'ai une douleur à la poitrine. *zhay ewn doo-luhr ah lah pwah-treen*

I had a heart attack _____ year(s) ago.	**J'ai eu une crise cardiaque il y a ___ ans.** _zhay ew ewn kreez kahr-dyahk eel yah ___ ahn_
I'm taking this medicine.	**Je prends ce médicament.** _zhuh prahn suh may-dee-kah-mahn_
I'm pregnant.	**Je suis enceinte.** _zhuh zwee zahn-sant_
I feel faint.	**Je vais m'évanouir.** _zhuh veh may-vah-nweer_
I'm dizzy.	**J'ai des vertiges.** _zhay day vehr-teezh_
I feel weak.	**Je me sens faible.** _zhuh muh sahn feh-bluh_
I want to sit down for a while.	**Je voudrais m'asseoir un moment.** _zhuh voo-dreh mah-sswahr uhn moh-mahn_
I feel all right now.	**Je vais bien maintenant.** _zhuh veh byan mant-nahn_
I feel better.	**Je vais mieux.** _zhuh veh myuh_
I feel worse.	**Je me sens moins bien.** _zhuh muh sahn mwan byan_
Do I have _____?	**Est-ce que j'ai _____?** _ehss kuh zhay_
■ appendicitis	**l'appendicite** _lah-pahn-dee-sseet_
■ the flu	**la grippe** _lah greep_
■ tonsilitis	**une amygdalite** _ewn nah-meeg-dah-leet_
Is it serious (contagious)?	**C'est grave (contagieux)?** _seh grahv (kohn-tah-zhyuh)_

| Do I have to go to the hospital? | **Dois-je aller à l'hôpital?** *dwahzh ah-lay ah loh-pee-tahl* |
| When can I continue my trip? | **Quand pourrai-je pour-suivre mon voyage?** *kahn poo-rayzh poor-swee-vruh mohn vwah yahzh* |

DOCTOR'S INSTRUCTIONS

Open your mouth.	**Ouvrez la bouche.** *oo-vray lah boosh*
Stick out your tongue.	**Tirez la langue.** *tee-ray lah lahng*
Cough.	**Toussez.** *too-ssay*
Breathe deeply.	**Respirez profondément.** *rehss-pee-ray proh-fohn-day-mahn*
Take off your clothing (to the waist)	**Déshabillez-vous (jusqu'à la ceinture).** *day-zah-bee-yay voo (zhewss-kah lah san-tewr)*
Lie down.	**Étendez-vous.** *ay-tahn-day voo*
Stand up.	**Levez-vous.** *luh-vay voo*
It is necessary to do a blood test.	**Il faut faire une analyse de sang.** *eel foh fehr ewn ah-nah-leez duh sahn*
Get dressed.	**Habillez-vous.** *ah-bee-yay voo*

PATIENT

| Are you going to give me a prescription? | **Allez-vous me donner une ordonnance?** *ah-lay voo muh doh-nay ewn ohr-doh-nahnss* |
| How often must I take this medicine (these pills)? | **Combien de fois par jour dois-je prendre ce médicament (ces pilules)?** *kohn-byan duh fwah pahr zhoor dwahzh prahn-druh suh may-dee-kah-mahn (seh pee-lewl)* |

(How long) do I have to stay in bed?	**(Combien de temps) dois-je garder le lit?** *(kohn-byan duh tahn) dwahzh gahr-day luh lee*
Thank you (for everything), doctor.	**Merci bien (pour tout), docteur.** *mehr-ssee byan (poor too) dohk-tuhr*
What is your fee?	**Quels sont vos honoraires?** *kehl sohn voh zoh-noh-rehr*
I have medical insurance.	**J'ai une assurance médicale.** *zhay ewn ah-ssew-rahnss may-dee-kahl*
Please fill out this medical form.	**Remplissez cette feuille de maladie, s'il vous plaît.** *rahn-plee-ssay seht fuhy duh mah-lah-dee seel voo pleh*
May I please have a receipt for my medical insurance?	**Puis-je avoir une quittance pour mon assurance médicale, s'il vous plaît?** *Pweezh ah-vwahr ewn kee-tahnss poor mohn nah-sew-rahnss may-dee-kahl seel voo pleh*

SPECIAL NEEDS

Where can I get _____?	**Où puis-je obtenir _____?** *oo pweezh ohb-tuh-neer*
■ a cane	**une canne** *ewn kahn*
■ crutches	**des béquilles (f.)** *day bay-kee*
■ a hearing aid	**un audiophone** *uhn noh-dyoh-fohn*
■ a walker	**un déambulateur** *uhn day-ahn-bew-lah-tuhr*
■ a wheelchair	**un fauteuil roulant** *uhn foh-tuhy roo-lahn*
What services are available for the handicapped?	**Quels services sont disponibles aux handicapés?** *kehl sehr-veess sohn deess-poh-nee-bluh oh zahn-dee-kah-pay*

IN THE HOSPITAL (ACCIDENTS)

Help!	**Au secours!**	*oh suh-koor*
Help me, please.	**Aidez-moi, s'il vous plaît.**	*eh-day mwah seel voo pleh*
Get a doctor, quick!	**Vite, appelez un médecin!**	*veet ah-play uhn mayd-ssan*
Call an ambulance!	**Faites venir une ambulance!**	*feht vuh-neer ewn ahn-bew-lahnss*
Take me (him, her) to the hospital.	**Emmenez-moi (le, la) à l'hôpital.**	*uhn-muh-nay mwah (luh, lah) ah loh-pee-tahl*
I need first aid.	**J'ai besoin de premiers soins.**	*zhay buh-zwan duh pruh-myay swan*
I fell.	**Je suis tombé(e).**	*zhuh swee tohn-bay*
I burned myself.	**Je me suis brûlé(e).**	*zhuh muh swee brew-lay*
I cut myself.	**Je me suis coupé(e).**	*zhuh muh swee koo-pay*
I'm bleeding.	**Je saigne.**	*zhuh seh-nyuh*
He's lost a lot of blood.	**Il a perdu beaucoup de sang.**	*eel ah pehr-dew boh-koo duh sahn*
My leg is swollen.	**Ma jambe est enflée.**	*mah zhahnb eh tahn-flay*
Is there out-patient surgery?	**Il y a de la chirurgie ambulatoire?**	*eel yah duh lah sheer-ewr-zhee ahn-bew-lah-twahr*

Is there a recovery room?	**Il y a une salle de repos?** *eel yah uhn sahl duh ruh-poh*
Is there home care?	**Il y a du soutien à domicile?** *eel yah dew soo-tyan ah doh-mee-sseel*
Is the wrist (ankle) sprained (twisted)?	**Le poignet (la cheville) est démis (démise) (tordu(e))?** *luh pwah-nyeh (lah shuh-vee) eh day-mee (day-meez) (tohr-dew)*
I can't move my elbow (knee).	**Je ne peux pas remuer le coude (le genou).** *zhuh nuh puh pah ruh-mew-ay luh kood (luh zhuh-noo)*

AT THE DENTIST

I have to go to the dentist.	**Il me faut aller chez le dentiste.** *eel muh foh tah-lay shay luh dahn-teesst*
Can you recommend a dentist?	**Pouvez-vous me recommander un dentiste?** *poo-vay voo muh ruh-koh-mahn-day uhn dahn-teesst*
I have a bad toothache.	**J'ai un mal de dents à tout casser. (J'ai une rage de dents.)** *zhay uhn mahl duh dahn ah too kah-ssay (zhay ewn rahzh duh dahn)*
What is your fee?	**Combien je vous dois?** *kohn-byan zhuh voo dwah*
I've lost a filling.	**J'ai perdu un plombage.** *zhay pehr-dew uhn plohn-bahzh*
I've broken a tooth.	**Je me suis cassé une dent.** *zhuh muh swee kah-ssay ewn dahn*

AT THE DENTIST • 195

My gums hurt me.	**Les gencives me font mal.** *lay zhah<u>n</u>-sseev muh foh<u>n</u> mahl*
Is there an infection?	**Il y a une infection?** *eel yah ewn a<u>n</u>-fehk-ssyoh<u>n</u>*
Will you have to pull the tooth?	**Faut-il arracher la dent?** *foh teel ah-rah-shay lah dah<u>n</u>*
Can you fill it ____?	**Pouvez-vous l'obturer ____?** *poo-vay voo lohb-tew-ray*
■ with amalgam	**avec une amalgame** *ah-vehk ewn ah-mahl-gahm*
■ with gold	**avec de l'or** *ah-vehk duh lohr*
■ with silver	**avec de l'argent** *ah-vehk duh lahr-zhah<u>n</u>*
■ for now	**pour le moment** *poor luh moh-mah<u>n</u>*
■ temporarily	**provisoirement** *proh-vee-zwahr-mah<u>n</u>*
Can you fix ____?	**Pouvez-vous réparer?** *poo-vay voo ray-pah-ray*
■ this bridge	**ce bridge** *suh breedzh*
■ this crown	**cette couronne** *seht koo-rohn*
■ this denture	**ce dentier** *suh dah<u>n</u>-tyay*
When should I come back?	**Quand faut-il revenir?** *kah<u>n</u> foh-teel ruh-vuh-neer*

COMMUNICATIONS

POST OFFICE

The letters P.T. (**Postes et Télécommunications**—for letters and telephones) identify the post offices. They are open from 8:00 A.M. to 7:00 P.M., with a two-hour break for lunch in many instances, and on Saturdays from 8:00 A.M. to noon. The main Paris post office never closes. Purchase stamps at post offices, at café-tabacs, or at your hotel. Look for the yellow mailbox.

Minitel, France's telephone-database network, provides an electronic telephone directory that allows for free assistance in most post offices.

I want to mail a letter.	**Je voudrais mettre cette lettre à la poste.** *zhuh voo-dreh meh-truh seht leh-truh ah lah pohsst*
Where's the post office?	**Où se trouve le bureau de poste?** *oo suh troov luh bew-roh duh pohsst*
Where's a mailbox?	**Où se trouve une boîte aux lettres?** *oo suh troov ewn bwaht oh leh-truh*
What is the postage on ＿＿ to the United States?	**Quel est l'affranchissement ＿＿ pour les États-Unis?** *kehl eh lah-frahn-sheess-mahn poor lay zay-tah zew-nee*
■ a letter	**d'une lettre** *dewn leh-truh*
■ an air mail letter	**pour une lettre envoyée par avion** *poor ewn leh-truh ahn-vwah-yay pahr ah-vyohn*
■ an insured letter	**pour une lettre recommandée** *poor ewn leh-truh ruh-koh-mahn-day*
■ a registered letter	**pour une lettre recommandée** *poor ewn leh-truh ruh-koh-mahn-day*

■ a special delivery letter	**pour une lettre par exprès**	*poor ewn leh-truh pahr ehkss-preh*
■ a package	**d'un colis**	*duhn koh-lee*
■ a postcard	**d'une carte postale**	*dewn kahrt pohss-tahl*
When will it arrive?	**Quand arrivera-t-il (t-elle)?**	*kahn tah-ree-vrah teel (tehl)*
Where is the ___ window?	**Où est le guichet ___?**	*oo eh luh gee-sheh*
■ general delivery	**pour la poste restante**	*poor lah pohsst rehss-tahnt*
■ money order	**pour les mandats-poste**	*poor lay muhn-dah pohsst*
■ stamp	**pour les timbres-poste**	*poor lay tan-bruh pohsst*
Are there any letters for me?	**Il y a des lettres pour moi?**	*eel yah day leh-truh poor mwah*
My name is ___.	**Je m'appelle ___.**	*zhuh mah-pehl*
I'd like ___.	**Je voudrais ___.**	*zhuh voo-dreh*
■ 10 post cards	**dix cartes postales**	*dee kahrt pohss-tahl*
■ 5 (air mail) stamps	**cinq timbres (courrier aérien)**	*sank tahn-bruh (koo-ryay ah-ay-ryan)*

TELEGRAMS

Where's the tele-graph window?	**Où est le guichet pour les télégrammes?** *oo eh luh gee-sheh poor lay tay-lay-grahm*
How late is it open?	**Il est ouvert jusqu'à quelle heure?** *eel eh too-vehr zhewss-kah kehl uhr*

I'd like to send a telegram (night letter) to _____.	**Je voudrais envoyer un télégramme (une lettre-télégramme) à _____.** *zhuh voo-dreh zahn-vwah-yay uhn tay-lay-grahm (ewn leh-truh tay-lay-grahm) ah*
How much is it per word?	**Quel est le tarif par mot?** *kehl eh luh tah-reef pahr moh*
Where are the forms?	**Où sont les formulaires (imprimés)?** *oo sohn lay fohr-mew-lehr (an-pree-may)*
I want to send it collect.	**Je voudrais l'envoyer en P.C.V.** *zhuh voo-dreh lahn-vwah-yay ahn pay say vay*
When will it arrive?	**Il arrivera quand?** *eel ah-ree-vrah kahn*

TELEPHONES

All telephone numbers in France have 10 digits and are given in pairs. The first two digits represent an area code:

Paris and surrounding regions	01
Northwest France	02
Northeast France	03
Southeast France and Corsica	04
Southwest France	05

The telephone system in France, France Télécom, is controlled by the government agency P.T.T. (**postes, télégraphes et téléphones**). You generally don't need operator assistance to place local or long-distance calls. Public pay phones are available in post offices, cafés, tobacconists, in some convenience stores, and on the streets of larger cities. To call the United States or Canada, dial **19 + 1 + area code + number.**

Hotels tend to charge exorbitant rates for international as well as domestic calls. It's an excellent idea, therefore, to purchase a **Télécarte,** available at the places listed above and in any location with a sign that reads "**Télécartes en vente ici,**" which enables you to buy 50 or 120 message units of calls. It is the only "coin" accepted in the public phone system. The number of message units required for the call depends on the total speaking time and the area phoned: One unit entitles you to one three-minute call during the normal rate period, and up to nine minutes of calls after 10:50 P.M. It also allows you to make 10 minutes worth of calls within France, or a four minute call to the United States. It can also connect you with an operator to call home. The pictures on these cards vary and change over time, so some of the **Télécartes** are already collectors' items that are on display at the market at Rond Point des Champs-Elysées.

TO CALL

You have to ____.	**Vous devez ____.** *voo duh-vay*
call back	**rappeler** *rah-play*
dial	**composer le numéro** *kohn-poh-zay luh new-may-roh*
hang up (the receiver)	**raccrocher** *rah-kroh-shay*
insert the card	**introduire la carte** *an-troh-dweer lah kahrt*
know the area code (of the country) (of the city)	**savoir l'indicatif (du pays) (de la ville)** *sah-vwahr lan-dee-kah-teef (dew pay-ee)(duh lah veel)*
leave a message	**laisser un message** *leh-say uhn meh-sahzh*
listen for the dial tone	**attendre la tonalité** *ah-tahndr lah toh-nah-lee-tay*
pick up (the receiver)	**décrocher** *day-kroh-shay*
telephone	**téléphoner** *tay-lay-foh-nay*

Where is ____?	**Où y a-t-il ____?** *oo ee ah-teel*
■ a public telephone	**un téléphone public** *uhn tay-lay-fohn pew-bleek*
■ a telephone booth	**une cabine téléphonique** *ewn kah-been tay-lay-foh-neek*
■ a telephone directory	**un annuaire téléphonique** *uhn nah-new-ehr tay-lay-foh-neek*
May I use your phone?	**Puis-je me servir de votre téléphone?** *pweezh muh sehr-veer duh voh-truh tay-lay-fohn*
I want to make a ____.	**Je voudrais téléphoner ____.** *zhuh voo-dreh tay-lay-foh-nay*
■ local call	**en ville** *ahn veel*
■ long-distance call	**à l'extérieur** *ah lehkss-tay-ryuhr*
■ person-to-person call	**avec préavis** *ah-vehk pray-ah-vee*
How do I get the ____?	**Que fait-on pour ____?** *kuh feh-tohn poor*
■ operator	**parler à la téléphoniste?** *pahr-lay ah lah tay-lay-foh-neesst*
■ area code	**obtenir le code régional** *ohp-tuh-neer luh kohd ray-zhyohn-nahl*
My number is ____.	**Mon numéro est ____.** *mohn new-may-roh eh*
I'd like to speak to ____.	**Je voudrais parler à ____.** *zhuh voo-dreh pahr-lay ah*
Is Mr. ____ in?	**Monsieur ____, est là?** *muh-ssyuh ____ eh lah*

This is ____.	**Ici ____.**	*ee-ssee*
Hello.	**Allô.**	*ah-loh*
Who is calling?	**Qui est à l'appareil?**	*kee eh tah lah-pah-rehy*
I can't hear.	**Je ne peux pas vous entendre.** *zhuh nuh puh pah voo zah<u>n</u>-tah<u>n</u>-druh*	
Speak louder.	**Parlez plus fort.**	*pahr-lay plew fohr*
Don't hang up.	**Ne quittez pas.**	*nuh kee-lay pah*
Do you have an answering machine?	**Avez-vous un répondeur automatique?** *ah-vay voo uh<u>n</u> ray-poh<u>n</u>-duhr oh-toh-mah-teek*	
I want to leave a message.	**Je voudrais laisser un message.** *zhuh voo-dreh leh-ssay uh<u>n</u> meh-ssahzh*	

Travel Tips Hotels often levy a service charge for calls made from a guest room. To avoid paying too much, make all calls from a telephone booth and use a Télécarte or telephone company calling card for long distance.

FAXES

Although the correct way to say "to fax" is **envoyer une télécopie** *(ahn-vwah-yay ewn tay-lay-koh-pee)*, informal French allows the use of the verb **faxer** *(fahk-ssay)* and the noun **un fax** *(uhn fahkss)*.

Do you have a fax machine?	**Avez-vous un fax?** *ah-vay voo uhn fahkss*
What is your fax number?	**Quel est le numéro de votre fax?** *kehl eh luh new-may-roh duh vohtr fahkss*
I'd like to send a fax.	**Je voudrais envoyer un fax.** *zhuh voo-dreh zahn-vwah-yay uhn fahkss*
May I fax this, please?	**Puis-je faxer ceci, s'il vous plaît?** *pweezh fahk-ssay suh-see seel voo pleh*
May I fax this letter (document) to you?	**Puis-je vous faxer cette lettre (ce document)?** *pweezh voo fahk-ssay seht lehtr (suh doh-kew-mahn)*
Fax it to me.	**Faxez-le (la) –moi.** *fahk-ssay-luh (lah) mwah.*
I didn't get your fax.	**Je n'ai pas reçu votre fax.** *zhuh nay pah ruh-sew vohtr fahkss.*

Did you receive my fax?	**Avez-vous reçu mon fax?** *voo ruh-sew mohn fahkss*	*ah-vay*
Your fax is illegible.	**Votre fax n'est pas lisible.** *fahkss neh pah lee-zee-bluh*	*vohtr*
Please send it again.	**Veuillez le (la) faxer de nouveau.** *vuh-yay luh (lah) fahk-ssay duh noo-voh*	

COMPUTERS

To get information on the Internet:
1. Go to the location box on your web browser
2. Type *http://www.altavista.digital.com* or *www.hotbot.com*
3. Click Enter
4. You will see a search screen. Click on "any language"
5. Select French
6. You can search for any subject

What kind of computer do you have?	**Quel système (type, genre) d'ordinateur avez-vous?** *kehl seess-tehm (teep, zhahn-ruh) dohr-dee-nah-tuhr ah vay voo*
What operating system are you using?	**Quel système opérant employez-vous?** *kehl sees-tehm oh-pay rahn ahn-plwah-yay-voo*
What word processing program are you using?	**Quel système de traitement de texte employez-vous?** *kehl sees-tehm duh treht-mahn duh tehkst ahn-plwah-yay-voo*
What spreadsheet program are you using?	**Quel tableur employez-vous?** *kehl tah-bluhr ahn-plwah-yay-voo*
What peripherals do you have?	**Quels périphériques avez-vous?** *kehl pay-ree-fay-reek ah-vay voo*

Are our systems compatible?	**Nos systèmes, sont-ils compatibles?**	*noh sees-tehm sohn teel kohn-pah-tee-bluh*
Do you have ____?	**Avez-vous ____?**	*ah-vay voo*
Do you use ____?	**Employez-vous ____?**	*ahn-plwah-yay-voo*
What is your e-mail address?	**Quelle est votre adresse e-mail?**	*kehl eh voh-truh ah-drehs ee-mehl*

MINI-DICTIONARY OF COMPUTER TERMS AND PHRASES

access	**l'accès (m.)**	*lahk-seh*
backup disk	**la copie de sauvegarde**	*lah koh-pee duh sohv-gahrd*
(to) boot	**démarrer**	*day-mah-ray*
brand name	**la marque**	*lah mahrk*
byte	**le byte**	*luh beet*
cable	**le câble**	*luh kahbl*
CD-ROM disk	**le disque optique numérique**	*luh deesk ohp-teek new-may-reek*
chip	**la puce**	*lah pews*
click (verb)	**cliquer**	*klee-kay*
clipboard	**le presse-papiers**	*luh prehs-pah-pyay*
CPU	**l'unité centrale (f.)**	*lew-nee-tay sahn-trahl*
to computerize	**informatiser**	*an-fohr-mah-tee-zay*

computer science	**l'informatique (f.)**	*lan-fohr-mah-teek*
computer scientist	**l'informaticien (ne)**	*lan-fohr-mah-tee-syan (syehn)*
cursor	**le curseur**	*luh kuhr-suhr*
database	**la base de données**	*lah bahz duh doh-nay*
disk drive	**le lecteur de disques**	*luh lehk-tuhr duh deesk*
diskette	**la disquette**	*lah dees-keht*
DOS	**le disque système opérant**	*luh deesk sees-tehm oh-pay-rahn*
(to) download	**décharger**	*day-shahr-zhay*
e-mail	**le e-mail**	*luh ee-mehl*
file	**le fichier**	*luh feesh-yay*
graphics	**la grafique**	*lah grah-feek*
Internet	**l'Internet**	*lan-tehr-neht*
joystick	**la manette de jeux**	*lah mah-neht duh zhuh*
key	**la touche**	*lah toosh*
keyboard	**le clavier**	*luh klah-vyay*
laptop computer	**l'ordinateur (m.) portable**	*lohr-dee-nah-tuhr pohr-tahbl*
memory	**la mémoire**	*lah may-mwahr*
modem	**le modem**	*luh moh-dehm*
monitor	**le moniteur**	*luh moh-nee-tuhr*
motherboard	**la carte-mère**	*lah kahrt mehr*
mouse	**la souris**	*lah soo-ree*
network	**le réseau**	*luh ray-zoh*

on-line service	**les serveurs en ligne (m.)**	*lay sehr-vuhr ahn lee-nyuh*
printer	**l'imprimante (f.)**	*lan-pree-mahnt*
laser	** laser**	* lah-zehr*
ink jet	** jet d'encre**	* zheh dahnkr*
scanner	**le scanneur**	*luh skah-nuhr*
screen	**l'écran (m.)**	*lay-krahn*
search engine	**le moteur de recherche**	*luh moh-tuhr duh ruh-shehrsh*
site	**le site**	*luh seet*
software	**le logiciel**	*luh loh-zhee-syehl*
speed	**la vitesse**	*lah vee-tehs*
spell checker	**le correcteur ortho- graphique**	*luh koh-rehk-tuhr ohr-toh-grah-feek*
thesaurus	**le thesaurus**	*luh tuh-soh-rewss*

WEB SITES AND SEARCH ENGINES

These web sites and search engines can give you the most up-to-date information on France and French-speaking countries:

www.nomade.fr —France and French-speaking countries

http://lokace.iplus.fr —France and French-speaking countries

www.yahoo.fr —France and French-speaking countries

www.pratique.fr —France and French-speaking countries

www.admifrance.fr —France and French-speaking countries

www.admin.ch —Switzerland

www.gouv.qc.ca —Quebec

www.primature.sn —Senegal

www.yweb.com/home-fr.html —a collection of European sites with a multilanguage interface

www.travelang.com —for worldwide travelers; you can reserve hotel accommodations, rent a car, book your flight, and figure currency conversions. There's also a travel calendar listing holidays and festivals

http://www.info-france-usa.org —the French embassy in Washington, D.C.; information in English on economic, political, scientific, and linguistic topics

http://www.francophonie.org —news and announcements in French pertaining to international relations, conferences, and English publications covering French government, the arts and sciences, and traveling

http://libraries.mit.edu/humanities/jtnews —foreign language news and newspapers, journals, and magazines

http://www.paris.org —information in English on Paris: maps, museums, monuments, travel

http://www.utm.edu/departments/french/french.html — 5,000 links to French-related sites

http://www.webfoot.com/travel/guides/france—comprehensive information for tourists in French or English

http://pariscope.fr —the French weekly *Pariscope* magazine, which gives current information about Paris: plays, festivals, flea markets, concerts

http://www.babelfish.altavista.com —an Internet language translator (works better for one word than a full sentence)

http://www.africaonline.co.ci —information about Africa

http://www.afp.com/ —site of L'Agence France-Presse; allows links with principal newspapers and magazines from France and French-speaking countries

http://www.admifrance.gouv.fr —directory of Internet services for French and French-speaking countries

www.cit.net —allows access to different cities of the world and gives links to official sites

GENERAL INFORMATION

TELLING TIME

What time is it?	**Quelle heure est-il?** *kehl uhr eh teel*
It is _____.	**Il est _____.** *eel eh*
■ noon	**midi** *mee-dee*
■ 8:00	**huit heures** *weet-uhr*
■ 1:05	**une heure cinq** *ewn-uhr sank*
■ 2:10	**deux heures dix** *duh-zuhr deess*
■ 3:15	**trois heures et quart** *trwah-zuhr ay kahr*
■ 4:20	**quatre heures vingt** *kahtruh-uhr van*
■ 5:25	**cinq heures vingt-cinq** *sank-uhr van-sank*
■ 6:30	**six heures et demie** *seez-uhr ay duh-mee*
■ 7:35	**sept heures trente-cinq** *seht-uhr trahnt-sank*
■ 8:40	**neuf heures moins vingt** *nuhv-uhr mwan van*
■ 9:45	**dix heures moins le quart** *deez-uhr mwan luh kahr*
■ 10:50	**onze heures moins dix** *ohnz-uhr mwan deess*
■ 11:55	**midi moins cinq** *mee-dee mwan sank*

EXPRESSIONS OF TIME

At what time?	**À quelle heure _____?**	*ah kehl-uhr*
When?	**Quand?** *kah<u>n</u>*	
at _____ o'clock	**à _____ heures** *ah _____ uhr*	
at exactly noon	**à midi précis** *ah mee-dee pray-ssee*	
at exactly 5 o'clock	**à cinq heures précises** *ah sa<u>n</u>k uhr pray-sseez*	
in an hour	**dans une heure** *dah<u>n</u> zewn-uhr*	
in 2 hours	**dans deux heures** *dah<u>n</u> duhz-uhr*	
not before 2:00 A.M.	**pas avant deux heures du matin** *pah zah-vah<u>n</u> duhz-uhr dew mah-ta<u>n</u>*	
after 3:00 P.M.	**après trois heures de l'après-midi** *ah-preh trwah-zuhr duh lah-preh mee-dee*	
at about 9:00 P.M.	**vers neuf heures du soir** *vehr nuhv-uhr dew swahr*	
between 8 and 9 o'clock	**entre huit et neuf heures** *ah<u>n</u>-truh weet ay nuhv-uhr*	
until 5 o'clock	**jusqu'à cinq heures** *zhewss-kah sa<u>n</u>k uhr*	
since what time _____?	**depuis quelle heure _____?** *duh-pwee kehl uhr*	

since 7 o'clock	**depuis sept heures**	*duh-pwee seht uhr*
per hour	**par heure**	*pahr uhr*
three hours ago	**il y a trois heures**	*eel yah trwah-zuhr*
early	**tôt**	*toh*
	de bonne heure	*duh bohn-uhr*
late	**tard**	*tahr*
late (in arriving)	**en retard**	*ah<u>n</u> ruh-tahr*
on, in time	**à l'heure**	*ah luhr*
noon	**midi**	*mee-dee*
midnight	**minuit**	*mee-nwee*
in the morning	**le matin**	*luh mah-ta<u>n</u>*
in the afternoon	**l'après-midi**	*lah-preh mee-dee*
in the evening	**le soir**	*luh swahr*

at night	**la nuit**	*lah nwee*
second	**une seconde**	*ewn suh-goh<u>n</u>d*
minute	**une minute**	*ewn mee-newt*
hour	**une heure**	*ewn uhr*
a quarter of an hour	**un quart d'heure**	*uh<u>n</u> kahr duhr*
a half hour	**une demi-heure**	*ewn duh-mee uhr*

Official time is based on the 24-hour clock. You will find schedules for planes, trains, radio and television programs, movies, sports events, and the like expressed in terms of a point within the 24-hour sequence. The time may be written as follows:

Noon	12 h 00	12.00
1:15 A.M.	01 h 15	1.15
1:15 P.M.	13 h 15	13.15
Midnight	00 h 00	00.00

To calculate the conventional time, subtract 12 from the official time for the hours between noon and midnight:

16 h 30   4:30 P.M.

The train leaves at 15:30.

Le train part à 15:30. *luh tran pahr ah kanz-uhr trahnt*

The time is now 21:15.

Il est maintenant 21 heures 15. *eel eh mant-nahn van-tay-ewn uhr kanz*

To calculate official time, add 12 to the conventional time for the hours between noon and midnight:

9:45 A.M.	09 h 45	9.45
9:45 P.M.	21 h 45	21.45

DAYS OF THE WEEK

What day is today?	**Quel jour est-ce aujourd' hui?** *kehl zhoor ess oh-zhoor-dwee* **Quel jour sommes-nous aujourd'hui?** *kehl zhoor sohm noo oh-zhoor-dwee*
Today is ____.	**C'est aujourd'hui ____.** *seh toh-zhoor-dwee* **Nous sommes ____.** *noo sohm*
Monday	**lundi** *luhn-dee*
Tuesday	**mardi** *mahr-dee*
Wednesday	**mercredi** *mehr-kruh-dee*
Thursday	**jeudi** *zhuh-dee*
Friday	**vendredi** *vahn-druh-dee*
Saturday	**samedi** *sahm-dee*
Sunday	**dimanche** *dee-mahnsh*

NOTE: In French, the names of the days and the months and seasons are written in small letters.

last Monday	**lundi dernier** *luhn-dee dehr-nyay*
the eve	**la veille** *lah vehy*
the day before yesterday	**avant-hier** *ah-vahn-tyehr*
yesterday	**hier** *yehr*

today	**aujourd'hui**	*oh-zhoor-dwee*
tomorrow	**demain**	*duh-ma<u>n</u>*
the day after tomorrow	**après-demain**	*ah-preh-duh-ma<u>n</u>*
the next day	**le lendemain**	*luh lah<u>n</u>-duh-ma<u>n</u>*
next Monday	**lundi prochain**	*lu<u>n</u>-dee proh-sha<u>n</u>*
the day	**le jour**	*luh zhoor*
2 days ago	**il y a deux jours**	*eel yah duh zhoor*
in 2 days	**dans deux jours**	*dah<u>n</u> duh zhoor*
every day	**tous les jours**	*too lay zhoor*
day off	**(le) jour de congé**	*(luh) zhoor duh koh<u>n</u>-zhay*
holiday	**(le) jour de fête**	*(luh) zhoor duh feht*
birthday	**l'anniversaire**	*lah-nee-vehr-ssehr*
per day	**par jour**	*pahr zhoor*
during the day	**pendant la journée**	*pah<u>n</u>-dah<u>n</u> lah zhoor-nay*
from this day on	**dès aujourd'hui**	*deh zoh-zhoor-dwee*
the week	**la semaine**	*lah suh-mehn*
a weekday	**un jour de semaine**	*uh<u>n</u> zhoor duh suh-mehn*
the weekend	**le week-end**	*luh week-ehnd*
last week	**la semaine passée**	*lah suh-mehn pah-ssay*
this week	**cette semaine**	*seht suh-mehn*

next week	**la semaine prochaine**	*lah suh-mehn proh-shehn*
a week from today	**dans une semaine**	*dahn-zewn suh-mehn*
2 weeks from tomorrow	**de demain en quinze**	*duh duh-man ahn kanz*
during the week	**pendant la semaine**	*pahn-dahn lah suh-mehn*

MONTHS OF THE YEAR

January	**janvier**	*zhan-vee-yay*
February	**février**	*fay-vree-yay*
March	**mars**	*mahrss*
April	**avril**	*ah-vreel*
May	**mai**	*meh*
June	**juin**	*zhwan*
July	**juillet**	*zhwee-yeh*
August	**août**	*oo or oot*
September	**septembre**	*sehp-tahn-bruh*
October	**octobre**	*ohk-toh-bruh*
November	**novembre**	*noh-vahn-bruh*
December	**décembre**	*day-ssahn-bruh*
the month	**le mois**	*luh mwah*
2 months ago	**il y a deux mois**	*eel yah duh mwah*
last month	**le mois dernier**	*luh mwah dehr-nyay*

this month	**ce mois** *suh mwah*
next month	**le mois prochain** *luh mwah proh-shan*
during the month of	**pendant le mois de** *pahn-dahn luh mwah duh*
since the month of	**depuis le mois de** *duh-pwee luh mwah duh*
for the month of	**pour le mois de** *poor luh mwah duh*
every month	**tous les mois** *too lay mwah*
per month	**par mois** *pahr mwah*
What is today's date?	**Quelle est la date d'aujourd'hui?** *kehl ay lah daht doh-zhoor-dwee*
Today is _____.	**C'est aujourd'hui _____.** *seht oh-zhoor-dwee*
Monday, May 1	**lundi, le premier mai** *luhn-dee luh pruh-myay meh*
Tuesday, June 2	**mardi, le deux juin** *mahr-dee luh duh zhwan*

NOTE: Use the ordinal number only for the first of the month.

the year	**l'an/l'année** *lahn/lah-nay*
per year	**par an** *pahr ahn*
all year	**toute l'année** *toot lah-nay*
every year	**chaque année** *shahk ah-nay*
during the year	**pendant l'année** *pahn-dahn lah-nay*

THE FOUR SEASONS

spring	**le printemps**	*luh pran-tahn*
summer	**l'été**	*lay-tay*
autumn	**l'automne**	*loh-tohn*
winter	**l'hiver**	*lee-vehr*
in the spring	**au printemps**	*oh pran-tahn*
in the summer	**en été**	*ahn-nay-tay*
in the autumn	**en automne**	*ahn-noh-tohn*
in the winter	**en hiver**	*ahn nee-vehr*

WEATHER

What is the weather like?	**Quel temps fait-il?**	*kehl tahn feh-teel*
It is beautiful.	**Il fait beau.**	*eel feh boh*
It is hot.	**Il fait chaud.**	*eel feh shoh*
It is sunny.	**Il fait du soleil.**	*eel feh dew soh-lehy*
It is bad.	**Il fait mauvais.**	*eel feh moh-veh*
It is cold.	**Il fait froid.**	*eel feh frwah*
It is cool.	**Il fait frais.**	*eel feh freh*
It is windy.	**Il fait du vent.**	*eel feh dew vahn*
It is foggy.	**Il fait du brouillard.**	*eel feh dew broo-yahr*
It is humid.	**Il fait humide.**	*eel feh ew-meed*
It is snowing.	**Il neige.**	*eel nehzh*
It is raining.	**Il pleut.**	*eel pluh*

TEMPERATURE

The average annual daily temperatures in Paris in Fahrenheit and Centigrade are:

MONTH	°F	°C	MONTH	°F	°C
January	42°	5°	July	77°	25°
February	45°	7°	August	75°	24°
March	54°	12°	September	70°	21°
April	61°	16°	October	61°	16°
May	68°	20°	November	50°	10°
June	73°	23°	December	44°	7°

| What heat! | **Quelle chaleur!** *kehl shah-luhr* |
| What cold! | **Quel froid!** *kehl frwah* |

RELIGIOUS SERVICES

France has many cathedrals and churches that you may wish to visit. There are churches and synagogues in major cities that do conduct some services in English. For more information, speak to the concierge at your hotel.

Is there a _____ near here?	**Y a-t-il _____ près d'ici?** *ee ah teel _____ preh dee-ssee*
■ Catholic church	**une église catholique** *ewn ay-gleez kah-toh-leek*
■ Protestant church	**un temple** *uhn tahn-pluh*
■ synagogue	**une synagogue** *ewn see-nah-gohg*
■ mosque	**une mosquée** *ewn mohss-kay*

At what time is the service (mass)?	**À quelle heure commence le service (la messe)?** *ah kehl uhr koh-mahnss luh sehr-veess (lah mehss)*

I would like to speak to a _____.	**Je voudrais parler à un _____.** *zhuh voo-dreh pahr-lay ah uhn*
■ priest	**prêtre** *preh-truh*
■ minister	**pasteur** *pahss-tuhr*
■ rabbi	**rabbin** *rah-ban*

PUBLIC HOLIDAYS AND CELEBRATIONS

Jan. 1	Le Jour de l'An Le Nouvel An	New Year's Day
May 1	La Fête du Travail	Labor Day
July 14	La Fête Nationale	Bastille Day
Aug. 15	L'Assomption	Assumption Day
Nov. 1	La Toussaint	All Saints' Day
Nov. 2	Le Jour des Morts	All Souls' Day
Nov. 11	L'Armistice	Armistice Day
Dec. 25	Noël	Christmas
February	Le Carnaval	Carnival
Last day of carnival	Le Mardi gras	Mardi-Gras
Mar./Apr.	Les Rameaux	Palm Sunday
Mar./Apr.	Le Vendredi-Saint	Good Friday

Mar./Apr.	Pâques	Easter
Mar./Apr.	Le Dimanche de Quasimodo	1st Sunday after Easter
40 days after Easter	L'Ascension	Ascension Thursday
7 Mondays after Easter	Lundi de la Pentecôte	Whit Monday
May	La Fête de Jeanne d'Arc	Feast of Joan of Arc

COUNTRIES AND NATIONALITIES

Where are you from?	**D'où êtes-vous?**	*doo eht voo*
I am (from) ____.	**Je suis de ____.**	*zhuh swee duh*
I am ____.	**Je suis ____.**	*zhuh swee*

NOTE: The feminine form of the adjective is indicated after the masculine form. For this form remember to pronounce the last consonant.

	COUNTRY	NATIONALITY
*Africa	**d'Afrique** *dah-freek*	**africain/e** *ah-free-kan/kehn*
Asia	**d'Asie** *dah-zee*	**asiatique** *ah-zyah-teek*
Australia	**d'Australie** *dah-strah-lee*	**australien/ne** *oh-strah-lyan/lyehn*
Europe	**d'Europe** *dew-rohp*	**européen/ne** *ew-roh-pay-an/ehn*

	COUNTRY	NATIONALITY
N. America	**d'Amérique du Nord** *dah-may-reek dew nohr*	**américain/e** *ah-may-ree-kan/ehn*
S. America	**d'Amérique du Sud** *dah-may-reek dew sewd*	**sud-américain/e** *sewd-ah-may-ree-kan/ehn*
Austria	**d'Autriche** *duh-treesh*	**autrichien/ne** *oh-tree-shyan/shyehn*
Belgium	**de Belgique** *duh behl-zheek*	**belge** *behlzh*
Canada	**(du) Canada** *(dew) kah-nah-dah*	**canadien/ne** *kah-nah-dyan/dyehn*
China	**(de) Chine** *(duh) sheen*	**chinois/e** *shee-nwah/nwahz*
Denmark	**(du) Danemark** *(dew) dahn-mahrk*	**danois/e** *dah-nwah/nwahz*
England	**d'Angleterre** *dahn-gluh-tehr*	**anglais/e** *ahn-gleh/glehz*
Finland	**(de) Finlande** *(duh) feen-lahnd*	**finlandais/e** *feen-lahn-deh/dehz*
France	**de France** *duh Frahnss*	**français/e** *frahn-sseh/sehz*
Germany	**d'Allemagne** *dahl-mah-nyuh*	**allemand/e** *ahl-mahn/mahnd*
Greece	**de Grèce** *duh grehss*	**grec/que** *grehk*
Haiti	**d'Haïti** *dahy-ee-tee*	**haïtien/ne** *ahy-ee-ssyan/ssyehn*

NOTE: When nationality refers to a person (noun) it is capitalized, i.e., **Un(e) Africain(e) parle français.** When the nationality is used as an adjective it begins with a lower case letter, i.e., **C'est un pays africain.**

	COUNTRY	NATIONALITY
India	**d'Inde (f.)** *da__n__d*	**indien/ne** *a__n__-dya__n__/dyehn*
Ireland	**d'Irlande (f.)** *deer-lah__n__d*	**irlandais/e** *eer-lah__n__-deh/dehz*
Israel	**d'Israël (m.)** *deez-rah-ehl*	**israélite** *eez-rah-ay-leet*
Italy	**d'Italie (f.)** *dee-tah-lee*	**italien/ne** *ee-tah-lya__n__/lyehn*
Japan	**du Japon** *dew zhah-poh__n__*	**japonais/e** *zhan-poh-neh/nehz*
Luxembourg	**du Luxembourg** *dew lewkss-ah__n__-boor*	**luxembourgeois/e** *lewkss-ah__n__-boor-zhwah/zhwahz*
Morocco	**du Maroc** *dew mah-rohk*	**marocain/e** *mah-roh-ka__n__/kehn*
Norway	**de Norvège** *duh norh-vehzh*	**norvégien/ne** *nohr-vay-zhya__n__/zhyehn*
Portugal	**du Portugal** *dew pohr-tew-gahl*	**portugais/e** *pohr-tew-geh/gehz*
Russia	**de Russie** *duh roo-se__e__*	**russe** *r__oo__ss*
Scotland	**d'Ecosse** *day-kohss*	**écossais/e** *ay-koh-sseh/ssehz*
Senegal	**du Sénégal** *dew say-nay-gahl*	**sénégalais/e** *say-nay-gah-leh/lehz*
Spain	**d'Espagne** *dehss-pah-nyuh*	**espagnol/e** *ehss-pah-nyohl*
Sweden	**de Suède** *duh swehd*	**suédois/e** *sway-dwah/dwahz*

	COUNTRY	NATIONALITY
Switzerland	**de Suisse** *duh sweess*	**suisse** *sweess*
Tunisia	**de Tunisie** *duh tew-nee-zee*	**tunisien/ne** *tew-nee-zyan/zyehn*
U.S.	**des États-Unis** *dayz ay-tah-zew-nee*	**américain/e** *ah-may-ree-kan/ kehn*
Wales	**du pays de Galles** *dew pay-ee duh gahl*	**gallois/e** *gahl-wah/wahz*

DIRECTIONS

the north	**le nord**	*luh nohr*
the south	**le sud**	*luh sewd*
the east	**l'est**	*lehsst*
the west	**l'ouest**	*lwehsst*

IMPORTANT SIGNS

À louer	*ah loo-ay*	For rent, hire
Ascenseur	*ah-sahn-ssuhr*	Elevator
Attention	*ah-tahn-ssyohn*	Careful
À vendre	*ah vahn-druh*	For sale
Dames	*dahm*	Ladies
Danger	*dahn-zhay*	Danger
Danger de mort	*dahn-zhay duh mohr*	Danger of death

Défense de _____	*day-fahnss duh*	Do not _____
Défense d'entrer	*day-fahnss dahn-tray*	Do not enter
Défense de cracher	*day-fahnss duh krah-shay*	No spitting
Défense de fumer	*day-fahnss duh few-may*	No smoking
Défense de marcher sur l'herbe	*day-fahnss duh muhr-shay sewr lehrb*	Keep off the grass
Eau non potable	*oh nohn poh-tah bluh*	Don't drink the water
École	*ay-kohl*	School
Entrée	*ahn-tray*	Entrance
Entrée interdite	*ahn-tray an-tehr-deet*	No Entrance
Entrée libre	*ahn-tray lee-bruh*	Free Admission
Fermé	*fehr-may*	Closed
Fumeurs	*few-muhr*	Smokers
Hommes	*ohm*	Men
Hôpital	*oh-pee-tahl*	Hospital
Horaire	*oh-rehr*	Schedule
Libre	*lee-bruh*	Free/Unoccupied
Messieurs	*meh-ssyuh*	Gentlemen
Ne pas toucher	*nuh pah too-shay*	Don't touch
Nonfumeurs	*nohn few-muhr*	Nonsmokers
Occupé	*oh-kew-pay*	Occupied

Ouvert	*oo-vehr*	Open
Passage souterrain	*pah-ssahzh soo-teh-ran*	Underground Passage
Poussez	*poo-ssay*	Push
Privé	*pree-vay*	Private
Quai/Voie	*kay/vwah*	Track, Platform
Renseignements	*rahn-sseh-nyuh-mahn*	Information
Réservé	*ray-zehr-vay*	Reserved
Salle d'attente	*sahl dah-tahnt*	Waiting room
Soldes	*sohld*	Sales
Sonnez	*soh-nay*	Ring
Sortie	*sohr-tee*	Exit
Sortie de secours	*sohr-tee duh-suh-koor*	Emergency exit
Stationnement inderdit	*stah-ssyohn-mahn an-tehr-dee*	No parking
Tirez	*tee-ray*	Pull
Toilettes	*twah-leht*	Toilets

COMMON ABBREVIATIONS

ACF	Automobile Club de France	Automobile Club of France
apr. J.-C.	après Jésus-Christ	A.D.
av. J.-C.	avant Jésus-Christ	B.C.
bd.	boulevard	boulevard
c.-à-d.	c'est-à-dire	that is to say, i.e.
CEE	Communauté économique européenne (Marché commun)	European Economic Community (Common Market)
CGT	Compagnie générale transatlantique	French Line
Cie.	compagnie	Company
EU	États-Unis	United States (U.S.)
h.	heure(s)	hour, o'clock
M.	Monsieur	Mr.
Mlle	Mademoiselle	Miss
MM	Messieurs	Gentlemen
Mme	Madame	Mrs.
ONU	Organisation des Nations Unies	United Nations (U.N.)
p.	page	page
p. ex.	par example	for example
P et T.	Postes et Télécommunications	Post Office and Telecommunications
RATP	Régie Autonome des Transports Parisiens	Paris Transport Authority
RD	Route Départementale	local road
RN	Route Nationale	national road
SA	Société anonyme	Ltd., Inc.
SI	Syndicat d'initiative	Tourist Information Office
SNCF	Société Nationale des Chemins de fer Français	French National Railways
s.v.p.	s'il vous plaît	please

CENTIMETERS/INCHES

It is usually unnecessary to make exact conversions from your customary inches to the metric system used in France, but to give you an approximate idea of how they compare, we give you the following guide.

Centimètres

Pouces

To convert centimeters into inches, multiply by .39.
To convert inches into centimeters, multiply by 2.54.

METERS/FEET

1 meter (**mètre**) = 39.37 inches
3.28 feet
1.09 yards

1 foot = 0.3 meters
1 yard = 0.9 meters

How tall are you in meters? See for yourself.

FEET	METERS	FEET	METERS
5'	1.52	5'7"	1.70
5'1"	1.54	5'8"	1.73
5'2"	1.57	5'9"	1.75
5'3"	1.59	5'10"	1.78
5'4"	1.62	5'11"	1.80
5'5"	1.64	6'	1.83
5'6"	1.68	6'1"	1.85

WHEN YOU WEIGH YOURSELF

1 kilogram (kilo) = 2.2 pounds
1 pound = 0.45 kilograms

KILOS	POUNDS	KILOS	POUNDS
40	88	75	165
45	99	80	176
50	110	85	187
55	121	90	198
60	132	95	209
65	143	100	220
70	154	105	231

LIQUID MEASUREMENTS

1 liter = 1.06 quarts
4 liters = 1.06 gallons
For quick, approximate conversions multiply the number
of gallons by 4 to get liters (**litres**). Divide the number of
liters by 4 to get gallons.

MINI-DICTIONARY FOR BUSINESS TRAVELERS

amount	le montant	*luh moh<u>n</u>-tah<u>n</u>*
appraise	évaluer	*ay-vah-lew-ay*
authorize	autoriser	*oh-toh-ree-zay*
authorized edition	l'édition autorisée (f.)	*lay-dee-ssyoh<u>n</u> oh-toh-ree-zay*
bill (noun)	la facture	*lah fahk-tewr*

bill of exchange	la lettre de change	*lah leh-truh duh shah<u>n</u>zh*
bill of lading	le connaissement	*luh koh-nehss-mah<u>n</u>*
bill of sale	la lettre de vente	*lah leh-truh duh vah<u>n</u>t*
business operation	■ l'affaire (f.) ■ le commerce	*lah-fehr* *luh koh-mehrss*
cash (noun)	l'argent (m.)	*lahr-zhah<u>n</u>*
to buy for cash	payer comptant	*peh-yay koh<u>n</u>-tah<u>n</u>*
to sell for cash	vendre au comptant	*vah<u>n</u>-druh oh koh<u>n</u>-tah<u>n</u>*
to cash a check	toucher un chèque	*too-shay uh<u>n</u> shehk*
certified check	le chèque assuré	*luh shehk ah-ssew-ray*
chamber of commerce	la chambre de commerce	*lah shah<u>n</u>-bruh duh koh-mehrss*
compensation for damage	le dédommagement	*luh day-doh-mahzh-mah<u>n</u>*
competition	la concurrence	*lah koh<u>n</u>-kew-rah<u>n</u>ss*
competitive price	le prix de concurrence	*luh pree duh koh<u>n</u>-kew-rah<u>n</u>ss*
contract	le contrat	*luk koh<u>n</u>-trah*
contractual obligations	les obligations du contrat	*lay-zoh-blee-gah-ssyoh<u>n</u> dew koh<u>n</u>-trah*
controlling interest	le droit d'autorité	*luh drwah doh-toh-ree-tay*

co-owner	le co-propriétaire	*luh koh-proh-pree-ay-tehr*
copartner	le co-associé	*luh koh-ah-ssoh-ssyay*
down payment	■ l'acompte (m.) ■ payer en compte	*lah kohnt* *peh-yay ahn-kohnt*
due	■ échu ■ arrivé à l'écheance	*ay-shew* *ah-ree-vay ah lay-shay-ahnss*
enterprise	l'entreprise (f.)	*lahn-truh-preez*
expedite delivery (of letters)	expédier la livraison	*ehkss-pay-dee-ay lah lee-vreh-zohn*
expedite delivery (of goods)	expédier la distribution	*ehkss-pay-dee-ay lah deess-tree-bew-ssyohn*
expenses	les frais (m. pl.)	*lay freh*
goods	■ les produits ■ les biens (m. pl.)	*lay proh-dwee* *lay byan*
infringement of patent rights	l'infraction de brevet d'invention	*lan-frahk-ssyohn duh bruh-veh dan-vahn-ssyohn*
insurance against all risks	l'assurance contre tous risques	*lah-ssew-rahnss kohn-truh too reessk*
international law	le droit international	*luh drwah an-tehr-nah-ssyohn-nahl*
lawful possession	la possession légitime	*lah poh-sseh-ssyohn lay-zhee-teem*

lawsuit	le procès	*luh proh-sseh*
lawyer	l'avocat	*lah-voh-kah*
letter of credit	la lettre de crédit	*lah leh-truh duh kreh-dee*
mail-order business	l'établissement de vente par correspondance (m.)	*lay-tah-bleess-mahn duh vahnt pahr koh-rehss-pohn-dahnss*
market value	le cours du marché	*luh koor dew mahr-shay*
manager	le gérant	*luh zhay-rahn*
payment	le versement	*luh vehrss-mahn*
partial payment	l'acompte (m.)	*lah-kohnt*
past due	■ arriéré ■ en retard	*ahr-yay-ray* *ahn ruh-tahr*
post office box	la boîte postale	*lah bwaht pohss-tahl*
property	■ la propriété ■ les biens	*lah proh-pree-ay-tay* *lay byan*
purchasing agent	l'acquéreur	*lah-kay-ruhr*
to put on the American market	mettre au marché américain	*meh-truh oh mahr-shay ah-may-ree-kan*
sale	la vente	*lah vahnt*
to sell	vendre	*vahn-druh*
to send	envoyer	*ahn-vwah-yay*
to send back	renvoyer	*rahn-vwah-yay*

to send C.O.D.	envoyer payable à l'arrivée	*ahn-vwah-yay peh-yah-bluh ah lah-ree-vay*
shipment	l'expédition (f.)	*lehkss-pay-dee-ssyohn*
tax	l'impôt (m.)	*lan-poh*
tax-exempt	exempt d'impôts	*ehg-zahn dan-poh*
sales tax	la taxe de luxe	*lah tahkss duh lewkss*
value-added tax	la taxe sur la valeur ajoutée	*lah tahkss sewr lah vah-luhr ah-zhoo-tay*
trade	le commerce	*luh koh-mehrss*
transact business	faire des affaires	*fehr day-zah-fehr*
to transfer	transférer	*trahnss-fay-ray*
transportation charges	les frais de transport	*lay freh duh trahnss-pohr*
via	par	*pahr*
yield a profit	rendre un bénéfice	*rahn-druh uhn bay-nay-feess*

QUICK GRAMMAR GUIDE

NOUNS

1. All nouns in French have a gender (masculine or feminine) and a number (singular or plural).
2. There is no easy way to determine gender, so a noun must be learned with its identifying article and its gender memorized.
3. To change a singular noun to the plural, an unpronounced **S** is usually added. Add nothing if the noun ends in **S, X,** or **Z.**

ARTICLES

Articles agree in gender and number with the nouns they modify.

DEFINITE ARTICLES (THE)			
	MASC. (THE)		FEM. (THE)
SING.	LE	**le livre** the book	LA **la carte** the map
PLUR.	LES	**les livres** the books	LES **les cartes** the maps

NOTE: LE and LA become L' before a noun beginning with a vowel or an H: **l'avion, l'homme.**

INDEFINITE ARTICLES (A, AN, SOME)			
	MASC. (A, AN, SOME)		FEM. (A, AN, SOME)
SING.	UN	**un restaurant** a restaurant	UNE **une voiture** a car
PLUR.	DES	**des restaurants** some restaurants	DES **des voitures** some cars

THE PARTITIVE (SOME, ANY)		
SINGULAR		
DU (de + le) + masc. sing. noun with consonant	**du pain**	some bread
DE LA + fem. sing. noun with consonant	**de la glace**	some ice cream
DE L' + masc. or fem. sing. noun with vowel or "H"	**de l'eau**	some water
PLURAL		
DES (de + les) + all plural nouns	**des glaces**	some ice creams
NEGATIVE		
DE is used in negative sentences	**Je n'ai pas d'argent.** **Elle n'a pas de cartes.**	I don't have any money. She doesn't have any maps.

NOTE: DE becomes D' before a vowel or a vowel sound (II, Y).

ADJECTIVES

1. Adjectives agree in number and gender with the nouns they modify.
2. To form the feminine of most adjectives, add **E** to the masculine form. If the masculine form ends in **E,** add nothing to get the feminine form.
3. To form the plural of most adjectives, add **S** to the singular form. If the singular form ends in **S,** add nothing to get the plural form.

un livre intéressant
des livres intéressants

une femme intéressante
des femmes intéressantes

4. Adjectives usually follow the nouns they modify. A few common exceptions that precede the noun are: **bon/bonne** good; **grand/grande** big; **jeune** young; **joli/jolie** pretty; **petit/petite** small.

un grand appartement

POSSESSIVE ADJECTIVES

Possessive adjectives agree in number and gender with the object possessed, not with the possessor. They precede the noun.

ENGLISH	MASC. SING. OR FEM. SING. WITH VOWEL	FEM. SING. WITH CONS.	ALL PLURALS
my	mon	ma	mes
your	ton	ta	tes
his/her/its	son	sa	ses
our	notre	notre	nos
your	votre	votre	vos
their	leur	leur	leurs

EXAMPLES:

mon ami(e)	my friend	*ami(e) starts with vowel
ma chemise	my shirt	*chemise is fem. sing. with cons.
mes chemises	my shirts	
ton gant	your glove	*gant is masc. sing.
tes gants	your gloves	

NOTE: **sa valise** can mean his or her valise
son argent can mean his or her money
ses parents can mean his or her parents.

Another way to show possession is by using the preposition DE (OF) or any of its forms:

SINGULAR	PLURAL
DU masculine noun with consonant	DES all nouns
DE LA feminine noun with consonant	
DE L' masculine or feminine noun with vowel	
DE proper noun (name)	

EXAMPLES:

la valise de Paul	Paul's valise
l'argent de la femme	the woman's money
la soupe du garçon	the boy's soup
la chemise de l'homme	the man's shirt
les cartes des touristes	the tourists' maps

DEMONSTRATIVE ADJECTIVES
(THIS/THAT; THESE/THOSE)

SINGULAR	
CE masc. noun with consonant	THIS/THAT
CET masc. noun with vowel or H	THIS/THAT
CETTE fem. noun	THIS/THAT
PLURAL	
CES all nouns	THESE/THOSE

EXAMPLES:

ce livre	this/that book
cet hôtel	this/that hotel
cette fille	this/that girl
cette eau	this/that water (**eau** is fem.)
ces arbres	these/those trees

PRONOUNS

Subject pronouns come at the beginning of the sentence before the verb.

Je parle   I speak

Nous sommes   We are

Direct object pronouns come before the verb except in an affirmative command when they come after the verb.

Il la voit.   He sees **it**.

Prenez-les!   Take **them**!

Indirect object pronouns come before the verb except in an affirmative command when they come after the verb.

Elle lui parle.   She speaks **to him** (**to her**).

Écrivez-leur!   Write **to them**!

Object of a preposition is a pronoun that comes after a preposition.

Après vous.   After you.

Avec eux.   With them.

SUBJECT	DIRECT OBJECT	INDIRECT OBJECT	OBJECT OF A PREPOSITION
Je I	**me** me	**me** to me	**moi** me
Tu You*	**te** you	**te** to you	**toi** you
Il He	**le** him	**lui** to him	**lui** him
Elle She	**la** her	**lui** to her	**elle** her
Nous We	**nous** us	**nous** to us	**nous** us
Vous You*	**vous** you	**vous** to you	**vous** you
Ils They m.	**les** them	**leur** to them	**eux** them
Elles They f.	**les** them	**leur** to them	**elles** them
On One			

*NOTE: Use **tu** for familiar conversation with a relative, a young child or a friend; **tu** is a singular subject pronoun only.

Use **vous** to be polite and to show respect when speaking to people with whom you are not intimate. **Vous** is a singular or plural subject or object pronoun and is used when addressing a group of people.

Use **ils** to refer to a group of males or to a mixed group consisting of males and females.

REGULAR VERBS

Regular verbs follow a specific pattern of conjugation (changing the verb to agree with the subject pronoun) depending upon the infinitive ending.

PRESENT TENSE			
	-ER ENDING	-IR ENDING	-RE ENDING
SUBJECT	PARLER	FINIR	VENDRE
	to speak	to finish	to sell
Je	parle	finis	vends
Tu	parles	finis	vends
Il/Elle	parle	finit	vend
Nous	parlons	finissons	vendons
Vous	parlez	finissez	vendez
Ils/Elles	parlent	finissent	vendent
COMMANDS	Parlez!	Finissez!	Vendez!

In order to conjugate a verb, the infinitive ending (-ER, -IR, -RE) must be removed and replaced by the appropriate ending found in the above table.

EXAMPLES:

désirer to desire, want	I desire	**Je désire**
choisir to choose	We choose	**Nous choisissons**
attendre to wait for	You wait for	**Vous attendez**

COMMON VERBS IN THE –ER FAMILY

admirer to admire
aider to help
aimer to like, to love
chercher to look for
coûter to cost
déjeuner to eat lunch
demander to ask
dépenser to spend money
désirer to wish, to desire
diner to eat dinner

donner to give
écouter to listen to
entrer to enter
fermer to close
fumer to smoke
marcher to walk
montrer to show
penser to think
regarder to look at
tourner to turn
trouver to find

COMMON VERBS IN THE -IR FAMILY

agir to act
avertir to warn
choisir to choose
finir to finish
grandir to grow

grossir to become fat
maigrir to become thin
nourrir to feed
obéir to obey
remplir to fill

COMMON VERBS IN THE -RE FAMILY

attendre to wait for
correspondre to correspond
défendre to defend
descendre to descend
entendre to hear

pendre to hang
perdre to lose
rendre to give back
répondre (à) to answer
vendre to sell

NOTE: Je + verb beginning with a vowel = J'

Je + écoute = J'écoute

Tu + vowel never drops the **u** from **tu**

Tu aimes le français

HELPING VERBS

The auxiliary verbs **avoir** (to have) and **être** (to be) must be memorized. They are used by themselves in the present or with other verbs to form compound tenses.

AVOIR—to have		
J'ai I have		**Nous avons** We have
Tu as you have		**Vous avez** You have
Il a he has		**Ils ont** They have
Elle a she has		**Elles ont** They have

Etre—to be		
Je suis I am		**Nous sommes** We are
Tu es You are		**Vous êtes** You are
Il est He is		**Ils sont** They are
Elle est She is		**Elles sont** They are

IRREGULAR VERBS

Irregular verbs must be memorized. Here are some common irregular verbs that you will find helpful.

PRESENT TENSE			
SUBJECT	ALLER to go	FAIRE to make, do	POUVOIR can, be able to
Je	vais	fais	peux
Tu	vas	fais	peux
Il/Elle	va	fait	peut
Nous	allons	faisons	pouvons
Vous	allez	faites	pouvez
Ils/Elles	vont	font	peuvent
COMMAND	Allez!	Faites!	

PRESENT TENSE	
VOIR to see	**VOULOIR** to wish, want
vois	**veux**
vois	**veux**
voit	**veut**
voyons	**voulons**
voyez	**voulez**
voient	**veulent**
Voyez!	

The following verbs will also be helpful to you in a more limited sense.

SUBJECT	BOIRE to drink	DIRE to say	ÉCRIRE to write
Je	**bois**	**dis**	**écris**
Vous	**buvez**	**dites**	**écrivez**
COMMAND	**Buvez!**	**Dites!**	**Écrivez!**

SUBJECT	METTRE to put (on)	OUVRIR to open	RECEVOIR to receive
Je	**mets**	**ouvre**	**reçois**
Vous	**mettez**	**ouvrez**	**recevez**
COMMAND	**Mettez!**	**Ouvrez!**	**Recevez!**

REFLEXIVE VERBS

Reflexive verbs show that the subject is acting upon itself. Reflexive verbs consist of a reflexive pronoun and a conjugated verb. Reflexive pronouns agree with their subjects.

JE	**ME**		**NOUS**	**NOUS**
TU	**TE**		**VOUS**	**VOUS**

IL	SE	ILS	SE
ELLE	SE	ELLES	SE

NOTE: ME, TE, and SE become M', T', and S' before a vowel or an H.

Verbs that are reflexive in French are not necessarily reflexive in English. Common reflexive verbs are:

s'appeler	to call oneself, to be called
s'asseoir	to sit down
se coucher	to go to bed
se dépêcher	to hurry up
s'habiller	to get dressed
se laver	to wash oneself
se lever	to get up
se peigner	to comb one's hair
se promener	to go for a walk
se raser	to shave oneself
se réveiller	to wake up

Follow this formula:

SUBJECT	REFLEXIVE PRONOUN	VERB
Je	**m'**	**appelle** My name is (I call myself)
Nous	**nous**	**réveillons** We wake up
Tu NE	**te**	**rases PAS** You don't shave

NOTE: A verb is reflexive only if the subject is acting upon itself. If the subject is acting upon another person or thing, the verb is NOT reflexive.

EXAMPLE:

Je me lave.	I wash myself.
Je lave l'enfant.	I wash the child.
Je lave la voiture.	I wash the car.

The infinitive of a reflexive verb is always preceded by the pronoun SE.

NEGATIVES

Form the negative by putting NE before the conjugated verb, and PAS (not) after the verb.

OTHER NEGATIVE CONSTRUCTIONS

NE . . . RIEN nothing

NE . . . JAMAIS never

NE . . . PERSONNE nobody

NE . . . PLUS no longer

NOTE: NE becomes N' before a vowel or H.

Il parle anglais.	**Il ne parle pas anglais.**
He speaks English.	He doesn't speak English.
Je veux manger.	**Je ne veux plus manger.**
I want to eat.	I don't want to eat any more.
Elle écoute.	**Elle n'écoute rien.**
She listens.	She doesn't listen to anything.

QUESTIONS

The four most common ways to ask a yes/no question are:
1. Raise your voice at the end of a phrase.
   Vous parlez francais?

2. Add the tag n'est-ce pas (isn't that so?) at the end of a phrase:

Vous parlez français, n'est-ce pas?

3. Put EST-CE QUE *(ehss-kuh)* in front of a phrase.

| **Vous parlez anglais.** | **Est-ce que vous parlez anglais?** |

4. Invert the order of the subject pronoun (ONLY) and the verb.

| **Vous parlez anglais.** | **Parlez-vous anglais?** |

NOTE: a) Do NOT invert with the pronoun JE. Use EST-CE QUE.

b) If the verb ends in a vowel and the pronoun begins with a vowel
(IL or elle) then –t- must separate the two vowels.

| **Il parle anglais.** | **Parle-t-il anglais?** |
| **Elle a une voiture.** | **A-t-elle une voiture?** |

To ask for information:

1. Put the information word at the end of the phrase:

Vous arrivez quand?

2. Use the information word + EST-CE QUE at the beginning of the sentence:

Quand est-ce que vous arrivez?

3. Use the information word followed by inversion:

Quand arrivez-vous?

PREPOSITIONS

Study the list of the following prepositions. The prepositions **à** (to, at) and **de** (of, from) have contracted forms.

a + le = au	**de + le = du**
à + les = aux	**de + les = des**
à la (no change)	**de la** (no change)
à l' (no change)	**de l'** (no change)

EXAMPLES:

to the movies	**au cinéma**
to the museums	**aux musées**
to the kitchen	**à la cuisine**
of the boy	**du garçon**
of the children	**des enfants**
of the year	**de l'année**

COMMON PREPOSITIONS

about	**de**	*duh*
according to	**selon**	*suh-lohn*
across	**à travers**	*ah trah-vehr*
after	**après**	*ah-preh*
among	**parmi**	*pahr-mee*
around	**autour de**	*oh-toor duh*
at	**à**	*ah*
at the house of	**chez**	*shay*
before	**avant**	*ah-vahn*
behind	**derrière**	*deh-ryehr*
between	**entre**	*ahn-truh*
by	**par**	*pahr*
down/downstairs	**en bas**	*ahn bah*
during	**pendant**	*pahn-dahn*
except	**sauf**	*sohf*
for	**pour**	*poor*
from	**de**	*duh*
in	**dans, en**	*dahn, ahn*
in front of	**devant**	*duh-vahn*

in order to	**pour**	*poor*
inside	**dedans**	*duh-dah<u>n</u>*
on	**sur**	*sewr*
opposite	**en face de**	*ah<u>n</u> fahss duh*
outside	**dehors**	*duh-ohr*
through	**à travers**	*ah trah-vehr*
to	**à**	*ah*
toward	**vers**	*vehr*
under	**sous**	*soo*
until	**jusqu'à**	*zhewss-kah*
up/upstairs	**en haut**	*ah<u>n</u> oh*
with	**avec**	*ah vehk*
without	**sans**	*sah<u>n</u>*

ENGLISH-FRENCH DICTIONARY*

A

a, an un (m.) *uhn*, une (f.) *ewn*

able: to be able pouvoir *poo-vwahr*

about à peu près *ah-puh-preh*; environ *ahn-vee-rohn*

above dessus *duh-ssew*

abroad à l'étranger *ah lay-trahn-zhay*

according to selon *suh-lohn*

accountant comptable *kohn-tah-bluh*

ache (noun) le mal *luh mahl*; **(head)** mal de tête *mahl duh teht*; **(stomach)** mal d'estomac *mahl dehss-toh-mah*; **(tooth)** mal de dents *mahl duh dahn*

acquaintance: make the . . . of faire la connaissance de *fehr lah koh-neh-ssahnss duh*

across à travers *ah trah-vehr*

add ajouter *ah-zhoo-tay*

address une adresse *ewn ah-drehss*

adjust arranger *ah-rahn-zhay*

advertisement une réclame *ewn ray-klahm*; une annonce *ewn ah-nohnss*

advice l'avis (m.) *lah-vee*; le conseil *luh kohn-ssehy*

aerobics de l'aérobic (m.) *duh lahy-roh-beek*

afraid: to be afraid of avoir peur de *ah-vwahr puhr duh*

after après *ah-preh*

afternoon l'après-midi (m.) *lah-preh mee-dee*

again encore une fois *ahn-kohr ewn fwah*

against contre *kohn-truh*

agency une agence *ewn ah-zhahnss*; **(travel)** une agence

de voyage *ewn ah-zhahnss duh vwah-yahzh*

ago il y a + time *eel yah*

agree être d'accord *eh-truh dah-kohr*

air conditioner le climatiseur *luh klee-mah-tee-zuhr*

air mail par avion *pahr ah-vyohn*

airplane un avion *uhn nah-vyohn*

airport un aéroport *uhn nahy-roh-pohr*

alcohol l'alcool (m.) *lahl-kol*

all tout (m.), toute (f.) *too*, *toot*

alley la ruelle *lah rew-ehl*

almond une amande *ewn ah-mahnd*

almost presque *prehss-kuh*

alone seul(e) *suhl*

already déjà *day-zhah*

also aussi *oh-ssee*

always toujours *too-zhoor*

ambulance une ambulance *ewn ahn-bew-lahnss*

among parmi *pahr-mee*

and et *ay*

ankle la cheville *lah shuh-vee*

annoy gêner *zheh-nay*; ennuyer *ahn-nwee-yay*

answer (noun) la réponse *lah ray-pohnss*; **(verb)** répondre *ray-pohn-druh*

answering machine le répondeur automatique *luh ray-pohn-duhr oh-toh-mah-teek*

antiseptic un antiseptique *uhn nahn-tee-ssehp-teek*

any ne . . . aucun(e) *nuh . . . oh-kuhn*, *oh-kewn*

appendicitis l'appendicite *lah-pahn-dee-sseet*

apple   la pomme *lah pohm*
apricot   un abricot *uhn nah bree-koh*
argument   la dispute *lah deess pewt*
arm   le bras *luh brah*
around   autour de *oh-toor duh*
arrival   l'arrivée (f.) *lah-ree-vay*
artichoke   l'artichaut *luhr-tee-shoh*
artificial sweetener   le sucre artificiel *luh sew kruh ahr-tee-fee-syehl*
artist (m. and f.)   artiste *ahr-leesst*
ashtray   le cendrier *luh ssahn-dree-yay*
ask   demander *duh-mahn-day*
asparagus   l'asperge (f.) *lahss-pehrzh*
asthma   l'asthme (m.) *lahs-muh*
at   à *ah*
August   août *oo*
author   l'auteur (m.) *loh-tuhr*
avoid   éviter *ay-vee tay*
awaken   réveiller *ray-veh-yay*

B

back (noun)   le dos *luh doh*; **in back of**   derrière *deh-ryehr*
backup disk   la copie de sauvegarde *lah kôh-pee duh sohv-gahrd*
backward   en arrière *ahn nah-ryehr*
bacon   le lard *luh lahr*
bad   mauvais(e) *moh-veh(z)*
badly   mal *mahl*
bag   le sac *luh sahk*
baggage room   la consigne *lah kohn-ssee-nyuh*
baked   au four *oh foor*
baked Alaska   l'omelette norvégienne *lohm-leht nohr-vay-zhyehn*
bakery   la boulangerie *lah boo-lahn-zhree*

balcony   le balcon *luh bahl-kohn*
ballet   le ballet *luh bah-leh*
banana   la banane *lah bah-nahn*
bandage (noun)   la bande *lah buhnd*
bank   la banque *lah bahnk*
bank [branch]   la succursale *luh sew-kewr ssakl*
banking window   le guichet *luh gee-sheh*
bar   le bistro *luh beess-troh*
barber   le coiffeur *luh kwah-fuhr*
bargain (noun)   l'occasion *loh-kah-zyohn*
basket   le panier *luh pah-nyay*
bath   le bain *luh ban*
bathe   se baigner *suh beh-nyay*
bathing suit   le maillot de bain *luh mah-yoh duh ban*
bathrobe   la robe de chambre *lah rohb duh shahn-bruh*
bathroom   la salle de bains *lah sahl duh ban*
battery   la batterie *lah bah-tree*; la pile *lah peel*
be   être *eh-truh*
beach   la plage *lah plahzh*
bean   le haricot *lah ah-ree-koh*
beard   la barbe *lah bahrb*
beautiful   beau (m.) *boh*, belle (f.) *behl*
beauty salon   le salon de beauté *luh sah-lohn duh boh-tay*
because   parce que *pahrss kuh*
become   devenir *duh-vuh-neer*
bed   le lit *luh lee*
bedroom   la chambre à coucher *lah shahn-bruh ah koo-shay*
beef (noun)   le boeuf *luh buhf*
beer   la bière *lah byehr*
beet   la betterave *lah beht-rahv*
before   avant *ah-vahn*
begin   commencer (à) *koh-mahn-ssay (ah)*

behind en arrière *ahn nah-ryehr*; derrière *deh-ryehr*

beige beige *behzh*

believe croire *krwahr*

bell la cloche *lah klohsh*

bellboy le chasseur *luh shah-ssuhr*

belong appartenir *ah-pahr-tuh-neer*

belt la ceinture *lah-san-tewr*; **seat belt** la ceinture de sécurité *lah san-tewr duh say-kew-ree-tay*

bench le banc *luh bahn*

beneath dessous *duh-ssoo*

berth la couchette *lah koo-sheht*

beside à côté de *ah koh-tay duh*

better (adj.) meilleur(e) *meh-yuhr*

better (adv.) mieux *myuh*

between entre *ahn-truh*

big grand(e) *grahn(d)*

bill la facture *lah fahk-tewr*; la note *lah noht*

birthday l'anniversaire (m.) *lah-nee-vehr-ssehr*

bitter amer(ère) *ah-mehr*

black noir(e) *nwahr*

blanket la couverture *lah koo-vehr-tewr*

blood le sang *luh sahn*

blood test analyse (f.) de sang *ah-nah-leez duh sahn*

blouse la blouse *lah blooz*

blue bleu *bluh*; **navy blue** bleu marine *bluh mah-reen*

boat le bateau *luh bah-toh*; **boating** le canotage *luh kah-noh-tahzh*

body le corps *luh kohr*

bodybuilding la musculation *lah mew-skew-lah syohn*

boiled bouilli(e) *boo-yee*

bone l'os (m.) *lohss*

book le livre *luh lee-vruh*

bookstore la librairie *lah lee-breh-ree*

boots les bottes (f.) *lay boht*

boot (v.) démarrer *day-mah-ray*

border la frontière *lah frohn-tyehr*

borrow emprunter *ahn-pruhn-tay*

boss le patron *luh pah-trohn*; le propriétaire *luh proh-pree-ay-tehr*

bother gêner *geh-nay*; ennuyer *ahn-nwee-yay*

bottle la bouteille *lah boo-tehy*

bowl un bol *uhn bohl*

box la boîte *lah bwaht*

box office le bureau de location *luh bew-roh duh loh-kah-ssyohn*

boy le garçon *luh gahr-ssohn*

bra le soutien-gorge *luh soo-tyan gohrzh*

braised braisé *breh-zay*

brakes les freins (m. pl.) *lay fran*

brand la marque *lah mahrk*

bread le pain *luh pan*; **French** la baguette *lah bah-geht*; **pumpernickel** le pain bis *luh pan bee*; **rye** le pain de seigle *luh pan duh seh-gluh*; **white** le pain blanc *luh pan blahn*; **whole wheat** le pain de froment *luh pan duh froh-mahn*

break briser *bree-zay*; casser *kah-ssay*

breakdown (auto) la panne *lah pahn*; **broken down** en panne *ahn pahn*

breakfast le petit déjeuner *luh puh-tee day-shuh-nay*

bridge le pont *luh pohn*

bring apporter *ah-pohr-tay*

broiled grillé *gree-yay*

brother le frère *luh frehr*

brown brun(e) *bruhn (brewn)*; marron *mah-rohn*; **browned** gratiné *grah-tee-nay*

bruise (noun) la contusion *lah kohn-tew-zyohn*

brush (noun) la brosse *lah brohss*; **(verb)** brosser *broh-ssay*; **toothbrush** la brosse à dents *lah brohss ah dahn*

Brussels sprouts les choux (m. pl.) de Bruxelles *lay shoo duh brew-ssehl*

building le bâtiment *luh bah-tee-mahn*

bulb (electric) l'ampoule (f.) *lahn-pool*

bumper le pare-choc *luh pahr-shohk*

bun (roll) la brioche *lah bree-ohsh*

burn (noun) la brûlure *luh brew-lewr*; **(verb)** brûler *brew-lay*

bus l'autobus *loh-toh-bewss*; **bus station** la gare routière *lah gahr roo-tyehr*; **bus stop** l'arrêt de bus (m.) *lah reh duh bewss*

businessperson homme (femme) d'affaires *ohm (fehm) dah-fehr*

busy occupé(e) *oh-kew-pay*

but mais *meh*

butcher shop la boucherie *lah boosh-ree*

butter le beurre *luh buhr*

button le bouton *luh boo-tohn*

buy acheter *ahsh-tay*

by par *pahr*; en *ahn*

C

cabbage le chou *luh shoo*

cake le gâteau *luh gah-toh*

call (verb) appeler *ah-play*

camera l'appareil (m.) photographique *lah-pah-rehy foh-toh-grah-feek*

can (verb) pouvoir *poo-vwahr*

candle la bougie *lah boo-zhee*

candy store la confiserie *lah kohn-feess-ree*

cane une canne *ewh kahn*

car la voiture *lah vwah-tewr*

carburetor le carburateur *luh kahr-bew-rah-tuhr*

card la carte *lah kahrt*; **credit card** la carte de crédit *lah kahrt duh kray dee*; **identification card** la carte d'identité *lah kahrt dee-dahn-tee-tay*

care le soin *luh swan*

carefully avec soin *ah-vehk swan*

carefulness la prudence *lah prew-dahnss*

carrot la carotte *lah kah-roht*

carry porter *pohr-tay*, **carry away** emporter *ahn-pohr-tay*

cashier le caissier *luh kehss-yay*

cash register la caisse *lah kehss*

castle le château *luh shah-toh*

cat le chat *luh shah*

catch attraper *ah-trah-pay*

caution attention *ah-tahn-ssyohn*

CD player le lecteur de CD *luh lehk-tuhr duh say-day*

CD-ROM disk le disque optique numérique *luh deesk ohp-teek new-may reek*

ceiling le plafond *luh plah-fohn*

cellar la cave *lah kahv*

cemetery le cimetière *luh seem-tyehr*

chain (jewelry) la chaînette *lah sheh ncht*

chair la chaise *lah shehz*

chambermaid la femme de chambre *lah fahm duh shahn-bruh*

change (noun) le changement *luh shahnzh-mahn*; **money** la monnaie *lah moh-nay*

change (verb) changer *shahn-zhay* **change plane or train** faire la correspondance *fehr lah koh-rehss-pohn-dahnss*

charge (noun) les frais (m. pl.) *lay freh*

charge (verb) charger *shahr-zhay*

charm (noun) le porte-bonheur *luh pohrt boh-nuhr*

cheap bon marché *bohn mahr-shay*; **cheaper** meilleur marché *meh-yuhr mahr-shay*

check (noun) (restaurant) l'addition (f.) *lah-dee-ssyohn*; **(money)** le chèque *luh shehk*; **traveler's check** le chèque de voyage *luh shehk duh vwah-yahzh*; **cash a check** toucher un chèque *too-shay uhn shehk*

check (verb) vérifier *vay-ree-fyay*; **check bags** enregistrer *ahn-ruh-zheess-tray*

checked (material) à carreaux *ah kah-roh*

cheek la joue *lah zhoo*

cheese le fromage *luh froh-mahzh*

cherry la cerise *lah suh-reez*

chest la poitrine *lah pwah-treen*

chicken le poulet *luh poo-leh*

chick-peas les pois (m. pl.) chiches *lay pwah sheesh*

chiffon la mousseline de soie *lah mooss-leen duh swah*

child l'enfant (m./f.) *lahn-fahn*

chin le menton *luh mahn-tohn*

chip la puce *lah pews*

choose choisir *shwah-zeer*

chop (noun) la côtelette *lah koht-leht*

church l'église (f.) *lay-gleez*; le temple (Prot.) *luh tahn-pluh*

cigar le cigare *luh see-gahr*

cigarette la cigarette *lah see-gah-reht*

cigarette lighter le briquet *luh bree-keh*

city la ville *la veel*

clam la palourde *lah pah-loord*

clean (verb) nettoyer *neh-twah-yay*

clean (adj.) propre *proh-pruh*; **dry cleaner's** la teinturerie *lah tan-tew-ruh-ree*; **dry-clean** nettoyer à sec *neh-twah-yay ah-sehk*

click (verb) cliquer *klee-kay*

clipboard le presse-papiers *luh prehss-pah-pyay*

clock la pendule *lah pahn-dewl*; l'horloge (f.) *lohr-lohzh*; **alarm clock** le réveil *luh ray-vehy*

close (verb) fermer *fehr-may*

closet l'armoire (f.) *lahr-mwahr*

clothes les habits (m. pl.) *lay zah-bee*; les vêtements (m. pl.) *lay veht-mahn*

coast la côte *lah koht*

coat le manteau *luh mahn-toh*; **coat check** le vestiaire *luh vehss-tyehr*

coconut la noix de coco *lah nwah duh koh-koh*

coffee le café *luh kah-fay*; **black** le café noir *luh kah-fay nwahr*; **with cream** le café crème *luh kah-fay krehm*; **decaffeinated** décaféiné *day-kah-fay-ee-nay*; **iced** le café glacé *luh kah-fay glah-ssay*; **with milk** le café au lait *luh kah-fay oh leh*; **espresso** le café express *luh kah-fay ehkss-prehss*

cold (noun) (weather) le froid *luh frwah*; **(verb) to be cold (weather)** faire froid *fehr frwah*; **to be cold (person)** avoir froid *ah-vwahr frwah*

cold (noun) (respiratory) le rhume *luh rewm*; **chest cold**

le rhume de poitrine *luh rewm duh pwah-treen*, **head cold** le rhume de cerveau *luh rewm duh sehr-voh*

cold cuts la charcuterie *lah shahr-kew-tree*

collar le col *luh kohl*

color la couleur *lah koo-luhr*

comb le peigne *luh peh-nyuh*

come venir *vuh-neer*; **come back** revenir *ruh vuh-neer*

company la compagnie *lah kohn pah-nyee*

complaint la plainte *lah plant*

computer l'ordinateur (m.) *lohr-dee-nah-tuhr*

computerize (verb) informatiser *an fohr mah-tee-zay*

computer science l'informatique (f.) *lan-fohr-mah-teek*

concert le concert *luh kohn-ssehr*; **concert hall** la salle de concert *lah sahl duh kohn-ssehr*

condom le préservatif *luh pray-zehr-vah-teef*

conductor le contrôleur *luh kohn-troh-luhr*

congratulations félicitations *fay-lee-ssee-tah-ssoyhn*

connect relier *ruh-lee-yay*

contact lense le verre de contact *luh vehr duh kohn-tahkt*

contagious contagieux(ieuse) *kohn-tah-zhuh(z)*

contain contenir *kohn-tuh-neer*

contents le contenu *luh kohnt-new*

cook (noun) le cuisinier *luh kwee-zee-nyay*

cooked cuit(e) *kwee(t)*

cookie le biscuit *luh bees-kwee*

cooking la cuisine *lah kwee-zeen*

corduroy le velours côtelé *luh vuh-loor koht-lay*

corkscrew le tire-bouchon *luh teer boo-shohn*

corn le maïs *luh mah-eess*

corner le coin *luh kwan*

cost coûter *koo tay*

costly coûteux(euse) *koo-tuh(z)*

cotton le coton *luh koh-tohn*; **absorbent cotton** l'ouate (f.) *lwaht*

cough (noun) la toux *lah too*; **cough drops** les pastilles contre la toux *lay pahss-teey kohn-truh lah too*; **cough syrup** le sirop contre la toux *luh see-roh kohn-truh lah too*

cough (verb) tousser *too-ssay*

count (verb) compter *kohn-tay*

country (nation) le pays *luh pay-ee*; la campagne *lah kahn-pah-nyuh*

countryside le paysage *luh pay-ee-zhahzh*

courtyard la cour *lah koor*

cover (verb) couvrir *koo-vreer*

cover charge le couvert *luh koo-vehr*

crab le crabe *luh krahb*

cramp la crampe *lah krahnp*

cream la crème *lah krehm*; **whipped cream** la crème fouettée *lah krehm foo-eh-tay*

CPU l'unité centrale (f.) *lew-nee-tay sahn-trahl*

cross (verb) traverser *trah-vehr-ssay*

crust la croûte *lah kroot*

crutches les béquilles (f.) *lay bay-kee*

cry pleurer *pluh-ray*

cucumber le concombre *luh kohn-kohn-bruh*

cup la tasse *lah tahss*

cursor le curseur *luh kuhr-suhr*

custard le flan *luh flahn*

customer le client *luh klee-ahn*
customs la douane *lah dwahn*
customs official le douanier *luh dwah-nyay*
cut couper *koo-pay*

D

daily quotidien(ne) *koh-tee-dyan (yehn)*
dance (noun) la danse *lah dahnss*
dance (verb) danser *dahn-ssay*
dark (color) foncé(e) *fohn-ssay*
database la base de données *lah bahz duh doh-nay*
date la date *lah daht*
date (fruit) la datte *lah daht*
daughter la fille *lah fee*
day le jour *luh zhoor*; **day before yesterday** avant-hier *ah-vahn-tyehr*; **day after tomorrow** après-demain *ah-preh-duh-man*
dear cher, chère *shehr*
deceive tromper *trohn-pay*
decide décider *day-ssee-day*
declare déclarer *day-klah-ray*
delay le retard *luh ruh-tahr*
delicatessen la charcuterie *lah shahr-kew-tree*
deliver livrer *lee-vray*
denim jean *zheen*
dentist dentiste *dahn-teesst*
deodorant le déodorant *luh day-oh-doh-rahn*
department (in store) le rayon *luh ray-ohn*
deserve mériter *may-ree-tay*
desire désirer *day-zee-ray*
desk le bureau *luh bew-roh*
detective story le roman policier *luh roh-mahn poh-lee-ssyay*
diabetes la diabète *lah dee-yah-beht*

diaper la couche *lah koosh*
dictionary le dictionnaire *luh deek-ssyoh-nehr*
different différent(e) *dee-fay-rahn(t)*
difficult difficile *dee-fee-sseel*
digital digital *dee-zhee-tahl*
diminish diminuer *dee-mee-new-ay*
dine dîner *dee-nay*
dining car le wagon-restaurant *luh vah-gohn rehss-toh-rahn*
dining room la salle à manger *lah sahl ah mahn-zhay*
dirty sale *sahl*
disappointed déçu(e) *day-ssew*
disco(theque) la disco(thèque) *lah deess-koh(tehk)*
dish (of food) le plat *luh plah*; **plate** l'assiette *lah-ssyeht*; **disposable** jetable *zheh-tah-bluh*
disk drive le lecteur de disques *luh lehk-tuhr duh deesk*
diskette la disquette *lah dees-keht*
distance le trajet *luh trah-zheh*
district le quartier *luh kahr-tyay*
diving le plongeon *luh plohn-zhohn*; **diving suit** le scaphandre *luh skah-fahn-druh*
do faire *fehr*
doctor le docteur *luh dohk-tuhr*; le médecin *luh mayd-ssan*
dog le chien *luh shyan*
door la porte *lah pohrt*
DOS le disque système opérant *luh deesk sees-tehm oh-pay-rahn*
down: to go down descendre *day-ssahn-druh*
download décharger *day-shahr-zhay*
downstairs en bas *ahn bah*
dozen la douzaine *lah doo-zehn*
dress (noun) la robe *lah rohb*
dress (verb) s'habiller *sah-bee-yay*

drink (noun) la boisson *lah bwah ssohn*; la consommation *lah kohn-ssoh-mah-ssyohn*; **soft drink** la boisson non-alcoolisée *lah bwah-ssohn nohn nahl-koh-lee-zay*

drink (verb) boire *bwahr*

drinkable potable *poh-tah-bluh*; **undrinkable** non potable *nohn poh-tah-bluh*

drive conduire *kohn-dweer*

drunk ivre *ee-vruh*; soûl(e) *soo*

dry (adj.) sec, sèche *sehk, sehsh*

dry (verb) sécher *say-shay*

duck le canard *luh kah-nahr*

during pendant *pahn-dahn*

E

each chaque *shahk*

each one chacun(e) *shah-kuhn (kewn)*

ear l'oreille (f.) *loh-rehy*

early tôt *toh*; de bonne heure *duh bohn-uhr*

earn gagner *gah-nyay*

earring la boucle d'oreille *lah boo-kluh doh-rehy*

east l'est *lehsst*

easy facile *fah-sseel*

eat manger *mahn-zhay*

egg l'oeuf *luhf*, **eggs** les oeufs *lay zuh*; **fried** au plat *oh plah*; **hard-boiled** durs *dewr*; **medium-boiled** mollets *moh-leh*; **poached** pochés *poh-shay*; **soft-boiled** à la coque *ah lah kohk*; **sunny-side up** poêlés *pwah-lay*; **scrambled** brouillés *broo-yay*

eggplant l'aubergine (f.) *loh-behr-zheen*

eight huit *weet*

eighteen dix-huit *deez weet*

eighty quatre-vingts *kah-truh van*

elbow le coude *luh kood*

elevator l'ascenseur (m.) *lah-ssahn-ssuhr*

eleven onze *ohnz*

elsewhere ailleurs *ah-yuhr*

e-mail le e-mail *luh ee-mehl*

emergency le cas urgent *luh kah zewr-zhahn*; **in case of emergency** en cas d'urgence *ahn kah dewr-zhahnss*

empty vide *veed*

end (noun) la fin *lah fan*

end (verb) finir *fee-neer*

endorse endosser *ahn doh ssay*

English anglais (m.) *ahn-gleh*

enlarge élargir *ay-lahr-zheer*

enough assez (de) *ah-ssay (duh)*

enter entrer *ahn-tray*

entire entier(ière) *ahn-tyay (yehr)*

entrance l'entrée (f.) *lahn-tray*

envelope l'enveloppe (f.) *lahn-vlohp*

eraser la gomme *lah gohm*

especially surtout *sewr-too*

evening la soirée *lah swah-ray*

evening gown la robe de soir *lah rohb duh swahr*

every tout(e) *too(t)*; chaque *shahk*; **everybody** tout le monde *too luh mohnd*; **every day** tous les jours *too lay zhoor*; **everywhere** partout *pahr-too*

example l'exemple (m.) *lehg-zahn-pluh*; **for example** par exemple *pahr ehg-zahn-pluh*

excellent excellent(e) *ehkss-eh-lahn(t)*

exchange échanger *ay-shahn-zhay*; **exchange office** le bureau de change *luh bew-roh duh shahnzh*; **exchange rate** le cours du change *luh koor dew shahnzh*

excursion l'excursion (f.) *lehkss-kewr-zyohn*

excuse (verb)   pardonner
pahr-doh-nay; **excuse me**
pardon *pahr-dohn*; excusez-
moi *ehkss-kew-zay mwah*

exhaust   l'echappement (m.)
lay-shahp-mahn

exhausted   épuisé(e) *ay-pwee-
zay*

exit   la sortie *lah sohr-tee*

expense   les frais (m. pl.) *lay
freh*

expensive   cher, chère *shehr*

express   express *ehkss-prehss*

eye   l'oeil (m.) *luhy*; **eyes**   les
yeux (m. pl.) *lay zyuh*

eyebrow   le sourcil *luh soor-ssee*

eyeglasses   les lunettes (f. pl.)
lay lew-neht

eyelash   le cil *luh seel*

eyelid   la paupière *lah poh-
pyehr*

eyeliner   le traceur à paupières
luh trah-ssuhr ah poh-pyehr

eye shadow   le fard à paupierès
luh fahr ah poh-pyehr

F

face (noun)   la figure *lah fee-
gewr*; le visage *luh vee-zazh*

facing   en face de *ahn fahss duh*

factory   l'usine (f.) *lew-zeen*

fall   tomber *tohn-bay*; **fall sick**
tomber malade *tohn-bay
mah-lahd*

fair (market)   la foire *lah fwahr*

false   faux, fausse *foh, fohss*

family   la famille *lah fah-meey*

fan   le ventilateur *luh vahn-tee-
lah-tuhr*

fan belt   la courroie de
ventilateur *lah koor-wah duh
vahn-tee-lah-tuhr*

far (from)   loin de *lwan duh*

farm   la ferme *lah fehrm*

fast   rapide *rah-peed*; vite *veet*

fat   gros(se) *groh(ss)*

father   le père *luh pere*

faucet   le robinet *luh roh-bee-neh*

fax   le fax *luh fahkss*

fear   la peur *lah puhr*; **to be
afraid**   avoir peur *ah-vwahr
puhr*

February   février *fay-vree-yay*

feel   (se) sentir *(suh) sahn-teer*

felt   le feutre *luh fuh-truh*

fender   l'aile (f.) *lehl*

festival   la fête *lah feht*

fever   la fièvre *lah fyeh-vruh*;
hay fever   le rhume des
foins *luh rewm day fwan*

few   peu de *puh duh*; **a few**
quelques *kehl-kuh*

field   le champ *luh shahn*

fifteen   quinze *kanz*

fifty   cinquante *san-kahnt*

fig   la figue *lah feeg*

figure (body)   la taille *lah tahy*

file (noun)   le fichier *luh
feesh-yay*

fill (out)   remplir *rahn-pleer*

film   le film *luh feelm*; la
pellicule *lah peh-lee-kewl*

finger   le doigt *luh dwah*

finish   finir *fee-neer*; terminer
tehr-mee-nay

fire   le feu *luh fuh*; l'incendie
(m.) *lan-ssahn-dee*

first   premier(ière) *pruh-myay
(yehr)*; **at first**   d'abord
dah-bohr; **first aid**   le
premier secours *luh pruh-
myay suh-koor*

fish (noun)   le poisson *luh
pwah-ssohn*

fish (verb)   pêcher *peh-shay*

fishing   la pêche *lah pehsh*;
deep-sea fishing   la pêche
sous-marine *lah pehsh soo-
mah-reen*; **fishing rod**   la
canne à pêche *lah kahn ah
pehsh*

five   cinq *sank*

flannel   la flanelle *lah flah-nehl*

flashlight   la lampe de poche
lah lahnp duh pohsh

flat   plat(te) *plah(t)*

flavor   le parfum *luh pahr-fuhn*

flight   le vol *luh vohl*

floor   le plancher *luh plahn-shay*; **(story)** l'étage (m.) *lay-tahzh*

florist   le fleuriste *luh fluh-reesst*

flounder   la sole *lah sohl*

flower   la fleur *lah fluhr*

flu   la grippe *lah greep*

fly (verb)   voler *voh-lay*

follow   suivre *swee-vruh*; **following**   suivant(e) *swee-vahn(t)*

food   les aliments (m. pl.) *lay zah-lee-mahn*; la nourriture *lah noo-ree-tewr*

food processor   le robot ménager *luh roh-boh may-nah-zhay*

foot   le pied *luh pyay*

for   pour *poor*

forbid   interdire *an-tehr-deer*; défendre *day fahn druh*; **forbidden**   interdit(e) *an-tehr-dee(t)*; défendu(e) *day-fahn-dew*; **it is forbidden to**   défense de *day-fahnss duh*

forehead   le front *luh frohn*

foreign   étranger(ère) *ay-trahn-zhay (zhehr)*

forest   la forêt *lah foh-reh*

forget   oublier *oo-blee-yay*

fork   la fourchette *lah foor-sheht*

form (noun)   la fiche *lah feesh*; la formule *lah fohr-mewl*

former   ancien(ne) *ahn-ssyan(n)*

forty   quarante *kah-rahnt*

forward (adv.)   en avant *ahn nah-vahn*

fountain   la fontaine *lah fohn-tehn*

four   quatre *kah-truh*

fourteen   quatorze *kah-tohrz*

free   libre *lee-bruh*; **for free**   gratuit(e) *grah-twee(t)*; **free of**

charge (adv.)   gratuitement *grah-tweet-mahn*

French   le français *luh frahn-sseh*

fresh   frais, fraîche *freh, frehsh*

Friday   vendredi *vahn-druh-dee*

fried   frit(e) *free(t)*

friend   ami(e) *ah-mee*

frog's legs   les cuisses (f. pl.) de grenouille *lay kweess duh gruh-nuhy*

front: in front of   devant *duh-vahn*

fruit   le fruit *luh frwee*

fruit salad   la macédoine de fruits *lah mah-ssay-dwahn duh frwee*

fuel pump   la pompe à essence *lah pohmp ah eh-ssahnss*

function (verb)   fonctionner *fohnk-ssyoh-nay*

furnished   meublé(e) *muh-blay*

G

gabardine   la gabardine *lah gah-bahr-deen*

game   le jeu *luh zhuh*; la partie *lah pahr-tee*

game (meat)   le gibier *luh zhee-byay*

garden   le jardin *luh zhahr-dan*

garlic   l'ail (m.) *lahy*

gas   l'essence (f.) *leh-ssahnss*

gas station   le poste d'essence *luh pohsst deh-ssahnss*; la station-service *lah stah-ssyohn sehr-veess*

gas tank   le réservoir à essence *luh ray-zehr-vwahr ah eh-ssahnss*

gears   l'engrenage (m.) *lahn-gruh-nahzh*

gear shift   le changement de vitesse *luh shahnzh-mahn duh vee-tehss*

get up   se lever *suh luh-vay*

gift   le cadeau *luh kah-doh*

girl la fille *lah fee*

give donner *doh-nay*

gladly volontiers *voh-lohn-tyay*

glass le verre *luh vehr*

glove le gant *luh gahn*

glue la colle *lah kohl*

go aller *ah-lay*; **go down** descendre *day-ssahn-druh*; **go home** rentrer *rahn-tray*; **go in** entrer *ahn-tray*; **go out** sortir *sohr-teer*; **go shopping** faire des emplettes *fehr day zahn-pleht*; **go to bed** se coucher *suh koo-shay*; **go up** monter *mohn-tay*

gold l'or (m.) *lohr*

golf course le terrain de golf *luh teh-rahn duh gohlf*

good bon(ne) *bohn, bohn*

goose l'oie (f.) *lwah*

grape le raisin *luh reh-zan*

grapefruit le pamplemousse *luh pahn-pluh-mooss*

graphics la grafique *lah grah-feek*

grass l'herbe (f.) *lehrb*

grave (adj.) sérieux(ieuse) *say-ree-uh(z)*; **grave** *grahv*

gray gris(e) *gree(z)*

green vert(e) *vehr(t)*

greet saluer *sah-lew-ay*

grilled grillé(e) *gree-yay*

grocery store l'épicerie (f.) *lay-peess-ree*

ground le terrain *luh teh-ran*; la terre *lah tehr*; **campground** le terrain de camping *luh teh-ran duh kahn-peeng*; **golf course** le terrain de golf *luh teh-ran duh golf*; **playing field** le terrain de sport *luh teh-ran duh spohr*; **on the ground** par terre *pahr tehr*

ground floor le rez-de-chaussée *luh rayd shoh-ssay*

guava la goyave *lah goh-yahv*

guide le guide *luh geed*; **guidebook** le guide

touristique *luh geed too-reess-teek*

gums (mouth) les gencives (f.) *lay zhahn-sseev*

H

hair les cheveux (m. pl.) *lay shuh-vuh*

haircut la coupe de cheveux *lah koop duh shuh-vuh*

hairdresser le (la) coiffeur (-euse) *luh (lah) kwah-fuhr (fuhz)*

hair dryer le sèche-cheveux *luh sehsh shuh-vuh*

hairspray la laque *lah lahk*

half (noun) la moitié *lah mwah-tyay*

half (adj.) demi(e) *duh-mee*

ham le jambon *luh zhahn-bohn*

hamburger le hamburger *luh ahn-boor-gehr*

hand la main *lah man*

handicapped handicapé *ahn-dee-kah-pay*

handkerchief le mouchoir *luh moo-shwahr*

handmade fait à la main *feh tah lah man*

handsome beau (m.), belle (f.) *boh, behl*

hanger le cintre *luh san-truh*

hang up accrocher *ah-kroh-sshay*

happy heureux(euse) *uh-ruh(z)*

hardware store la quincaillerie *lah kahn-kahy-ree*

have avoir *ah-vwahr*; **have just** venir de *vuh-neer duh*; **have to** avoir à *ah-vwahr ah*; devoir *duh-vwahr*

he il *eel*

head la tête *lah teht*

headlight le phare *luh fahr*

health la santé *lah sahn-tay*

hear entendre *ahn-tahn-druh*

hearing aid l'audiophone (m.) *loh-dyoh-fohn*

heart le coeur *luh kuhr*

heat (noun) la chaleur *lah shah-luhr*

heat (verb) chauffer *shoh-fay*

heating le chauffage *luh shoh-fahzh*

heel le talon *luh tah-lohn*

height la hauteur (f.) *lah oh-tuhr*

hello bonjour *bohn-zhoor*

help (noun) le secours *luh suh-koor;* **help!** au secours! *oh suh-koor*

help (verb) aider *eh day*

here ici *ee-ssee*

here is, are voici *vwah-ssee*

herring les harengs (m. pl.) *lay ah-rahn;* **smoked herring** les harengs fumés *lay ah-rahn few may*

high haut(e) *oh(t)*

high school le lycée *luh lee-ssay*

highway l'autoroute (f.) *loh-toh-root*

hip la hanche *lah ahnsh*

hire louer *loo-ay*

hit frapper *frah-pay*

hockey le hockey *luh oh-kee*

hold tenir *tuh-neer*

hole le trou *luh troo*

holiday la fête *lah feht*

hood (car) le capot *luh ka-poh*

hope (verb) espérer *ehss-pay-ray*

horn le klaxon *luh klahk-ssohn*

horse le cheval *luh shuh-vahl;* les chevaux (pl.) *lay shuh-voh*

horseback riding l'équitation (f.) *lay-kee-tah-syohn*

horseradish le raifort *luh reh-fohr*

hospital l'hôpital (m.) *loh-pee-tahl*

host l'hôte (m.) *loht*

hostel (youth) l'auberge (f.) de jeunesse *loh-behrzh duh zhuh-nehss*

hostess l'hôtesse (f.) *loh-tehss*

hot chaud *shoh;* **be hot (person)** avoir chaud *ah-vwahr shoh;* **be hot (weather)** faire chaud *fehr shoh*

hotel l'hôtel (m.) *loh-tehl*

hour l'heure (f.) *luhr*

house la maison *lah meh-zohn;* **at the house of** chez *shay;* **boardinghouse** la pension *lah pahn-ssyohn*

house porter le concierge *luh kohn-ssyehrzh*

how comment *koh-mahn;* **how far** à quelle distance *ah kehl deess-tahnss;* **how long** depuis quand *duh-pwee kahn*

how many, much combien *kohn-byan*

hundred cent *sahn*

hunger la faim *lah fan;* **to be hungry** avoir faim *ah-vwahr fan*

hunting la chasse *lah shahss*

hurry se dépêcher *suh day-peh-shay;* **be in a hurry** être pressé *eh-truh preh-ssay*

husband le mari *luh mah-ree*

I

I je *zhuh*

ice la glace *luh glahss;* **ice cream** la glace *luh glahss;* **ice cubes** les glaçons (m. pl.) *lay glah-ssohn;* **ice-skating** le patin à glace *luh pah-tan ah glahss;* **ice water** l'eau (f.) glacée *loh glah-ssay*

if si *see*

ignition l'allumage (m.) *lah lew-mahzh*

ill malade *mah-lahd*

illness la maladie *lah mah-lah-dee*

immediately immédiatement *ee-may-dyaht-mahn*

important   important(e) *an-pohr-tahn(t)*
impossible   impossible *an-poh-ssee-bluh*
improbable   invraisemblable *an-vreh-sahn-blah-bluh*
in   dans *dahn*; en *ahn*
incapable   incapable *an-kah-pah-bluh*
included   compris(e) *kohn-pree(z)*
indefinite   imprécis(e) *an-pray-ssee(z)*
infection   l'infection (f.) *lan-fehk-ssyohn*
information   les renseignements *lay rahn-seh-nyuh-mahn*
inn   l'auberge (f.) *loh-behrzh*
inside   dedans *duh-dahn*
insomnia   l'insomnie (f.) *lan-ssohm-nee*
in spite of   malgré *mahl-gray*
instead of   au lieu de *oh lyuh duh*
insufficient   insuffisant(e) *an-ssew-fee-zahn(t)*
insurance   l'assurance (f.) *lah-ssew-rahnss*
insure   assurer *ah-ssew-ray*
intelligent   intelligent(e) *an-teh-lee-zhahn(t)*
interesting   intéressant(e) *an-tay-reh-ssahn(t)*
Internet   l'Internet *lan-tehr-neht*
interpret   interpréter *an-tehr-pray-tay*
interpreter   l'interprète (m.) *lan-tehr-preht*
intersection   le croisement *luh krawhz-mahn*
introduce   présenter *pray-zahn-tay*
invite   inviter *an-vee-tay*
invoice   la facture *lah fahk-tewr*
iron (noun)   le fer *luh fehr*

iron (verb)   repasser *ruh-pah-ssay*
island   l'île (f.) *leel*
itinerary   l'itinéraire *lee-tee-nay-rehr*

J

jack (auto)   le cric *luh kreek*
jacket   le veston *luh vehss-tohn*
jam (marmalade)   la confiture *lah kohn-fee-tewr*
January   janvier *zhahn-vyay*
jar   la jarre *lah zhahr*
jaw   la mâchoire *lah mah-shwahr*
jewel   le bijou *luh bee-zhoo*
jeweler   le bijoutier *luh bee-zhoo-tyay*
jewelry shop   la bijouterie *lah bee-zhoo-tree*
jogging suit   le survet *luh sewr-veh*; le jogging *luh zhoh-geengh*
joystick   la manette de jeux *lah mah-neht duh zhuh*
joke   la plaisanterie *lah pleh-zahn-tree*
journey   le voyage *luh vwah-yahzh*; le trajet *luh trah-zheh*
judge (noun)   le juge *luh zhewzh*
judge (verb)   juger *zhew-zhay*
juice   le jus *luh zhew*
July   juillet *zhwee-yeh*
June   juin *zhwan*
just: have just   venir de *vuh-neer duh*

K

keep   garder *gahr-day*
ketchup   le ketchup *luh keht-shuhp*
key   la clef *lah klay*; (computer) la touche *lah toosh*

keyboard   le clavier *luh klah-vyay*

kiss (verb)   embrasser *ahn-brah-ssay*

kitchen   la cuisine *lah kwee-zeen*

knee   le genou *luh zhuh-noo*; **kneepads**   les genouillères *lay zhuh-noo-yehr*

knife   le couteau *luh koo-toh*

knock (verb)   frapper *frah-pay*

know (facts)   savoir *sah vwahr*, **(people)**   connaître *koh-neh-truh*

L

label   l'étiquette (f.) *lay-tee-keht*

lace   la dentelle *lah dahn-tehl*

lack (noun)   le manque *luh mahnk*

lack (verb)   manquer *mahn kay*

lake   le lac *luh lahk*

lamb   l'agneau *lah-nyoh*

lamp   la lampe *lah lahnp*

land (noun)   la terre *lah tehr*

land (verb) (plane)   atterrir *ah-teh-reer*; débarquer *day-bahr-kay*

landing   l'atterrissage (m.) *lah-teh-ree-ssahzh*; le débarquement *luh day-bahrk-mahn*

lane   la ruelle *lah rew-ehl*

language   la langue *lah lahng*

laptop computer   l'ordinateur (m.) portable *lohr-dee-nah-tuhr pohr-tahbl*

last (adj.)   dernier(ière) *dehr-nyay(nyehr)*

last (verb)   durer *dew-ray*

late   tard *tahr*; **(to be) late**   (être) en retard *(eh-truh) ahn ruh-tahr*

laugh   rire *reer*

launderette   la laverie automatique *lah lah-vree oh-toh-mah-teek*

laundering   le blanchissage *luh blahn-shee-ssahzh*

laundry   la blanchisserie *lah blahn-sheess-ree*

lawyer   l'avocat (m.), l'avocate (f.) *lah-voh-kah, lah-voh-kaht*

learn   apprendre *ah prahn-druh*

least: at least   au moins *oh mwan*

leather   le cuir *luh kweer*

leave (behind)   laisser *leh-ssay*

leave (depart)   partir *pahr-teer*; **to go out**   sortir *sohr-teer*; **to leave + (place or person)**   quitter *kee-tay*

left   gauche *gohsh*; **to the left**   à gauche *ah gohsh*

leg   la jambe *lah zhahnb*

lemon   le citron *luh see-trohn*

lemonade   la citronnade *luh see-troh-nahd*

lend   prêter *preh-tay*

less   moins *mwan*

letter   la lettre *lah leh-truh*

lettuce   la laitue *lah leh-tew*

library   la bibliothèque *lah bee-blee-oh-tehk*

life   la vie *lah vee*

life preserver   la ceinture de sauvetage *lah san-tewr duh sohv-tahzh*

light (noun)   la lumière *lah lew-myehr*

light (color)   clair(e) *klehr*

light (weight)   léger(ère) *lay-zhay(zhehr)*

light (verb)   allumer *ah-lew-may*

lighter   le briquet *luh bree-keh*

like (prep.)   comme *kohm*

like (verb)   aimer *eh-may*

lime   la limette *lah lee-meht*

line   la ligne *lah lee-nyuh*; la voie *lah vwah*

line (of people)   la queue *lah kuh*; **form a line**   faire la queue *fehr lah kuh*

linen (cloth) le lin *luh lan*
lip la lèvre *lah leh-vruh*
lipstick le rouge à lèvres *luh roozh ah leh-vruh*
list la liste *lah leesst*
listen écouter *ay-koo-tay*
little (adj.) petit(e) *puh-tee(t)*; **(adv.)** peu (de) *puh (duh)*
live vivre *vee-vruh*
live in demeurer *duh-muh-ray*; habiter *ah-bee-tay*
liver le foie *luh fwah*
lobster le homard *luh oh-mahr*
lock (noun) la serrure *lah seh-rewr*
lodging le logis *luh loh-zhee*
long long, longue *lohn, lohng*
look at regarder *ruh-gahr-day*
look for chercher *shehr-shay*
lose perdre *pehr-druh*
loss la perte *lah pehrt*
lost: get lost s'égarer *say-gah-ray*
lot beaucoup de *boh-koo duh*
loudspeaker le haut-parleur *luh oh pahr-luhr*
love (noun) l'amour (m.) *lah-moor*
love (verb) aimer *eh-may*
low bas(se) *bah(ss)*
luck la chance *lah shahnss*; **Good luck!** Bonne chance! *bohn shahnss*
lunch (noun) le déjeuner *luh day-zhuh-nay*
lunch (verb) déjeuner *day-zhuh-nay*
lung le poumon *luh poo-mohn*
luxurious luxueux(euse) *lewk-ssew-uh(uhz)*
luxury le luxe *luh lewkss*

M

magazine le magazine *luh mah-gah-zeen*
mail le courrier *luh koo-ryay*

mailbox la boîte à lettres *lah bwaht ah leh-truh*
mailman le facteur *luh fahk-tuhr*
make faire *fehr*
man l'homme (m.) *lohm*
manager le gérant *luh zhay-rahn*
mango la mangue *lah mahng*
many beaucoup de *boh-koo duh*; **too many** trop de *troh duh*
map la carte *lah kahrt*; **road map** la carte routière *lah kahrt roo-tyehr*
March mars *mahrss*
margarine la margarine *lah mahr-gah-reen*
market le marché *luh mahr-shay*
marvelous merveilleux(euse) *mehr-veh-yuh(z)*
mashed en purée *ahn pew-ray*
match (noun) l'allumette (f.) *lah-lew-meht*
material le tissu *luh tee-ssew*
matter (noun) l'affaire (f.) *lah-fehr*; **it doesn't matter** n'importe *nan-pohrt*; **What's the matter?** Qu'est-ce qu'il y a? *Kehss keel yah*
May mai *meh*
may (verb) pouvoir *poo-vwahr*
maybe peut-être *puh-teh-truh*
mayonnaise la mayonnaise *lah may-yoh-nehz*
meal le repas *luh ruh-pah*
mean (verb) vouloir dire *voo-lwahr deer*; signifier *see-nee-fyay*
mean (adj.) méchant(e) *may-shahn(t)*
meaning la signification *lah see-nee-fee-kah-ssyohn*
measure (noun) la mesure *lah muh-zewr*
measure (verb) mesurer *muh-zew-ray*

meat la viande *lah vee-ahnd*

meatballs les boulettes *lay boo-leht*

mechanic le mécanicien *luh may-kah-nee-ssyan*

medicine la médecine *lah mayd-sseen*

medium (cooking) à point *ah pwan*

meet rencontrer *rah-kohn-tray*

meeting le rendez-vous *luh rahn-day-voo*

melon le melon *luh muh-lohn*

memory la mémoire *lah may-mwahr*

merchandise la marchandise *lah mahr-shahn-deez*

merchant le marchand *luh mahr shahn*

mezzanine le parterre *luh pahr-tehr*

microwave oven le four à micro-ondes *luh foor ah mee-kroh ohnd*

middle le milieu *luh meel-yuh*; **in the middle of** au milieu de *oh meel-yuh duh*

midnight minuit *mee nwee*

milk le lait *luh leh*

milk shake le frappé *luh fruh-pay*

million le million *luh mee-lyohn*

minute la minute *lah mee-newt*

mirror le miroir *luh mee-rwahr*; la glace *lah glahss*

miss (verb) manquer *mahn-kay*

miss mademoiselle *mahd-mwah-zehl*

mistake la faute *lah foht*; l'erreur (f.) *leh-ruhr*; **make a mistake** se tromper *suh trohn-pay*

mister monsieur *muh-ssyuh*

misunderstanding le malentendu *luh mahl-ahn-tahn-dew*

modem le modem *luh moh-dehm*

modify modifier *moh-dee-fyay*

Monday lundi *luhn-dee*

money l'argent (m.) *lahr-zhahn*

money (coins) la monnaie *lah moh-nay*

monitor le moniteur *luh moh-nee-tuhr*

month le mois *luh mwah*

monthly mensuel(le) *mahn-sswehl*

morning le matin *luh mah-tan*

mosque la mosquée *lah mohss-kay*

mother la mère *lah mehr*

motherboard la carte-mère *lah kahrt mehr*

motor le moteur *luh moh-tuhr*

mountain la montagne *lah mohn-tah-nyuh*

mouse (computer) la souris *lah soo-reé*

mouth la bouche *lah boosh*

mouthwash l'eau dentifrice *loh dahn-tee-freess*

movies le cinéma *luh see-nay-mah*

Mr. monsieur *muh-ssyuh*

Mrs. madame *mah-dahm*

museum le musée *luh mew-zay*

mushroom le champignon *luh shahn-pee-nyohn*

music la musique *lah mew-zeek*

mussels les moules (f. pl.) *lay mool*

mustard la moutarde *lah moo-tahrd*

mutton leg le gigot *luh zhee-goh*

N

nail l'ongle *lohn-gluh*

nail file la lime à ongles *lah leem ah ohn-gluh*

name le nom *luh nohn*; **family (last) name** le nom de famille *luh nohn duh fah-mee*; **first name** le prénom

luh pray-nohn; **last name**
le surnom *luh sehr-nohn;*
My name is Je m'appelle
zhuh mah-pehl

napkin la serviette *lah sehr-vyeht;* **sanitary napkin** la
serviette hygiénique *lah sehr-vyeht ee-zhyay-neek*

nationality la nationalité *lah
nah-ssyohn-nah-lee-tay*

nausea la nausée *lah noh-zay*

near (to) près de *preh duh*

nearby proche *prohsh*

nearly presque *prehss-kuh*

necessary nécessaire *nay-sseh-ssehr;* **it is necessary**
il est nécessaire *eel eh nay-sseh-ssehr;* il faut *eel foh*

neck le cou *luh koo*

necklace le collier *luh koh-lyay*

need (verb) avoir besoin de
ah-vwahr buhz-wan duh

needle l'aiguille (f.) *lay-gwee*

neighbor le voisin *luh vwah-san;* la voisine *lah vwah-zeen*

network le réseau *luh ray-zoh*

never jamais *zhah-meh;* ne . . .
jamais *nuh . . . zhah-meh*

new nouveau (m.), nouvelle
(f.) *noo-voh, noo-vehl*

newspaper le journal *luh
zhoor-nahl*

next prochain(e) *proh-shan
(shehn)*

night la nuit *lah nwee*

nightclub la boîte de nuit *lah
bwaht duh nwee*

nine neuf *nuhf*

nineteen dix-neuf *deez nuhf*

ninety quatre-vingt-dix *kah-truh van deess*

no non *nohn*

noise le bruit *luh brwee*

no longer ne . . . plus *nuh . . .
plew*

none ne . . . aucun(e) *nuh . . .
oh-kuhn(kewn)*

nonsmokers non-fumeurs
nohn few-muhr

noon midi *mee-dee*

north le nord *luh nohr*

nose le nez *luh nay*

not ne . . . pas *nuh . . . pah*

not any ne . . . aucun(e) *nuh . . .
oh-kuhn(kewn)*

notebook le cahier *luh kah-yay*

nothing ne . . . rien *nuh . . .
ryan*

notice (noun) l'avis (m.) *lah-vee*

notice (verb) remarquer *ruh-mahr-kay*

novel le roman *luh roh-mahn*

novelty la nouveauté *lah noo-voh-tay*

now maintenant *mant-nahn*

number le numéro *luh new-may-roh*

number (quantity) le nombre
luh nohn-bruh

nurse l'infirmière (f.) *lan-feer-myehr*

nut la noix *lah nwah*

nylon le nylon *luh nee-lohn*

O

observe observer *ohb-zehr-vay*

obtain obtenir *ohp-tuh-neer*

ocean l'océan (m.) *loh-ssay-ahn*

of de *duh*

of course bien entendu *byan
nahn-tahn-dew*

offer offrir *oh-freer*

office le bureau *luh bew-roh;*
box office le bureau de
location *luh bew-roh duh loh-kah-ssyohn;* **exchange office**
le bureau de change *luh bew-roh duh shahnzh;* **post
office** le bureau de poste
luh bew-roh duh pohsst

often souvent *soo-vahn*

oil l'huile (f.) *lweel*

O.K. d'accord *dah-kohr*

old vieux (m.), vieille (f.) *vyuh, vyay*; **How old are you?** Quel âge avez-vous? *kehl ahzh ah-vay voo?*

old-fashioned démodé(e) *day-moh-day*

olive l'olive (f.) *loh-leev*

olive oil l'huile d'olive *lweel doh-leev*

omelet l'omelette (f.) *lohm-leht*

on sur *sewr*

one un (m.), une (f.) *uhn, ewn*

onion l'oignon (m.) *loh-nyohn*

on-line service les serveurs en ligne (m.) *lay sehr-vuhr ahn lee-nyuh*

only ne . . . que *nuh . . . kuh*; seulement *suhl-mahn*

only (adj.) seul(e) *suhl*; unique *ew-neek*

open (verb) ouvrir *oo-vreer*

open (adj.) ouvert(e) *oo-vehr(t)*

opera l'opéra (m.) *loh-pay-rah*

operator la téléphoniste *lah tay-lay-foh-neesst*

opportunity l'occasion (f.) *loh-kah-zyohn*

opposite (noun) le contraire *luh kohn-trehr*

opposite (prep.) en face de *ahn fahss duh*

optician l'opticien (m.) *lohp-tee-ssyan*

or ou *oo*

orange l'orange (f.) *loh-rahnzh*

orangeade l'orangeade (f.) *loh-rahnzh-ahd*

orchestra l'orchestre (m.) *lohr-kehss-truh*

order (noun) la commande *lah koh-mahnd*

order (verb) commander *koh-mahn-day*

other autre *oh-truh*

outside dehors *duh-ohr*

over dessus *duh-ssew*

overcoat le manteau *luh mahn-toh*; le pardessus *luh pahr-duh-ssew*

overseas outre-mer *oo-truh mehr*

owe devoir *duh-vwahr*

own posséder *poh-ssay day*

owner le propriétaire *luh proh-pree-ay-tehr*

oyster l'huître (f.) *lwee-truh*

P

package le paquet *luh pah-keh*; le colis *luh koh-lee*

pad (writing) le bloc *luh blohk*

pain la douleur *lah doo-luhr*

painting le tableau *luh tah-bloh*

pair la paire *lah pehr*

pajamas le pyjama *luh pee-zhah-mah*

palace le palais *luh pah-leh*

panties la culotte *lah kew-loht*

pants le pantalon *luh pahn-tah-lohn*

panty hose les collants (m. pl.) *lay koh-lahn*

paper le papier *luh pah-pyay*; **toilet** le papier hygiénique *luh pah-pyay ee-zhyay-neek*; **typing** le papier à machine *luh pah-pyay ah mah-sheen*; **wrapping** le papier d'emballage *luh pah-pyay dahn-bah-lahzh*; **writing** le papier à lettres *luh pah-pyay ah leh-truh*

park (noun) le parc *luh pahrk*

park (verb) garer *gah-ray*; stationner *stah-ssyoh-nay*

part la partie *lah pahr-tee*

pass (verb) passer *pah-ssay*

pastry la pâtisserie *lah pah-teess-ree*

path le sentier *luh sahn-tyay*

pay payer *peh-yay*

pear la poire *lah pwahr*

peas les pois (m. pl.) *lay pwah*

pedestrian le piéton *luh pyay-tohn*

pen la plume *lah plewm*; **ball-point** le stylo à bille *luh stee-loh ah bee*

penalty l'amende (f.) *lah-mahnd*

pencil le crayon *luh kreh-yohn*; **pencil sharpener** le taille-crayon *luh tahy kreh-yohn*

people les gens *lay zhahn* [adj. before (f.); adj. after (m.)]

people (nation) le peuple *luh puh-pluh*

pepper le poivre *luh pwah-vruh*

perfect parfait(e) *pahr-feh(t)*

performance la représentation *lah ruh-pray-zahn-tah-ssyohn*

perfume le parfum *luh pahr-fuhn*

perhaps peut-être *puh-teh-truh*

permanent permanent(e) *pehr-mah-nahn(t)*

permanent press infroissable *an-frwah-ssah-bluh*

permit (noun) le permis *luh pehr-mee*

permit (verb) permettre *pehr-meh-truh*; **permitted** permis *pehr-mee*

person la personne *lah pehr-ssohn*

persuade persuader *pehr-sswah-day*

pharmacy la pharmacie *lah fahr-mah-ssee*

photocopy la photocopie *lah foh-toh-koh-pee*

photograph (noun) la photo *lah foh-toh*

photograph (verb) photographier *foh-toh-grah-fyay*

pickle le cornichon *luh kohr-nee-shohn*

picture (art) le tableau *luh tah-bloh*

pie la tarte *lah tahrt*

piece le morceau *luh mohr-ssoh*

pill la pilule *lah pee-lewl*

pillow l'oreiller (m.) *loh-reh-yay*

pin l'épingle (f.) *lay pan-gluh*

pineapple l'ananas (m.) *lah-nah-nah*

pink rose *rohz*

pipe (smoking) la pipe *lah peep*; **pipe tobacco** le tabac pour pipe *luh tah-bah poor peep*

pitcher la cruche *lah krewsh*

place (noun) l'endroit (m.) *lahn-drwah*; le lieu *lyuh*

place setting le couvert *luh koo-vehr*

plaid le tartan *luh tahr-tahn*

plan le plan *luh plahn*; **plan of the city** le plan de ville *luh plahn duh veel*

plate l'assiette (f.) *lah-ssyeht*

platform le quai *luh kay*

platinum le platine *luh plah-teen*

play (noun) la pièce *lah pyehss*

play (verb) jouer *zhoo-ay*; **play (a game)** jouer à *zhoo-ay ah*; **play (an instrument)** jouer de *zhoo-ay duh*

please s'il vous plaît *seel voo pleh*

pleasure le plaisir *luh pleh-zeer*

plum la prune *lah prewn*

pocket la poche *lah pohsh*

pocketbook le sac *luh sahk*

policeman l'agent (m.) de police *lah-zhahn duh poh-leess*; le gendarme *luh zhahn-dahrm*

police station le commissariat *luh koh-mee-ssah-ryah*

polka-dotted à pois *ah pwah*

polyester synthétique *san-tay-teek*

pool la piscine *lah pee-sseen*

poor pauvre *poh-vruh*

pork le porc *luh pohr*

portable portatif(tive) *pohr-tah-teef(teev)*

porter le porteur *luh pohr-tuhr*

possess posséder *poh-ssay-day*

postcard la carte postale *lah kahrt pohss-tahl*

poster l'affiche (f.) *lah-feesh*

postman le facteur *luh fahk-tuhr*

post office la poste *lah pohsst*; le bureau de poste *luh bew-roh duh pohsst*

postpone remettre *ruh-meh-truh*

potato la pomme de terre *lah pohm duh tehr*

pottery la poterie *luh poh tree*

pound (meas.) la livre *luh lee vruh*

practice (noun) l'usage (m.) *lew-zahzh*

prefer préférer *pray-fay-ray*; aimer mieux *eh may myuh*

pregnant enceinte *ahn-sant*

prepare préparer *pray-pah-ray*

prescription l'ordonnance (f.) *lohr-doh-nahnss*

pretty joli(e) *zhoh-lee*

price le prix *luh pree*

printer l'imprimante (f.) *lan-pree-mahnt*

  laser laser *luh-zehr*

  ink jet jet d'encre *zheh dahnkr*

private privé(e) *pree-vay*

prize le prix *luh pree*

profession la profession *lah proh-feh-ssyohn*

prohibit interdire *an-tehr-deer*; **prohibited** interdit(e) *an-tehr-dee(t)*

promise (verb) promettre *proh-meh-truh*

promise (noun) la promesse *lah proh-mehss*

pronounce prononcer *proh-nohn-ssay*

property la propriété *lah proh-pree-ay-tay*

protect protéger *proh-tay-zhay*

protest (verb) protester *proh-tehss-tay*

prune le pruneau *luh prew-noh*

public (adj.) public(ique) *pew-bleek*

public (noun) le public *luh pew-blook*

pull tirer *tee-ray*; arracher (tooth) *ah-rah-shay*

purchase (noun) l'achat (m.) *lah-shah*

purple violet *vee-oh-leht*; mauve *mohv*

purse le porte-monnaie *luh pohrt moh-nay*

push pousser *poo-ssay*

put mettre *meh-truh*; **to put on** mettre *meh-truh*; **to put back** remettre *ruh-meh-tr uh*

Q

quality la qualité *lah kah-lee-tay*

quantity la quantité *lah kahn-tee-tay*

quarter le quart *luh-kahr*

question la question *lah kehss-tyohn*

quickly vite *veet*; rapidement *rah-peed-mahn*

quickness la vitesse *lah vee-tehss*

R

rabbit le lapin *luh luh-pan*

radio la radio *lah rah-dyoh*

radish le radis *luh rah-dee*

railroad le chemin de fer *luh shuh-man duh fehr*

railroad station la gare *lah gahr*

rain la pluie *lah plwee*

raincoat l'imperméable (m.) *lan-pehr-may-ah-bluh*

raisin le raisin sec *luh reh-zan sehk*

rare rare *rahr*

rare (meat) saignant *seh-nyahn*

raspberry la framboise *lah frahn-bwahz*

rate le tarif *luh tah-reef*

rate of exchange le cours du change *luh koor dew shahnzh*

rather plutôt *plew-toh*

raw cru(e) *krew*

razor le rasoir *luh rah-zwahr*

read lire *leer*

ready prêt(e) *preh(t)*

really vraiment *vreh-mahn*

reason la raison *lah reh-zohn*

reasonable raisonnable *reh-zoh-nah-bluh*

receipt le reçu *luh ruh-ssew*

receive recevoir *ruh-ssuh-vwahr*

recently récemment *ray-sseh-mahn*

recommend recommander *ruh-koh-mahn-day*

record le disque *luh deessk*

recover (health) se remettre *suh ruh-meh-truh*

recovery room la salle de repos *lah sahl duh ruh-poh*

recuperate récupérer *ray-kew-pay-ray*

red rouge *roozh*

reduction le rabais *luh rah-beh*

refreshments les rafraîchisse-ments (m. pl.) *lay rah-freh-sheess-mahn*

refund rembourser *rahn-boor-ssay*

refuse (verb) refuser *ruh-few-zay*

regret regretter *ruh-greh-tay*

regular régulier(ière) *ray-gew-lyay(yehr)*

regularly régulièrement *ray-gew-lyehr-mahn*

reimburse rembourser *rahn-boor-ssay*

remain rester *rehss-tay*

remedy le remède *luh ruh-mehd*

remember se rappeler *suh rah-play*; se souvenir de *suh soo-vuh-neer duh*

rent (noun) le loyer *luh lwah-yay*

rent (verb) louer *loo-ay*

repair (verb) réparer *ray-pah-ray*

repeat répéter *ray-pay-tay*

replace remplacer *rahn-plah-ssay*

resemble ressembler à *ruh-ssahn-blay ah*

reservation la réservation *lay ray-zehr-vah-ssyohn*

reserve réserver *ray-zehr-vay*

resolve résoudre *ray-zoo-druh*

responsible responsable *rehss-pohn-ssah-bluh*

rest (noun) le repos *luh ruh-poh*

rest (verb) se reposer *suh ruh-poh-zay*

restaurant le restaurant *luh rehss-toh-rahn*

result le résultat *luh ray-zewl-tah*

retain retenir *ruh-tuh-neer*

retired en retraite *ahn ruh-treht*

return retourner *ruh-toor-nay*; **return (give back)** rendre *rahn-druh*

reward (noun) la récompense *lah ray-kohn-pahnss*

reward (verb) récompenser *ray-kohn-pahn-ssay*

rice le riz *luh ree*

right: to be right avoir raison *ah-vwahr reh-zohn*

right (direction) droit *drwah*; **to the right** à droite *ah drwaht*

ring (noun) la bague *lah bahg*

ring (verb) sonner *soh-nay*

river le fleuve *luh fluhv*; la rivière *lah ree-vyehr*

road le chemin *luh shuh-man*

roasted (adj.) rôti(e) *roh-tee*

roll   le petit pain *luh puh-tee pan*

roller skating   le patin à roulettes *luh pah-tan ah roo-leht*

roof   le toit *luh twah*

room   la pièce *lah pyehss*; la salle *lah sahl*; la chambre *lah shahn-bruh*; **single room** une chambre à un lit *ewn shahn-bruh ah uhn lee*; **double room** une chambre à deux lits *ewn shahn-bruh ah duh lee*

round   rond(e) *rohn(d)*

route   la route *lah root*

row (noun)   le rang *luh rahn*

rubber   le caoutchouc *luh kah-oo-tshoo*; **rubbers** les caoutchoucs *lay kah-oo-tshoo*

rug   le tapis *luh tah poo*

rule   la règle *lah reh-gluh*

ruler   la règle *lah reh-gluh*

run   courir *koo-reer*

runway   la piste *lah peesst*

S

sad   triste *treessl*

safe (strongbox)   le coffre-fort *luh koh-fruh fohr*

sailboat   le bateau à voiles *luh bah-toh ah vwahl*

sale   la vente *lah vahnt*; **for sale** en vente *ahn vahnt*

sale (bargain)   les soldes (m. pl.) *lay sohld*

salesman   le vendeur *luh vahn-duhr*

saleswoman   la vendeuse *lah vahn-duhz*

salmon   le saumon *luh soh-mohn*

salt   le sel *luh sehl*; **salty** salé *sah-lay*

salted   salé *sah-lay*

same   même *mehm*

sample   l'échantillon (m.) *lay-shahn-tee-yohn*

sand   le sable *luh sah-bluh*

sandals   les sandales (f.) *lay sahn-dahl*

sardine   la sardine *lah sahr-deen*

satin   le satin *luh sah-tan*

satisfied   satisfait(e) *sah-teess-feh(t)*

Saturday   samedi *sahm-dee*

sauerkraut   la choucroute *lah shoo-kroot*

sausage   la saucisse *lah soh-sseess*

say   dire *deer*

scanner   le scanneur *luh skah-nuhr*

scarf   l'écharpe (f.) *lay-shahrp*

schedule   l'horaire (m.) *loh-rehr*

school   l'école (f.) *lay-kohl*

scissors   les ciseaux (m. pl.) *lay see-zoh*

scrambled   brouillé(e) *broo-yay*

screen   l'écran (m.) *lay-krahn*

sea   la mer *lah mehr*

seafood   les fruits (m. pl.) de mer *lay frwee duh mehr*

search engine   le moteur de recherche *luh moh-tuhr duh ruh-shehsh*

season   la saison *lah seh-zohn*

seasoned   assaisonné *ah-sseh-zoh-nay*

seat   la place *lah plahss*; le siège *luh syehzh*

secondhand   usagé *ew-zah-zhay*

secondhand goods   la marchandise d'occasion *lah mahr-shahn-deez doh-kah-zyohn*

secretary   le (la) secrétaire *luh (lah) seh-kray tehr*

security   la sécurité *lah say-kew-ree-tay*

see   voir *vwahr*

seem   sembler *sahn-blay*; avoir l'air de *ah-vwahr lehr duh*

sell   vendre *vahn-druh*

send   envoyer *ahn-vwah-yay*; **send for** faire venir *fehr*

vuh-neer; **send back**
renvoyer *rahn-vwah-yay*
sentence la phrase *lah frahz*
serious sérieux(ieuse) *say-ryuh(z)*; grave *grahv*
serve servir *sehr-veer*
service le service *luh sehr-veess*
service station la station service *lah stah-ssyohn sehr-veess*
settle régler *ray-glay*; **settle an affair** régler une affaire *ray-glay ewn ah-fehr*
seven sept *seht*
seventeen dix-sept *dee seht*
seventy soixante-dix *swah-ssahnt deess*
several plusieurs *plew-zyuhr*
sew coudre *koo-druh*
shade l'ombre (f.) *lohn-bruh*
shampoo le shampooing *luh shahn-pwan*
share partager *pahr-tah-zhay*
shark le requin *luh ruh-kan*
shave (verb) raser *rah-zay*
shawl le châle *luh shahl*
she elle *ehl*
sheet la feuille *lah fuhy*
shelf le rayon *luh reh-yohn*
shellfish le coquillage *luh koh-kee-yahzh*
sherbet le sorbet *luh sohr-beh*
shine (verb) cirer *see-ray*
shirt la chemise *lah shuh-meez*
shoe le soulier *luh soo-lyay*; la chaussure *lah shoh-ssewr*
shoelaces les lacets (m. pl.) *lay lah-sseh*
shoemaker le cordonnier *luh kohr-doh-nyay*
shop (noun) la boutique *lah boo-teek*
shop (verb) faire des achats *fehr day zah-shah*; faire des emplettes *fehr day zahn-pleht*
shop window la vitrine *lah vee-treen*

shore (bank) la rive *lah reev*
short court(e) *koor(t)*
shorts (briefs) le caleçon *luh kahl-ssohn*
short story le conte *luh kohnt*
shoulder l'épaule (f.) *lay-pohl*
show (verb) montrer *mohn-tray*
show (noun) le spectacle *luh spehk-tah-kluh*
shower la douche *lah doosh*
shrimp la crevette *lah kruh-veht*
sick malade *mah-lahd*
sickness la maladie *lah mah-lah-dee*
side le côté *luh koh-tay*
sidewalk le trottoir *luh troh-twahr*
sightseeing le tourisme *luh too-reess-muh*
sign (noun) l'enseigne (f.) *lahn-sseh-nyuh*
sign (verb) signer *see-nyay*
signal (directional) le clignotant *luh klee-nyoh-tahn*
silk la soie *lah swah*
silver l'argent (m.) *lahr-zhahn*
since depuis *duh-pwee*
since when depuis quand *duh-pwee kahn*
sing chanter *shahn-tay*
single (unmarried) célibataire *say-lee-bah-tehr*
sir monsieur *muh-ssyuh*
sister la soeur *lah suhr*
sit s'asseoir *sah-sswahr*
site le site *luh seet*
six six *seess*
sixteen seize *sehz*
sixty soixante *swah-ssahnt*
size la taille *lah tahy*
skateboard la planche à roulettes *lah plahnssh ah roo-leht*
ski le ski *luh skee*; **water skis** les skis nautiques *lay skee-noh-teek*

ski lift le téléski *luh tay-lay-sskee*

ski slope la piste de ski *lah peesst duh skee*

skin la peau *lah poh*

skirt la jupe *lah zhewp*

sky le ciel *luh syehl*

skyscraper le gratte-ciel *luh graht syehl*

sleep (verb) dormir *dohr-meer*

sleep, sleepiness le sommeil *luh soy-mehy*; **to be sleepy** avoir sommeil *ah vwahr soh-mehy*; **sleeping car** le wagon-lit *luh vah-gohn lee*; **sleeping pill** le somnifère *luh sohm-nee-fehr*

sleeve la manche *lah mahnsh*

slice la tranche *lah trahnsh*

slide (pictures) la diapositive *lah dee-ah-poh-zee-teev*

slip (clothing) la combinaison *lah kohn-bee-neh-zohn*; le jupon *luh zhew-pohn*

slippers les pantoufles (f. pl.) *lay pahn-too fluh*

slope la piste *lah peesst*

slow (adj.) lent(e) *lahn(t)*

slowly (adv.) lentement *lahnt-mahn*

small petit(e) *puh-tee(t)*

smoke fumer *few-may*

smoker le fumeur *luh few-muhr*

snail l'escargot (m.) *lehss-kahr-goh*

snow (noun) la neige *lah nehzh*

snow (verb) neiger *neh-zhay*

so alors *ah-lohr*

soap le savon *luh sah-vohn*; **a bar of soap** une savonnette *ewn sah-voh-neht*

socket la prise de courant *lah preez duh koo-rahn*

socks les chaussettes (f. pl.) *lay shoh-sseht*

soda le soda *luh soh-dah*

soft doux, douce *doo(ss)*

softly doucement *dooss-mahn*

software le logiciel *luh loh-zhee-syehl*

sole (fish) la sole *lah sohl*

solid (colored) uni(e) *ew-nee*

some quelques *kehl-kuh*

some du *dew*; de la *duh lah*; de l' *duhl*; des *day*

someone quelqu'un *kehl-kuhn*

something quelque chose *kehl-kuh shohz*

sometimes quelquefois *kehl-kuh fwah*

somewhere quelque part *kehl-kuh pahr*

son le fils *luh feess*

song la chanson *lah shahn-ssohn*

soon bientôt *byan-toh*; **see you soon** à bientôt *ah byan-toh*

sore throat le mal de gorge *luh mahl duh gohrzh*

sorry: to be sorry être désolé(e) *eh-truh day-zoh-lay*; regretter *ruh-greh-tay*

soup la soupe *lah soop*; le potage *luh poh-tahzh*

south le sud *luh sewd*

space l'espace (m.) *lehss-pahss*

spark plugs les bougies (f.) *lay boo-zhee*

speak parler *pahr-lay*

speed la vitesse *lah vee-tehss*

spell épeler *ay-play*

spell checker le correcteur orthographique *luh koh-rehk-tuhr ohr-toh-grah-feek*

spend (money) dépenser *day-pahn-ssay*

spend (time) passer *pah-ssay*

spicy épicé *ay-pee-say*

spinach les épinards (m. pl.) *lay zay-pee-nahr*

spoon la cuiller *lah kwee-yehr*; **teaspoon** la cuiller à café *lah kwee-yehr ah kah-fay*; **tablespoon** la cuiller à

soupe *lah kwee-yehr ah soop*;
teaspoonful la cuillerée à
café *lah kwee-yuh-ray ah
kah-fay*; **tablespoonful** la
cuillerée à soupe *lah kwee-
yuh-ray ah soop*

spouse l'époux (m.), l'épouse
(f.) *lay-poo, lay-pooz*

spring le printemps *luh pran-
tahn*

square (adj.) carré(e) *kah-ray*

square (public) la place *lah
plahss*

stadium le stade *luh stahd*

stain la tache *lah tahsh*

staircase l'escalier (m.) *lehss-
kah-lyay*

stamp le timbre *luh tan-bruh*

stand (noun) le kiosque *luh
kee-ohssk*; **newsstand** le
kiosque à journaux *luh kee-
ohssk ah zhoor-noh*

starter le démarreur *luh day-
mah-ruhr*

state l'état (m.) *lay-tah*

station la gare *lah gahr*

stay, sojourn le séjour *luh
say-zhoor*

stay (verb) rester *rehss-tay*

stay at loger *loh-zhay*

steak le bifteck *luh beef-tehk*

steal voler *voh-lay*

steamed à la vapeur *ah lah
vah-puhr*

steering wheel le volant *luh
voh-lahn*

stew le ragoût *luh rah-goo*

stewed en cocotte *ahn koh-koht*

stewardess l'hôtesse de l'air
loh-tehss duh lehr

still encore *ahn-kohr*

stockings les bas (m. pl.) *lay bah*

stock market la bourse *lah
boorss*

stomach l'estomac (m.) *lahss-
toh-mah*; le ventre *luh van-truh*

stomachache mal à l'estomac
mahl ah lehss-toh-mah

stone la pierre *lah pyehr*

stop (noun) l'arrêt (m.) *lah-reh*

stop (verb) arrêter *ah-reh-tay*

stop light le feu *luh fuh*

store le magasin *luh mah-gah-
zan*; **book** la librairie *lah
lee-breh-ree*; **camera** le
magasin de photographie *luh
mah-gah-zan duh foh-toh-
grah-fee*; **clothing** le
magasin de vêtements *luh
mah-gah-zan duh veht-
mahn*; **department** le
grand magasin *luh grahn
mah-gah-zan*; **drug** la
pharmacie *lah fahr-mah-ssee*;
grocery l'épicerie (f.) *lay-
peess-ree*; **hardware** la
quincaillerie *lah kahn-kahy-
ree*; **jewelry** la bijouterie
lah bee-zhoo-tree; **liquor** le
magasin de spiritueux *luh
mah-gah-zan duh spee-ree-
tew-uh*; **record** le magasin
de disques *luh mah-gah-zan
duh deessk*; **shoe** le magasin
de chaussures *luh mah-gah-
zan duh shoh-ssewr*;
tobacco le bureau de tabac
luh bew-roh duh tah-bah; **toy**
le magasin de jouets *luh
mah-gah-zan duh zhoo-eh*

storm la tempête *lah tahn-
peht*; l'orage (m.) *loh-rahzh*

story l'histoire (f.) *leess-twahr*

straw la paille *lah pahy*

strawberry la fraise *lah frehz*

stream la rivière *lah ree-
vyehr*

street la rue *lah rew*

string la ficelle *lah fee-ssehl*

string beans les haricots (m.
pl.) verts *lay ah-ree-koh vehr*

stripe la rayure *lah rah-yewr*;
striped à rayures *ah rah-
yewr*

strong fort(e) *fohr(t)*

stuffed farci(e) *fahr-ssee*

style la mode *lah mohd*; **in style** à la mode *ah lah mohd*

subtitles les sous-titres (m. pl.) *lay soo-tee-truh*

suburb la banlieue *lah bahn-lyuh*; le faubourg *luh foh boor*

subway le métro *luh may-troh*

suede le daim *luh dan*

sugar le sucre *luh sew-kruh*

suit (man's) le complet *luh kohn-pleh*; **(woman's)** le tailleur *luh tah-yuhr*

suitcase la valise *lah vah-leez*

sum total le montant *luh mohn-tahn*

summer l'été (m.) *lay-tay*

sun le soleil *luh soh-lehy*

sunburn les coups (m. pl.) de soleil *lay kood soh-lehy*

Sunday dimanche *dee-mahnsh*

sunglasses les lunettes (f. pl.) de soleil *lay lew-neht duh soh-lehy*

suntan lotion la lotion à bronzer *lah loh ssyohn ah brohn zay*

supermarket le supermarché *luh sew-pehr-mahr-shay*

supper le dîner *luh dee-nay*; le souper *luh soo-pay*; **to have supper** dîner *dee-nay*; souper *soo-pay*

sure sûr(e) *sewr*

surfboard la planche de surf *lah plahnsh duh sewrf*

surgeon le chirurgien *luh sheer-ewr-zhyan*

sweater le chandail *luh shahn-dahy*

sweet doux, douce *doo, dooss*

sweetener, artificial saccharine *sahk-a-ran*

swim nager *nah-zhay*

swimming pool la piscine *lah pee-sseen*

synagogue la synagogue *lah see-nah-gohg*

synthetic synthétique *san-tay-teek*

T

table la table *lah tah-bluh*

tablecloth la nappe *lah nahp*

tablet (pill) le comprimé *luh kohn-pree-may*

taillight le feu arrière *luh fuh ah-ryehr*

tailor le tailleur *luh tah-yuhr*

take prendre *prahn-druh*

take off (clothing) ôter *oh-tay*; enlever *ahn-luh-vay*

talcum powder le talc *luh tahlk*

tampon le tampon périodique *luh tahn-pohn pay-ree-oh-deek*

tangerine la mandarine *lah mahn-dah-reen*

taste (noun) le gout *luh goo*

taste (verb) goûter *goo-tay*

taxi le taxi *luh tahk-ssee*

tea le thé *luh lay*; **iced** le thé glacé *luh tay glah-ssay*; **with lemon** au citron *oh see-trohn*; **with milk** au lait *oh leh*; **with sugar** sucré *sew-kray*

team l'équipe (f.) *lay-keep*

telegram le télégramme *luh tay-lay-grahm*

telephone le téléphone *luh tay-lay-fohn*; **telephone book** l'annuaire (m.) *luh-new-ehr*; **telephone booth** la cabine téléphonique *luh kah-been tay-lay-foh-neek*; **telephone call** le coup de téléphone *luh koo duh tay-lay-fohn*; **to call** donner un coup de téléphone *doh-nay uhn koo duh tay-lay-fohn*

television la télévision *lah tay-lay-vee-zyohn*

tell raconter *rah-kohn-tay*

temporary provisoire *proh-veez-wahr*

ten dix *deess*

tent la tente *lah tahnt*

terrific formidable *fohr-mee-dah-bluh*

terrycloth le tissu-éponge *luh tee-ssew ay-pohnzh*

thank remercier *ruh-mehr-ssyay*

thanks to grâce à *grahss ah*

thank you merci *mehr-ssee*

that ça *sah*; cela *suh-lah*

the le(m.), la (f.), les (m./f. pl.) *luh, lah, lay*

there là *lah*; **over there** là-bas *lah bah*

there is, are il y a *eel yah*; voilà *vwah-lah*

they ils (m. pl.) *eel*, elles (f. pl.) *ehl*

thief le voleur *luh voh-luhr*

thin mince *manss*

thing la chose *lah shohz*

think penser *pahn-ssay*

thirst la soif *lah swahf*; **be thirsty** avoir soif *ah-vwahr swahf*

thirteen treize *trehz*

thirty trente *trahnt*

this ceci *suh-ssee*

thousand mille *meel*

three trois *trwah*

throat la gorge *lah gohrzh*

through à travers *ah trah-vehr*

thumb le pouce *luh pooss*

Thursday jeudi *zhuh-dee*

ticket le billet *luh bee-yeh*; **entrance ticket** le billet d'entrée *luh bee-yeh dahn-tray*

ticket collector le contrôleur *luh kohn-troh-luhr*

ticket window le guichet *luh gee-sheh*

tie (neck) la cravate *lah krah-vaht*

time l'heure (f.) *luhr*; le temps *luh tahn*; **at what time?** À quelle heure? *ah kehl uhr*; **on time** à l'heure *ah luhr*

time (in a series) la fois *la fwah*; **one time** une fois *ewn fwah*; **two times** deux fois *duh fwah*

timetable l'horaire (m.) *loh-rehr*; l'indicateur (m.) *lan-dee-kah-tuhr*

tip (end) le bout *luh boo*

tip (gratuity) le pourboire *luh poor-bwahr*

tire (car) le pneu *luh pnuh*

tire (verb) fatiguer *fah-tee-gay*

tired fatigué(e) *fah-tee-gay*

tiring fatigant(e) *fah-tee-gahn(t)*

tissue le mouchoir en papier *luh moo-shwahr ahn pah-pyay*

title le titre *luh tee-truh*

to à *ah*

toast le pain grillé *luh pan gree-yay*

tobacco le tabac *luh tah-bah*; **tobacco shop** le bureau de tabac *luh bew-roh duh tah-bah*

today aujourd'hui *oh-zhoor-dwee*

toe l'orteil (m.) *lohr-tehy*

together ensemble *ahn-ssahn-bluh*

toilet la toilette *lah twah-leht*

token le jeton *luh zhuh-tohn*

tolerate supporter *sew-pohr-tay*

tomato la tomate *lah toh-maht*

tomorrow demain *duh-man*

tonsilitis l'amygdalite (f.) *lah-meeg-dah-leet*

tooth la dent *lah dahn*; **toothache** le mal de dents *luh mahl duh dahn*

toothpaste la pâte dentifrice *lah paht dahn-tee-freess*

toothpick le cure-dents *luh kewr dahn*

touch toucher *too-shay*

touch-up une retouche *ewn ruh-toosh*

tough dur *dewr*

tourist le touriste *luh too-reesst*

tourist office le syndicat d'initiative *luh san-dee-kah dee-nee-ssyah-teev*

toward   vers *vehr*

towel   la serviette *lah sehr-vyeht*

tower   la tour *lah toor*

town hall   la mairie *lah meh-ree*

track   la voie *lah vwah*

traffic   la circulation *lah seer-kew-lah-ssyohn*

traffic light   le feu *luh fuh*

train   le train *luh trahn*

translate   traduire *trah-dweer*

travel (verb)   voyager *vwah-yah-zhay*

travel agency   l'agence (f.) de voyage *lah-zhahnss duh vwah-yahzh*

traveler   voyageur *vwah-yah-zhuhr*

treatment   le traitement *luh treht-mahn*

tree   l'arbre (m.) *lahr-bruh*

trick (verb)   tromper *trohn-pay*

trip   le voyage *luh vwah-yahzh*; l'excursion (f.) *lehkss-kewr-zyohn*; **business trip**   le voyage d'affaires *luh vwah-yahzh dah-fehr*

trouble   la difficulté *lah dee-fee-kewl tay*

trout   la truite *lah trweet*

truck   le camion *luh kah-myohn*

true   vrai(e) *vreh*

trunk   la malle *lah mahl*; **car trunk**   le coffre *luh koh-fruh*

truth   la vérité *lah vay-ree-tay*

try (to)   essayer (de) *eh-sseh-yay duh*

try (on)   essayer *eh-sseh-yay*

Tuesday   mardi *mahr-dee*

tuna (fish)   le thon *luh tohn*

turkey   la dinde *lah dand*

turn (noun)   le tour *luh toor*

turn (verb)   tourner *toor-nay*

twelve   douze *dooz*

twenty   vingt *van*

tweezers   la pince à épiler *lah panss ah ay-pee-lay*

two   deux *duh*

U

ugly   laid(e) *leh(d)*

umbrella   le parapluie *luh pah-rah-plwee*

unbearable   insupportable *an-ssew-pohr-tah-bluh*

unbelievable   incroyable *an-krwah-yah-bluh*

undecided   indécis(e) *an-day-ssee(z)*

under   sous *soo*; dessous *duh-ssoo*

undershirt   le maillot de corps *luh mah-yoh duh kohr*

understand   comprendre *kohn-prahn-druh*

underwear   les sous-vêtements (m. pl.) *lay soo veht mahn*

unfair   injuste *an-zhewsst*

unhappy   malheureux(euse) *mahl uh-ruh(z)*

unimportant   insignifiant(e) *an-ssee-nee-fee-ahn(t)*

United States   les Etats-Unis *lay zay-tah zew-nee*

until   jusqu'à *zhewss-kah*

up, upstairs   en haut *ahn oh*

urgent   urgent(e) *ewr-zhahn(t)*; **urgently**   d'urgence *dewr-zhahnss*

us   nous *noo*

use (verb)   utiliser *ew-tee-lee-zay*; employer *ahn-plwah-yay*

use (noun)   l'emploi (m.) *lahn-plwah*

used up   épuisé(e) *ay-pwee-zay*

useful   utile *ew-teel*

useless   inutile *een-ew-teel*

V

vacation   les vacances (f. pl.) *lay vah-kahnss*

valid   valable *vuh-lah-bluh*

value   la valeur *lah vah-luhr*

varied   varié(e) *vah-ree-yay*

veal   le veau *luh voh*

vegetable   le légume *luh lay-gewm*
velvet   le velours *luh vuh-loor*
very   très *treh*
vest   le gilet *luh zhee-leh*
vicinity   les environs (m. pl.) *lay zahn-vee-rohn*
view   la vue *lah vew*
village   le village *luh vee-lahzh*
vinegar   le vinaigre *luh vee-neh-gruh*
vitamin   la vitamine *lah vee-tah-meen*

W

waist   la taille *lah tahy*
waiter   le garçon *luh gahr-ssohn*
wait for   attendre *ah-tahn-druh*
waiting room   la salle d'attente *lah sahl dah-tahnt*
waitress   la serveuse *lah sehr-vuhz*
walk (noun)   la promenade *lah prohm-nahd*; **to take a walk**   faire une promenade *fehr ewn prohm-nahd*
walk (verb)   marcher *mahr-shay*
walker   le déambulateur *luh day-ahn bew-lah-tuhr*
wall   le mur *luh mewr*
wallet   le portefeuille *luh pohr-tuh-fuhy*
want   désirer *day-zee-ray*; vouloir *voo-lwahr*; avoir envie de *ah-vwahr ahn-vee duh*
war   la guerre *lah gehr*
warm   chaud *shoh*
wash   laver *lah-vay*; **wash oneself**   se laver *suh lah-vay*
wash and wear   ne pas repasser *nuh pah ruh-pah-ssay*
washroom   le lavabo *luh lah-vah-boh*
watch (noun)   la montre *lah mohn-truh*

watch (verb); (look at)   regarder *ruh-gahr-day*; **(supervise)**   surveiller *sewr-veh-yay*
watchband   un bracelet de montre *uhn brahs-leh duh mohn-truh*
watchmaker's shop   l'horlogerie (f.) *lohr-lohzh-ree*
waterfall   la cascade *lah kahss-kahd*
water   l'eau *loh*
watermelon   la pastèque *lah pahss-tehk*
waxing   l'épilation (f.) *lay-pee-lah-syohn*
way   le moyen *luh mwah-yan*; la façon *lah fah-ssohn*
weak   faible *feh-bluh*
wear   porter *pohr-tay*
weather   le temps *luh tahn*
Wednesday   mercredi *mehr-kruh-dee*
week   la semaine *lah suh-mehn*
weigh   peser *puh-zay*
weight   le poids *luh pwah*; **weights**   les haltères *lay zahl-tehr*
welcome: you're welcome   de rien *duh ryan*; il n'y a pas de quoi *eel nyah pah duh kwah*
well   bien *byan*
well-done (cooking)   bien cuit *byan kwee*
west   l'ouest (m.) *lwehsst*
wet   mouillé(e) *moo-yay*
wet suit   la combinaison (f.) de plongée *lah kohn-bee-neh-zohn duh plohn-zhay*
what   que, quoi *kuh, kwah*
wheelchair   le fauteuil roulant *luh foh-tuhy roo-lahn*
when   quand *kahn*
where   où *oo*
which   quel(le) *kehl*
white   blanc(he) *blahn(sh)*
who   qui *kee*

whole entier(ière) *ahn-tyay (ahn-tyehr)*

why pourquoi *poor-kwah*

wife la femme *lah fahm*

willingly volontiers *voh-lohn-tyay*

win gagner *gah-nyay*

wind le vent *luh vahn*

window la fenêtre *lah fuh-neh-truh*; **ticket window** le guichet *luh gee-sheh*

window display l'étalage (m.) *lay-tah-lahzh*

windshield wipers les essuie-glaces (m.) *lay zeh sswee glahss*

wine le vin *luh van*; **red** rouge *roozh*; **rosé** rosé *roh-zay*; **sparkling** mousseux *moo-ssuh*; **white** blanc *blahn*

wine glass le verre à vin *luh vehr ah van*

wine merchant le négociant en vins *luh nay-gohss-yahn ahn van*

wine waiter le sommelier *luh soh-muh-lyay*

winter l'hiver (m.) *lee-vehr*

wish (verb) désirer *day-zee-ray*; vouloir *voo-lwahr*; avoir envie de *ah-vwahr ahn-vee duh*

wish (someone something) souhaiter *sweh-tay*

with avec *ah-vehk*

without sans *sahn*

woman la femme *lah fahm*

wood(s) le(s) bois *luh (lay) bwah*

wool la laine *lah lehn*

word le mot *luh moh*

work (noun) le travail *luh trah-vahy*

work (verb) travailler *trah-vah-yay*; **function** fonctionner *fohnk-ssyoh-nay*; marcher *mahr-shay*

workshop l'atelier (m.) *lah-tuh-lyay*

world le monde *luh mohnd*

worn out (things) usé(e) *ew-zay*; **(people)** épuisé(e) *ay-pwee-zay*

wound (noun) la blessure *lah bleh-ssewr*

wound (verb) blesser *bleh-ssay*

wounded blessé *bleh-ssay*

wrapper l'enveloppe (f.) *lahn-vlohp*

wrap up emballer *ahn-bah-lay*; envelopper *ahn-vloh-pay*

wrist le poignet *luh pwah-nyeh*

write écrire *ay-kreer*

wrong: to be wrong avoir tort *ah-vwahr tohr*

X

X-ray la radio *lah rah-dyoh*

Y

year l'an (m.) *lahn*, l'année (f.) *lah-nay*

yellow jaune *zhohn*

yes oui *wee*

yesterday hier *yehr*

yet encore *ahn-kohr*

yogurt le yaourt *luh yah-oort*

you tu *tew*; vous *voo*

young jeune *zhuhn*

Z

zero zéro *zay-roh*

zipper la fermeture éclair *lah fehr-muh-tewr ay-klehr*

zone la zone *lah zohn*

zoo le zoo *luh zoh*; le jardin zoologique *luh zhahr-dan zoh-oh-loh-zheek*

FRENCH-ENGLISH DICTIONARY

A

à   to, at; **à peu près**   about, approximately; **à prix fixe** fixed price meal; **à travers** across, through

abricot (m.)   apricot

accord (m.)   agreement; **d'accord**   agreed, O.K.

accrocher   to hang up

achat (m.)   purchase

acheter   to buy

addition (f.)   check, restaurant bill

adresse (f.)   address

aérobic (m.)   aerobics

affaire (f.)   matter, concern

affiche (f.)   poster

agence (f.)   agency, bureau; **une agence de voyage** travel agency

agent (de police) (m.) policeman

agneau (m.)   lamb

aider   to help

aiguille (f.)   needle

ail (m.)   garlic

aile (f.)   fender

ailleurs   elsewhere

aimer   to like, love; **aimer mieux**   to prefer

ajouter   to add

alcool (m.)   alcohol

aliments (m. pl.)   food

aller   to go; **aller à**   to fit

allumage (m.)   ignition

allumer   to light

allumette (f.)   match

alors   then

amande (f.)   almond

ambulance (f.)   ambulance

amende (f.)   fine, penalty

amer, amère   bitter

ami(e) (m./f.)   friend

amour (m.)   love (noun)

ampoule (f.)   bulb (electric)

amygdalite (f.)   tonsilitis

an (m.)   year

analyse (f.) de sang   blood test

ananas (m.)   pineapple

ancien(ne)   former, old

anglais (m.)   English

année (f.)   year

anniversaire (m.)   birthday

annonce (f.)   advertisement

annuaire (m.)   telephone book

antiseptique (m.)   antiseptic

août   August

appareil de photo (m.)   camera

appartenir   to belong

appeler   to call; **s'appeler**   to be called, named

appendicite (f.)   appendicitis

apporter   to bring

apprendre   to learn

après   after; **après-demain** day after tomorrow; **après-midi**   afternoon

arbre (m.)   tree

argent (m.)   money, silver

armoire (f.)   closet

arracher   to pull (tooth)

arranger   to adjust

arrêt (m.)   a stop; **arrêt obligatoire**   regular bus stop

arrêter   to stop

arrière   back; **en arrière** backward, behind

arrivée (f.)   arrival

artichaut (m.)   artichoke

artiste (m. or f.)   artist

ascenseur (m.)   elevator

asperge (f.) asparagus

assaisonné(e) seasoned

asseoir (s' . . .) to sit down; **asseyez-vous** sit down

assez (de) enough

assiette (f.) plate

assurance (f.) insurance

assurer (faire assurer) to insure

asthme (m.) asthma

atelier (m.) workshop, studio

attendre to wait for

attention caution

atterrir to land (plane)

atterrissage (m.) landing (plane)

attraper to catch

au to the, **au lieu de** instead of; **au milieu de** in the middle of; **au moins** at least; **au secours** help

auberge (f.) inn; **auberge de jeunesse** youth hostel

aubergine (f.) eggplant

aucun(e) any; **ne (verb) aucun(e)** not any

audiophone (m.) hearing aid

aujourd'hui today

aussi also, too

auteur (m.) author

autoroute (f.) highway

autour de around

autre other

aux to the

avant (de, que) before; **avant-hier** day before yesterday; **en avant** forward, ahead

avec with

avion (m.) airplane; **par avion** air mail, by plane

avis (m.) notice

avocat (m.), avocate (f.) lawyer

avoir to have; **avoir l'air de** to seem to; **avoir besoin de** to need; **avoir chaud** to be hot; **avoir envie de** to want to; **avoir faim** to be hungry;

avoir froid to be cold; **avoir peur de** to be afraid of; **avoir raison** to be right; **avoir soif** to be thirsty; **avoir sommeil** to be sleepy; **avoir tort** to be wrong

B

bague (f.) ring

baguette (f.) French bread

baigner (se . . .) to bathe

bain (m.) bath

balcon (m.) balcony

ballet (m.) ballet

banane (f.) banana

banc (m.) bench

bande (f.) bandage

banlieue (f.) suburb

banque (f.) bank

barbe (f.) beard

bas (m. pl.) stockings

bas (se) low; **en bas** downstairs

base de données (f.) database

bateau (m.) boat; **bateau à voile** sailboat

bâtiment (m.) building

batterie (f.) battery (car)

beau (m.) beautiful

beaucoup (de) many, much, a lot, a great deal of

beige beige

belle (f.) beautiful

béquilles (f.) crutches

besoin (m.) need; **avoir besoin de** to need

betterave (f.) beet

beurre (m.) butter

bibliothèque (f.) library

bien well; **bien entendu** of course

bientôt soon; **à bientôt** see you soon

bière (f.) beer

bifteck (m.) steak

bijou (m.) jewel

bijouterie (f.) jewelry shop
bijoutier (m.) jeweler
billet (m.) ticket; **billet d'entrée** admission ticket
biscuit (m.) cookie
bistro (m.) bar, tavern, saloon
blanc(he) white
blanchissage (m.) laundering, washing
blanchisserie (f.) laundry
blessé(e) wounded
blesser to wound, hurt
blessure (f.) wound
bleu(e) blue
bleu marine navy blue
bloc (m.) writing pad
blouse (f.) blouse
boeuf (m.) beef, ox
boire to drink
bois (m.) wood; **bois (m. pl.)** woods
boisson (f.) drink; **une boisson non-alcoolisée** soft drink
boîte (f.) box; **boîte aux lettres** mailbox; **boîte de nuit** nightclub
bol (m.) bowl
bon(ne) good
bonjour hello
bon marché cheap
bottes (f.) boots
bouche (f.) mouth
boucherie (f.) butcher shop
boucle (f.) curl; **boucles d'oreille** earrings
bougie (f.) candle, spark plug
bouilli(e) boiled
boulangerie (f.) bakery
boulette (f.) meatball
bourse (f.) stock market
bout (m.) tip, point, end
bouteille (f.) bottle
boutique (f.) shop
bouton (m.) button
bracelet de montre (m.) watchband
braisé(e) braised

bras (m.) arm
brioche (f.) breakfast bun
briquet (m.) cigarette lighter
briser to break
brosse (f.) brush; **brosse à dents** toothbrush
brosser (se ...) to brush
brouillé(e) scrambled; **les oeufs brouillés** scrambled eggs
bruit (m.) noise
brûler to burn
brûlure (f.) a burn
brun(e) brown
bureau (m.) office, desk; **bureau de location** theater box office; **bureau des objets trouvés** lost and found; **bureau de poste** post office; **bureau de renseignements** information desk; **bureau de tabac** tobacco shop

C

ça that; **ça ne fait rien** it doesn't matter
cabine téléphonique (f.) telephone booth
cadeau (m.) gift, present
café (m.) coffee, café; **café au lait** coffee with milk; **café crème** coffee with cream; **café express** espresso; **café décaféiné** decaffeinated coffee; **café glacé** iced coffee; **café noir** black coffee
cahier (m.) notebook
caisse (f.) cash register
caissier (m.) cashier
caleçon (m.) men's shorts, undergarments
camion (m.) truck
campagne (f.) country (outside city)
canne (f.) cane
canne à pêche (f.) fishing rod

canard (m.) duck

canotage (m.) boating

caoutchouc (m.) rubber; **caoutchoucs (m. pl.)** rubbers

capot (m.) hood (car)

carburateur (m.) carburetor

carotte (f.) carrot

carré(e) square

carreaux (à carreaux) checked (material)

carrefour (m.) crossroad

carte (f.) map, card; **cartes à jouer** playing cards; **carte de crédit** credit card; **carte postale** postcard; **carte routière** road map

carte-mère (f.) motherboard

cas (m.) case; **en cas d'urgence** in case of emergency

cascade (f.) waterfall

casser to break; **casser la croûte** to get a bite to eat

cave (f.) cellar

ceci this, it

ceinture (f.) belt; **ceinture de sauvetage** life preserver; **ceinture de sécurité** seat belt

célibataire single (unmarried)

cendrier (m.) ashtray

cent one hundred

cerise (f.) cherry

chacun(e) each one

chaînette (f.) chain (jewelry)

chaise (f.) chair

châle (m.) shawl

chaleur (f.) heat

chambre (f.) room; **chambre à coucher** bedroom; **chambre à un lit** single room; **chambre à deux lits** double room

champignon (m.) mushroom

champ (m.) field

chance (f.) luck; **Bonne chance!** Good luck!

chandail (m.) sweater

changement (m.) change; **changement de vitesse** gearshift

changer to change

chanson (f.) song

chanter to sing

chaque each

charcuterie (f.) cold cuts, delicatessen

chasse (f.) hunting

chasseur (m.) bellboy, bellhop

chat (m.) cat

château (m.) castle

chaud hot; **avoir chaud** to be hot (person); **faire chaud** to be hot (weather)

chauffage (m.) heating

chauffer to heat

chaussettes (f.) socks

chaussures (f.) shoes

chemin (m.) road, way

chemin de fer (m.) railway, railroad

chemise (f.) shirt

chèque (m.) check; **toucher un chèque** to cash a check

cher, chère dear, expensive

chercher to look for

cheval (m.) (pl. chevaux) horse

cheveux (m. pl.) hair

cheville (f.) ankle

chez at the house (shop, business) of

chien (m.) dog

chirurgien (m.) surgeon

choisir to choose

chose (f.) thing

chou (m.) cabbage

choucroute (f.) sauerkraut

choux de Bruxelles (m. pl.) Brussels sprouts

ciel (m.) sky

cigare (m.) cigar

cigarette (f.) cigarette

cil (m.) eyelash

cimetière (m.) cemetery

cinéma (m.) movies

cinq five
cinquante fifty
cintre (m.) hanger
circulation (f.) traffic
cirer to shine, wax
ciseaux (m. pl.) scissors
citron (m.) lemon
citronnade (f.) lemonade
clair(e) clear, light (color)
clavier (m.) keyboard
clef (f.) key
client (m.) customer
clignotant (m.) directional signal
climatiseur (m.) air conditioner
cliquer (to) click
cloche (f.) bell
coco (m.) coconut
cocotte (en) stewed
coeur (m.) heart
coffre (m.) trunk (car)
coffre-fort (m.) safe, strongbox
coiffeur (m.), coiffeuse (f.), barber, hairdresser
coin (m.) corner
col (m.) collar
colis (m.) package, parcel
collants (m. pl.) panty hose
colle (f.) glue
collier (m.) necklace
combien (de) how much, how many
combinaison (f.) slip (clothing); **combinaison de plongée** wet suit
commande (f.) order
commander to order
comme like, as
commencer to begin
comment how
commissariat (m.) police station
compagnie (f.) company
complet (m.) suit (man's)
comprendre to understand
comprimé (m.) tablet

compris(e) included
comptable (m.) accountant
compter to count
concert (m.) concert; **la salle de concert** concert hall
concierge (m. or f.) house porter, caretaker, doorman
concombre (m.) cucumber
conduire to drive, take a person somewhere
confiserie (f.) confectionery store
confiture (f.) jam, marmalade
connaître to know, be acquainted
conseil (m.) advice
consigne (f.) baggage checkroom
consommation (f.) drink
contagieux(ieuse) contagious
conte (m.) short story
contenir to contain
contenu (m.) contents
contraire (m.) opposite
contre against
contrôleur (m.) ticket collector
contusion (f.) bruise
copie (f.) de sauvegarde backup disk
coquillage (m.) shellfish
cordonnier (m.) shoemaker
cornichon (m.) pickle
corps (m.) body
correcteur (m.) orthographique spell checker
costume (m.) suit (woman's)
côte (f.) coast
côté (m.) side; **à côté de** beside, next to
côtelette (f.) cutlet, chop
coton (m.) cotton
cou (m.) neck
couche (f.) diaper
couchette (f.) berth
coude (m.) elbow
coudre to sew
couleur (f.) color

coup de téléphone (m.) phone call
coupe de cheveux (f.) haircut
coupe de glace (f.) sundae
couper to cut
cour (f.) courtyard
courir to run
courrier (m.) mail
courroie (f.) de ventilateur fan belt
cours du change (m.) exchange rate
court(e) short
couteau (m.) knife
coûter to cost
coûteux(euse) costly
couvert (m.) cover charge; place setting
couverture (f.) blanket
couvrir to cover
crabe (m.) crab
crampe (f.) cramp
cravate (f.) tie
crayon (m.) pencil
crème (f.) cream; **la crème anglaise** custard; **la crème fouettée** whipped cream
crêpe (f.) thin French pancake
crevette (f.) shrimp
cric (m.) jack (auto)
croire to believe
croisement (m.) intersection
croissant (m.) crescent-shaped breakfast pastry
croûte (f.) crust; **casser la croûte** to get a bite to eat
cru(e) raw, uncooked
cruche (f.) pitcher
cuiller (f.) spoon; **cuiller à soupe** tablespoon; **cuiller à café** teaspoon
cuillerée (f.) spoonful; **cuillerée à soupe** tablespoonful; **cuillerée à café** teaspoonful
cuir (m.) leather
cuisine (f.) cooking, kitchen
cuisinier (m.) the cook

cuisse (f.) thigh; **les cuisses de grenouille** frog's legs
cuit(e) cooked
cure-dent (m.) toothpick
curseur (m.) cursor

D

d'abord at first
d'accord agreed, O.K.
daim (m.) suede
dans in
danse (f.) the dance
danser to dance
date (f.) date
datte (f.) date (fruit)
de of; **de bonne heure** early
déambulateur (m.) walker
débarquement (m.) landing (boat)
débarquer to land (boat)
décharger (to) download
décider to decide
déclarer to declare
déçu(e) disappointed
dedans inside
défendre to forbid; **défense de cracher** no spitting; **défense d'entrer** no entry; **défense de fumer** no smoking
défendu(e) forbidden
dehors outside
déjà already
déjeuner (m.) lunch
déjeuner to eat lunch
demain tomorrow
demander to ask (for)
démarrer to boot
démarreur (m.) starter
demeurer to live, reside
demi(e) half
démodé(e) old-fashioned
dent (f.) tooth; **mal (m.) de dent** toothache
dentelle (f.) lace
dentiste (m. or f.) dentist
déodorant (m.) deodorant

dépêcher (se . . .) to hurry up;
dépêchez-vous hurry up
dépenser to spend money
déranger to bother
dernier(ière) last
derrière behind
des some
descendre to go down, get off
désirer to desire, wish, want
désolé(e) sorry; **être
désolé(e)** to be sorry
dessous under, beneath
dessus over, above
deux two
devant in front of
devenir to become
devoir to owe, have to, ought to
diapositive (f.) slide (photo)
dictionnaire (m.) dictionary;
dictionnaire de poche
pocket dictionary
Dieu God
différent(e) different
difficile difficult
dimanche Sunday
diminuer to diminish
dinde (f.) turkey
dîner (m.) dinner
dîner to dine
dire to say
discothèque (f.) discotheque
dispute (f.) dispute, argument
disque (m.) record
**disque optique numérique
(m.)** CD-ROM disk
disque (m.) système opérant
DOS
disquette (f.) diskette
dix ten
dix-huit eighteen
dix-neuf nineteen
dix-sept seventeen
docteur (m.) doctor
doigt (m.) finger
donner to give
dormir to sleep
dos (m.) back
douane (f.) customs

douanier (m.) customs official
doucement softly
douche (f.) shower
douleur (f.) pain
doux, douce sweet, mild, soft
douzaine (f.) dozen
douze twelve
droit (m.) right; **à droite** to
the right
du some
dur hard, tough
durer to last

E

eau (f.) water; **eau courante**
running water; **eau chaude**
hot water; **eau froide** cold
water; **eau glacée** ice water;
eau minérale mineral water
eau dentifrice (f.) mouthwash; **la pâte dentifrice**
toothpaste
échanger to exchange
échantillon (m.) sample
échappement (m.) exhaust
écharpe (f.) scarf
école (f.) school
écouter to listen to
écran (m.) screen
écrire to write
égarer (s' . . .) to lose one's
way, to get lost
église (f.) church
élargir enlarge
elle she
elles they
e-mail (m.) e-mail
emballer to wrap up
embrasser to kiss
emploi (m.) employ, use
employer to use
emporter to carry, take away
emprunter to borrow
en in; **en arrière** behind; **en
avant** ahead; **en bas**
downstairs; **en ce moment**
right now; **en face de**

opposite, facing; **en retard** late; **en voiture** all aboard
enceinte pregnant
encore yet, still; **encore une fois** again
endosser to endorse
endroit (m.) place
enfant (m./f.) child
engrenage (m.) gears
ennuyer to annoy, bother
enregistrer to check bags
enseigne (f.) sign
ensemble together
entendre to hear
entier (entière) entire, whole
entre between
entrée (f.) entrance
entrer to enter
enveloppe (f.) envelope, wrapper, cover
envelopper to wrap up
environ about
environs (m. pl.) vicinity
envoyer to send
épaule (f.) shoulder
épeler to spell
épicerie (f.) grocery store
épicé spicy
épilation (f.) waxing
épinards (m. pl.) spinach
épingle (f.) pin
époux (épouse) spouse
épuisé(e) exhausted, used up
équipe (f.) team
équitation (f.) horseback riding
escalier (m.) stairs
escargot (m.) snail
espace (f.) space
espérer to hope
essayer (de) to try (to)
essence (f.) gas; **le réservoir à essence** gas tank
essuie-glaces (m. pl.) windshield wipers
est (m.) east
estomac (m.) stomach
et and

étage (m.) story, floor
étalage (m.) window display
état (m.) state
Etats-Unis (m. pl.) United States
été (m.) summer
étiquette (f.) label
étranger(ère) foreign; **à l'étranger** abroad
être to be; **être d'accord** to agree; **être de retour** to be back; **être en difficulté** to be in trouble
éviter to avoid
excellent(e) excellent
excursion (f.) excursion, trip
exemple (m.) example; **par exemple** for example
express (m.) express

F

facile easy
façon (f.) way, style, fashion
facteur (m.) mailman
facture (f.) bill, invoice
faible weak
faim (f.) hunger; **avoir faim** to be hungry
faire to make, do; **faire beau** to be beautiful weather; **faire chaud** to be hot weather; **faire des achats** to go shopping; **faire des emplettes** to go shopping; **faire du soleil** to be sunny; **faire du vent** to be windy; **faire froid** to be cold weather; **faire la connaissance de** to make the acquaintance of; **faire la correspondance** to change trains or planes; **faire la queue** to form a line; **faire une promenade** to take a walk; **faire venir** to send for
fait(e) à la main handmade
famille (f.) family

farci(e) stuffed
fard (m.) à paupières eye shadow
fatigant(e) tiring
fatigué(e) tired
fatiguer to tire
faubourg (m.) suburb
faut: il faut it is necessary
faute (f.) mistake, error
fauteuil (m.) roulant wheelchair
faux, fausse false
félicitations (f.) congratulations
femme (f.) woman, wife; **femme de chambre** chambermaid
fenêtre (f.) window
fer (m.) iron
ferme (f.) farm
fermer to close
fermeture éclair (f.) zipper
fête (f.) festival, feast, holiday
feu (m.) fire, traffic light; **feu arrière** taillight
feuille (f.) sheet, leaf
feutre (m.) felt
février February
ficelle (f.) string
fiche (f.) form
fichier (m.) file
fièvre (f.) fever
figue (f.) fig
figure (f.) face
fille (f.) girl, daughter
film (m.) film
fils (m.) son
fin (f.) end
finir to finish, end
flan (m.) custard
flanelle (f.) flannel
fleur (f.) flower
fleuriste (m.) florist
fleuve (m.) river
foie (m.) liver
foire (f.) fair, market

fois (f.) time in a series; **une fois** one time, once; **deux fois** two times, twice
foncé(e) dark (color)
fonctionner to function, work
fontaine (f.) fountain
forêt (f.) forest
formidable terrific
formule (f.) form
fort(e) strong
four (m.) oven; **four à micro-ondes** microwave oven
fourchette (f.) fork
frais, fraîche fresh
frais (m. pl.) expense, charge, cost
fraise (f.) strawberry
framboise (f.) raspberry
français (m.) French
frappé (m.) milk shake
frapper to knock, hit, strike
freins (m. pl.) brakes
frère (m.) brother
frit(e) fried
froid (m.) cold; **avoir froid** to be cold (person); **faire froid** to be cold (weather)
fromage (m.) cheese
front (m.) forehead
frontière (f.) border
fruit (m.) fruit
fruits de mer (m. pl.) seafood
fumer to smoke
fumeur (m.) smoker, smoking compartment

G

gabardine (f.) gabardine
gagner to earn, win
gant (m.) glove
garçon (m.) boy, waiter
garder to keep
gare (f.) station
garer to park a car
gare routière (f.) bus station
gâteau (m.) cake

gauche left; **à gauche** to the left
gencives (f. pl.) gums
gendarme (m.) policeman
gêner to bother, annoy
genou (m.) knee
genouillères (f.) kneepads
gens (m./f. pl.) people
gérant (m.) manager
gibier (m.) game (meat)
gigot (m.) leg of mutton
gilet (m.) vest
glace (f.) ice, ice cream
glacé(e) iced
glaçon (m.) ice cube
gomme (f.) eraser
gorge (f.) throat; **avoir mal à la gorge** to have a sore throat
goût (m.) taste
goûter to taste
goyave (f.) guava
grâce à thanks to
grafique (f.) graphics
grand(e) big
gratiné browned
gratte-ciel (m.) skyscraper
gratuit(e) (adj.) free
gratuitement (adv.) free of charge
grave grave, serious
grillé(e) grilled, broiled
grippe (f.) the flu
gris(e) gray
gros(se) fat
guerre (f.) war
guichet (m.) ticket window; banking window
guide (m.) guide; **guide touristique** guidebook

H

habiller (s'...) to dress oneself
habiter to live in
habits (m. pl.) clothes
haltères (m.) weights

hamburger (m.) hamburger
hanche (f.) hip
handicapé handicapped
hareng (m.) herring; **hareng fumé** smoked herring
haricot (m.) bean
haricots verts (m. pl.) string beans
haut(e) high
hauteur (f.) height, elevation
haut-parleur (m.) loudspeaker
herbe (f.) grass
heure (f.) hour; **à l'heure** on time; **de bonne heure** early
heureux(euse) happy
hier yesterday
histoire (f.) story
hiver (m.) winter
hockey (m.) hockey
homard (m.) lobster
homme (m.) man
homme (femme) d'affaires businessperson
hôpital (m.) hospital
horaire (m.) schedule, timetable
horloge (f.) clock
horlogerie (f.) watchmaker's shop
hôte (m.) host
hôtel (m.) hotel
hôtesse (f.) hostess
huile (f.) oil; **l'huile d'olive** olive oil
huit eight
huître (f.) oyster

I

ici here
il he
île (f.) island
ils they
il y a there is, are; **il y a + time** ago
immédiatement immediately
imperméable (m.) raincoat
important(e) important

impossible impossible
imprécis(e) indefinite
imprimante (f.) printer;
  laser laser; **jet d'encre**
  ink jet
incapable incapable
incendie (m.) fire
incroyable unbelievable
indécis(e) undecided
infection (f.) infection
informaticien(ne) computer
  scientist
informatique (f.) computer
  science
informatiser to computerize
infirmière (f.) nurse
infroissable permanent press
injuste unfair
insignifiant(e) unimportant
insomnie (f.) insomnia
insuffisant(e) insufficient
insupportable unbearable
intelligent(e) intelligent
interdire to prohibit, forbid
interdit(e) prohibited,
  forbidden
intéressant(e) interesting
interprète (m./f.) interpreter
interpréter to interpret
inutile useless
inviter to invite
invraisemblable improbable,
  unlikely
itinéraire (m.) itinerary, route
ivre drunk

J

jamais never; **ne . . . jamais**
  never
jambe (f.) leg
jambon (m.) ham
janvier January
jardin (m.) garden
jarre (f.) jar
jaune yellow
je I
jean denim

jetable disposable
jeton (m.) token
jeu (m.) game
jeudi Thursday
jeune young
jogging (m.) jogging suit
joli(e) pretty
joue (f.) cheek
jouer to play; **jouer à** to play
  a game, sport; **jouer de** to
  play a musical instrument
jour (m.) day
journal (m.) newspaper
juge (m.) judge
juger to judge
juillet July
juin June
jupe (f.) skirt
jupon (m.) slip
jus (m.) juice
jusqu'à until

K

ketchup (m.) ketchup
kiosque (m.) stand; **le
  kiosque à journaux**
  newsstand
klaxon (m.) horn

L

là there; **là-bas** over there
lac (m.) lake
lacet (m.) lace (shoe)
laid(e) ugly
laine (f.) wool
laisser to let, leave behind
lait (m.) milk
laitue (f.) lettuce
lampe (f.) lamp; **la lampe de
  poche** flashlight
langue (f.) language, tongue
lapin (m.) rabbit
laque (f.) hairspray
lard (m.) bacon
lavabo (m.) washroom

laver to wash; **se laver** to wash oneself

laverie automatique (f.) launderette

lecteur (m.) de CD CD player

leger(ère) light (weight)

légume (m.) vegetable

lent(e) slow

lentement slowly

lettre (f.) letter

lever: se lever to get up

lèvre (f.) lip; **rouge à lèvres (m.)** lipstick

librairie (f.) bookstore

libre free

ligne (f.) line

limette (f.) lime

lin (m.) linen (material)

lire to read

liste (f.) list

lit (m.) bed

livre (m.) book

livre (f.) pound (weight)

livrer to deliver

loger to stay at

logiciel (m.) software

logis (m.) lodging

loin far; **loin de** far from

long(ue) long

lotion (f.) lotion; **la lotion à bronzer** suntan lotion

louer to rent, hire

loyer (m.) the rent

lumière (f.) light

lundi Monday

lunettes (f. pl.) eyeglasses; **les lunettes de soleil** sunglasses

luxe (m.) luxury

luxueux(euse) luxurious

lycée (m.) high school

M

macédoine de fruits (f.) fruit salad

mâchoire (f.) jaw

madame Mrs.

mademoiselle Miss

magasin (m.) store; **de chaussures** shoe store; **de disques** record store; **un grand magasin** department store; **de jouets** toy store; **de photographie** camera store; **de souvenirs** gift shop; **de spiritueux** liquor store; **de vêtements** clothing store

magazine (m.) magazine

mai May

maillot (m.) de bain bathing suit; **de corps** undershirt

main (f.) hand

maintenant now

mairie (f.) town hall

mais but

maïs (m.) corn

maison (f.) house; **à la maison** at home

mal (m.) ache; **mal de dents** toothache; **mal d'estomac** stomachache; **mal de gorge** sore throat; **mal de tête** headache

malade sick

maladie (f.) sickness, illness

malentendu (m.) misunderstanding

malgré in spite of

malheureux(euse) unhappy

malle (f.) trunk; **malle arrière** auto trunk

manche (f.) sleeve

mandarine (f.) tangerine

manette (f.) de jeux joystick

manger to eat

mangue (f.) mango

manque (m.) lack

manquer to lack, miss

manteau (m.) overcoat

marchand (m.) merchant

marchandise (f.) merchandise

marché (m.) market

marcher to walk

mardi Tuesday

margarine (f.) margarine
mari (m.) husband
marque (f.) brand (of product)
marron brown
marron (m.) chestnut
mars March
matin (m.) morning
mauvais(e) bad
mauve purple
mayonnaise (m.) mayonnaise
mécanicien (m.) mechanic
médecin (m.) doctor
médecine (f.) medicine
meilleur(e) better (adj.)
melon (m.) melon
même same; **le/la même** the same
mémoire (f.) memory
menton (m.) chin
mer (f.) sea; **au bord de la mer** at the seashore
merci thank you
mercredi Wednesday
mère (f.) mother
mériter to deserve
merveilleux(euse) marvelous
mesure (f.) measurement
mesurer to measure
métro (m.) subway
mettre to put, put on
meublé(e) furnished
midi noon
mieux better (adv.)
milieu (m.) middle; **au milieu de** in the middle of
mille thousand
million (m.) million; **un million de + noun** a million
mince thin
minuit midnight
minute (f.) minute
miroir (m.) mirror
mode (f.) style; **à la mode** stylish, in style
modem (m.) modem
modifier to modify, change
moins less
mois (m.) month

moitié (f.) half
monde (m.) world; **tout le monde** everybody
moniteur (m.) monitor
monnaie (f.) coin money, change
monsieur (m.) mister, Mr., sir
montagne (f.) mountain
montant (m.) sum total
monter to go up
montre (f.) watch
montrer to show
morceau (m.) piece
mosquée (f.) mosque
mot (m.) word
moteur (m.) motor
moteur (m.) de recherche search engine
mouchoir (m.) handkerchief; **le mouchoir en papier** tissue
mouillé(e) wet
moule (f.) mussel
mousseline de soie (f.) chiffon
moutarde (f.) mustard
moyen (m.) way
mur (m.) wall
musculation (f.) bodybuilding
musée (m.) museum
musique (f.) music

N

nager to swim
nappe (f.) tablecloth
nationalité (f.) nationality
nausée (f.) nausea
ne; ne . . . aucun(e) not . . . any; **ne . . . jamais** never; **ne . . . pas** not; **ne . . . plus** no longer, not . . . anymore; **ne . . . que** only; **ne . . . rien** nothing
nécessaire necessary
neige (f.) snow
neiger to snow
nettoyer to clean

nettoyer à sec to dry-clean
neuf nine
nez (m.) nose
noir(e) black
noix (f.) nut
nom (m.) name; **nom de famille** family name, **prénom (m.)** first name; **surnom (m.)** last name, nickname
nombre (m.) number (quantity)
non no
non-fumeurs non-smoking
nord (m.) north
note (f.) bill (hotel)
nourriture (f.) food
nous us
nouveau (m.) new
nouveauté (f.) novelty
nouvelle (f.) new
nuit (f.) night
numéro (m.) number; **le numéro de téléphone** telephone number
nylon (m.) nylon

O

observer to observe
obtenir to obtain
occasion (f.) opportunity, bargain; **marchandise d'occasion (f.)** secondhand (used) goods; **une véritable occasion** a genuine bargain
occupé(e) busy
océan (m.) ocean
oeil (m.) eye; **(pl.) les yeux** eyes
oeuf (m.) egg; **au plat** fried; **brouillé** scrambled, **dur** hard-boiled; **frit** fried; **mollet** medium-boiled; **à la coque** soft-boiled; **pochés** poached; **poelé** sunny-side up
offrir to offer
oie (f.) goose

oignon (m.) onion
olive (f.) olive; **l'huile (f.) d'olive** olive oil
ombre (f.) shade (tree)
omelette (f.) omelet; **l'omelette norvégienne** baked Alaska
omnibus (m.) local bus
ongle (m.) nail (finger); **la lime à ongle** nail file
onze eleven
opéra (m.) opera, opera hall
opticien (m.) optician
or (m.) gold; **en or** of gold
orage (m.) storm
orange (f.) orange
orangeade (f.) orangeade
orchestre (m.) orchestra
ordinateur (m.) computer
ordinateur (m.) portable laptop computer
ordonnance (f.) prescription
oreille (f.) ear, **boucle (f.) d'oreille** earring
oreiller (m.) pillow
orteil (m.) toe
os (m.) bone
ôter to take off, remove
ou or
où where
ouate (f.) absorbent cotton
oublier to forget
ouest (m.) west
oui yes
outre-mer overseas
ouvert(e) open (adj.)
ouvrir to open

P

paille (f.) straw (material)
pain (m.) bread; **baguette (f.)** French bread; **pain blanc** white bread; **pain bis** pumpernickel; **pain de froment** whole wheat; **pain grillé** toast; **pain de seigle** rye bread; **petit pain** roll

paire (f.) pair
palais (m.) palace
palourde (f.) clam
pamplemousse (m.) grapefruit
panier (m.) basket
panne (f.) breakdown, mishap;
en panne broken down
pantalon (m.) pants
pantoufle (f.) slipper
papier (m.) paper; **papier à
lettres** note paper; **papier
à machine** typing paper;
papier d'emballage
wrapping paper; **papier
hygiénique** toilet paper
paquet (m.) package
par by; per; **par avion** air
mail, by plane; **par exemple**
for example; **par ici** this
way; **par jour** per day
parapluie (m.) umbrella
parc (m.) park
parce que because
pardessus (m.) overcoat
pardon excuse me
pardonner to excuse
pare-choc (m.) bumper
parfait(e) perfect
parfum (m.) perfume, flavor
parler to speak
parmi among
partager to share
parterre (m.) mezzanine
partie (f.) part
partir to leave
partout everywhere
pastèque (f.) watermelon
pâte (f.) paste; **la pâte
dentifrice** toothpaste
patin (m.) à glace ice-skating;
patin à roulettes roller
skating
pâtisserie (f.) pastry, pastry
shop
patron (m.) boss
pauvre poor
payer to pay

pays (m.) country (nation)
paysage (m.) countryside
peau (f.) skin
pêche (f.) peach; fishing; **la
pêche sous-marine** deep-
sea fishing
pêcher to fish
peigne (m.) comb
pellicule (f.) roll of film
pendant during
pendule (f.) clock
penser to think
pension (f.) boardinghouse
perdre to lose
père (m.) father
permanent(e) permanent
permettre to permit; **permis**
permitted
permis (m.) permit
personne (f.) person
persuader to persuade
perte (f.) loss
peser to weigh
petit(e) small
petit déjeuner (m.) breakfast
peu (adv.) little, not much
peuple (m.) people (nation)
peur (f.) fear; **avoir peur de**
to be afraid of
peut-être maybe, perhaps
phare (m.) headlight
pharmacie (f.) pharmacy
photo (f.) photograph
photocopie (f.) photocopy
photographier to photograph
phrase (f.) sentence
pièce (f.) room, play
pied (m.) foot; **à pied** on foot
pierre (f.) stone
piéton (m.) pedestrian
pile (f.) battery (watch)
pilule (f.) pill
pince (f.) à épiler tweezers
pipe (f.) pipe; **le tabac
pour pipe** pipe
tobacco
piscine (f.) swimming pool

piste (f.) runway; **piste de ski** ski slope

place (f.) square (public); seat in conveyance

plafond (m.) ceiling

plage (f.) beach

plainte (f.) complaint

plaisanterie (f.) joke

plaisir (m.) pleasure

plan (m.) plan; **plan de ville** street map of city; **plan à vue d'oiseau** bird's-eye view of the city

planche de surf (f.) surfboard; **planche (f.) à roulettes** skateboard

plancher (m.) floor

plat (m.) dish of food

plat(e) flat

platine (m.) platinum

pleurer to cry

plongeon (m.) diving

pluie (f.) rain

plume (f.) pen

plusieurs several

plutôt rather

pneu (m.) tire; **pneu crevé** flat tire

poche (f.) pocket; **livre de poche** paperback

poids (m.) weight

poignet (m.) wrist

poire (f.) pear

pois (m.) pea; **pois chiches (m. pl.)** chick-peas; **à pois** polka-dotted

poisson (m.) fish

poitrine (f.) chest

poivre (m.) pepper

pomme (f.) apple

pomme de terre (f.) potato

pompe (f.) à essence fuel pump

pont (m.) bridge

porc (m.) pork

portatif(ive) portable

porte (f.) door

porte-bonheur (m.) charm

portefeuille (m.) wallet

porte-monnaie (m.) purse

porter to carry, wear

porteur (m.) porter

posséder to possess, own

poste (f.) post office; **poste aérienne** air mail

poste (m.) station; **poste d'essence** gas station

potable drinkable; **eau potable** drinking water

potage (m.) soup

poterie (f.) pottery

pouce (m.) thumb

poulet (m.) chicken

poumon (m.) lung

pour for, in order to

pourboire (m.) tip (gratuity)

pourquoi why

pousser to push

pouvoir to be able to, can

préférer to prefer

premier(ière) first; **premier secours (m.)** first aid

prendre to take

prénom (m.) first name

préparer to prepare

présenter to present, introduce

préservatif (m.) condom

presque almost

pressé(e) hurried, rushed

presse-papiers (m.) clipboard

prêt(e) ready

prêter to lend

printemps (m.) spring

prise de courant (f.) socket

privé(e) private

prix (m.) price, prize

prochain(e) next

proche near, neighboring

profession (f.) profession

promenade (f.) walk; **faire une promenade** to take a walk

promesse (f.) promise

promettre to promise

prononcer to pronounce
propre clean
propriétaire (m.) owner
propriété (f.) property
protéger to protect
protester to protest
provisoire temporary
provisoirement temporarily
prudence (f.) carefulness
prune (f.) plum
pruneau (m.) prune
public(ique) public
puce (f.) chip
purée (en) mashed
pyjama (m.) pajamas

Q

quai (m.) platform
qualité (f.) quality
quand when
quantité (f.) quantity
quarante forty
quart (m.) quarter
quartier (m.) district
quatorze fourteen
quatre four
quatre-vingt-dix ninety
quatre-vingts eighty
que that
que? what?
quel(le) which
quelque chose something
quelquefois sometimes
quelque part somewhere
quelques some
quelqu'un someone
question (f.) question
queue (f.) line (of people); tail; **faire la queue** to form a line
qui who
quincaillerie (f.) hardware store
quinze fifteen
quitter + place *or* person to leave
quoi what
quotidien(ne) daily

R

rabais (m.) reduction
raconter to tell
radio (f.) radio, X-ray
radis (m.) radish
rafraîchissements (m. pl.) refreshments
ragoût (m.) stew
raifort (m.) horseradish
raisin (m.) grape; **raisin sec** raisin
raison (f.) reason; **avoir raison** to be right
raisonnable reasonable
rang (m.) row
rapide fast, express train
rapidement quickly
rappeler: se rappeler to remember
rare rare
raser: se raser to shave oneself
rasoir (m.) razor; **le rasoir électrique** electric razor
rayon (m.) shelf; department (of a store)
rayure (f.) stripe; **à rayures** striped
récemment recently
recevoir to receive
réclame (f.) advertisement
recommander to recommend
récompense (f.) reward
récompenser to reward
reçu (m.) receipt
récupérer to recuperate
refuser to refuse
regarder to look at
règle (f.) rule, ruler
régler to settle, adjust, regulate; **régler une affaire** to settle an affair
regretter to regret, be sorry
regulier(ière) regular
regulièrement regularly
relier to connect
remarquer to notice

rembourser to reimburse, refund
remède (m.) remedy
remercier to thank
remettre to put back; **se remettre** to recover (health)
remplacer to replace
remplir to fill (out)
rencontrer to meet
rendez-vous (m.) meeting
rendre to return, give back
renseignement (m.) a piece of information; **les renseignements** information
renvoyer to send back
réparer to repair
repas (m.) meal
repasser to iron; **ne pas repasser** wash and wear
répéter to repeat
répondeur (m.) automatique answering machine
répondre to answer
réponse (f.) the answer
repos (m.) rest, relaxation
reposer: se reposer to rest
représentation (f.) performance
requin (m.) shark
réseau (m.) network
réservation (f.) reservation
réserver to reserve
résoudre to resolve
responsable responsible
ressembler à to resemble, look like
restaurant (m.) restaurant
rester to stay, remain
résultat (m.) result
retard (m.) delay; **en retard** late
retenir to retain
retouche (f.) touch-up
retourner to return, go back
retraite (en) retired
réveil (m.) alarm clock

réveiller: se réveiller to wake up
revenir to come back, return
rez-de-chaussée (m.) ground floor
rhume (m.) cold; **rhume de cerveau** head cold; **rhume des foins** hay fever; **rhume de poitrine** chest cold
rien nothing, **ne . . . rien** nothing; **de rien** you're welcome
rire to laugh
rive (f.) bank, shore
rivière (f.) river, stream
riz (m.) rice
robe (f.) dress; **robe de chambre** bathrobe; **robe de soir** evening gown
robinet (m.) faucet
robot (m.) ménager food processor
roman (m.) novel; **roman policier** detective story
rond(e) round
rose pink, rose
rôti(e) roasted
rouge red
route (f.) route, road
rue (f.) street
ruelle (f.) lane, alley

S

sable (m.) sand
sac (m.) bag, pocketbook
saignant(e) rare (food)
saison (f.) season
salade (f.) salad
sale dirty
salé(e) salted; salty
salle (f.) room; **salle à manger** dining room; **salle d'attente** waiting room; **salle de bains** bathroom; **salle de concert** concert hall; **salle de repos** recovery room

salon (m.) de beauté beauty salon
saluer to greet
samedi Saturday
sandales (f.) sandals
sang (m.) blood
sans without
santé (f.) health
sardine (f.) sardine
satin (m.) satin
satisfait(e) satisfied
saucisse (f.) sausage
saumon (m.) salmon
savoir to know (facts)
savon (m.) soap
scanneur (m.) scanner
scaphandre (m.) diving suit
sec, sèche dry
sèche-cheveux (m.) hair dryer
sécher to dry
secours (m.) help; **au secours!** help!
secrétaire (m. or f.) secretary
sécurité (f.) security; **la ceinture de sécurité** seat belt
seize sixteen
séjour (m.) stay, sojourn
sel (m.) salt
selon according to
semaine (f.) week
sembler to seem
sentier (m.) path
sentir: se sentir to feel
sept seven
sérieux(ieuse) serious
serrure (f.) lock
serveur (m.) en ligne on-line service
serveuse (f.) waitress
service (m.) service
serviette (f.) towel, napkin, briefcase; **serviette hygiénique (f.)** sanitary napkin
servir to serve
seul(e) alone, only (adj.)
seulement (adv.) only

shampooing (m.) shampoo
si if; yes (to a negative question)
siège (m.) seat
signer to sign
signification (f.) meaning
signifier to mean
s'il vous plaît please
six six
ski (m.) ski; **les skis nautiques** water skis
slip (m.) panties
soda (m.) soda
soeur (f.) sister
soie (f.) silk
soif (f.) thirst; **avoir soif** to be thirsty
soin (m.) care; **avec soin** carefully
soir (m.) evening
soixante sixty
soixante-dix seventy
soldes (m. pl.) sales, bargains
sole (f.) sole, flounder
soleil (m.) sun; **il fait du soleil** it is sunny; **les coups (m. pl.) de soleil** sunburn
sommeil (m.) sleep, sleepiness; **avoir sommeil** to be sleepy
sommelier (m.) wine waiter
somnifère (m.) sleeping pill
sonner to ring
sorbet (m.) sherbert
sortie (f.) exit
sortir to leave
souhaiter to wish (someone something)
soûl(e) drunk
soulier (m.) shoe
souper (m.) supper
souper to have supper
souris (f.) mouse
sous under
sous-titre (m.) subtitle
sous-vêtement (m.) undergarment; **les sous-vêtements (m. pl.)** underwear

soutien-gorge (m.) bra
souvent often
spectacle (m.) show
stade (m.) stadium
station-service (f.) service station; gas station
stylo à bille (m.) ball-point pen
succursale (f.) branch of a bank, etc.
sucre (m.) sugar
sucre artifiel (m.) artifical sweetener
sud (m.) south
suivant(e) following, next
suivre to follow
supermarché (m.) supermarket
supporter to tolerate
sur on
sûr(e) sure
surnom (m.) last name, nickname
surtout especially
surveiller to watch, supervise
survêt (m.) jogging suit
synagogue (f.) synagogue
syndicat (m.) d'initiative tourist office
synthétique synthetic, polyester

T

tabac (m.) tobacco
table (f.) table
tableau (m.) picture, painting
tache (f.) stain
taille (f.) size, figure (body), waist
taille-crayon (m.) pencil sharpener
tailleur (m.) tailor, woman's suit
talc (m.) talcum powder
talon (m.) heel (of foot)
tampon (m.) périodique tampon

tapis (m.) rug
tard late
tarif (m.) rate
tartan (m.) plaid
tarte (f.) pie
tasse (f.) cup
taxi (m.) taxi
teinturerie (f.) dry cleaner's
télégramme (m.) telegram
téléphone (m.) telephone; **cabine (f.) téléphonique** telephone booth
téléphoner to call on the phone
téléphoniste (f.) operator
téléski (m.) ski lift
télévision (f.) television
tempête (f.) storm
temple (m.) church (Protestant)
temps (m.) weather, time; **de temps en temps** from time to time
tenir to hold
tente (f.) tent
terminer to finish
terrain (m.) ground; **terrain de camping** camping grounds; **terrain de golf** golf course; **terrain de sport** playing field
terre (f.) land, earth; **par terre** on the ground
tête (f.) head
thé (m.) tea; **au citron** with lemon; **au lait** with milk; **glacé** iced; **sucré** with sugar
thon (m.) tuna (fish)
timbre (m.) stamp
tire-bouchon (m.) corkscrew
tirer to pull
tissu (m.) material
tissu-éponge (m.) terry cloth
titre (m.) title
toit (m.) roof
tomate (f.) tomato
tomber to fall; **tomber malade** to become ill

tort: avoir tort to be wrong
tôt early
touche (f.) key (computer)
toucher to touch; **toucher un chèque** to cash a check
toujours always
tour (f.) tower
tour (m.) trip, turn
touriste (m./f.) tourist
tourner to turn
tout (m. s.); tous (m. pl.); toute (f. s.); toutes (f. pl.) all, every; **tous les jours** every day; **tout le monde** everybody; **tout le temps** all the time
tousser to cough
toux (f.) the cough; **la pastille contre la toux** cough drop; **le sirop contre la toux** cough syrup
traceur à paupieres eyeliner
traduire to translate
train (m.) train; **être en train de** to be in the act of
traitement (m.) treatment
trajet (m.) distance, journey, trip
tranche (f.) slice
travail (m.) work
travailler to work
travers: à travers across, through
traverser to cross, go across
treize thirteen
trente thirty
très very; **très bien** very well
triste sad
trois three
tromper to deceive, trick; **se tromper** to be mistaken, make a mistake
trop (de) too much, many (of)
trottoir (m.) sidewalk
trou (m.) hole
trouver to find
truite (f.) trout
tu you

U

un (m.) a, an, one
une (f.) a, an, one
uni(e) solid (color)
unique (adj.) only
unité centrale (f.) CPU
urgent(e) urgent; **cas urgent (m.)** emergency; **d'urgence** urgently
usage (m.) custom, practice
usagé(e) secondhand
usé worn out, threadbare, hackneyed
usine (f.) factory
utile useful
utiliser to use

V

vacances (f. pl.) vacation
valable valid
valeur (f.) value
valise (f.) suitcase
vapeur (à la) steamed
varié(e) varied
veau (m.) veal
velours (m.) velvet; **velours côtelé** corduroy
vendeur(euse) salesman, saleswoman
vendre to sell
vendredi Friday
venir to come; **venir de** to come from; **faire venir** to send for
vent (m.) wind; **il fait du vent** it is windy
vente (f.) sale; **en vente** for sale
ventilateur (m.) fan, blower
verglas (m.) ice, frost
vérifier to check
vérité (f.) truth
verre (m.) glass; **le verre à vin** wineglass; **le verre de contact** contact lens

vers towards
vert(e) green
vestiaire (m.) coat checkroom
veston (m.) jacket
vêtements (m. pl.) clothing
viande (f.) meat
vide empty
vie (f.) life
vieille (f.) old
vieux (m.) old
village (m.) village
ville (f.) city
vin (m.) wine; **vin blanc**
white wine; **vin mousseux**
sparkling wine; **vin rosé**
rosé wine; **vin rouge** red
wine; **le négociant en vins**
wine merchant
vinaigre (m.) vinegar
vingt twenty
violet purple
virage (m.) turn, bend, corner
visage (m.) face
vitamine (f.) vitamin
vite quickly
vitesse (f.) speed
vitrine (f.) shop window
vivre to live
voici here is, are
voie (f.) route, path, track
voilà there is, are
voir to see
voisin(e) neighbor
voiture (f.) car
vol (m.) flight
volant (m.) steering wheel

voler to fly, steal
voleur (m.) thief, robber
volontiers gladly, with
pleasure, willingly
vouloir to wish, want; **vouloir
dire** to mean, signify
vous you
voyage (m.) trip; **voyage
d'affaires** business trip
voyager to travel
voyageur (m.) traveler
vrai(e) true
vraiment really
vue (f.) view

W

wagon (m.) railroad car
wagon-lit (m.) sleeping car
wagon-restaurant (m.)
dining car
W.C. toilet

Y

y there
yaourt (m.) yogurt
yeux (m. pl.) eyes

Z

zéro zero
zone (f.) zone
zoo (m.) zoo

INDEX

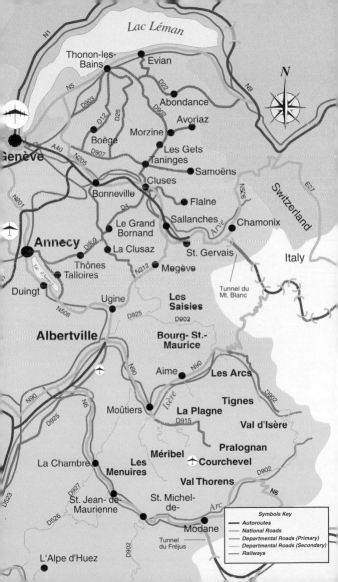

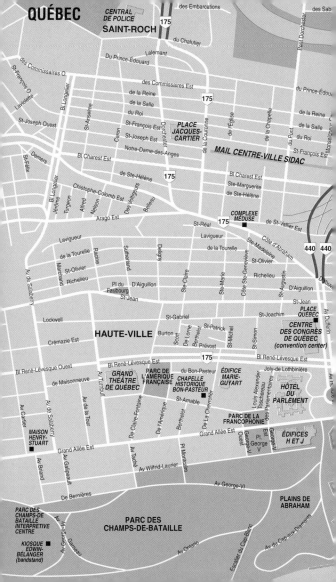

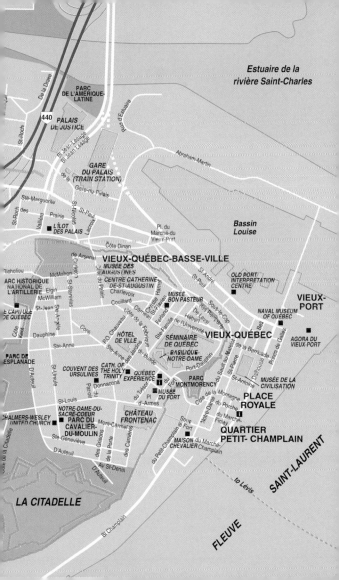

Estuaire de la
rivière Saint-Charles

PARC
DE L'AMÉRIQUE-
LATINE

440

PALAIS
DE JUSTICE

De la Dame
St-Roch

Bl Jean-Lesage
Bl Jean Lesage

de la

GARE
DU PALAIS
(TRAIN STATION)

Gare-du-Palais

Rue d'Estuaire

Abraham-Martin

Ste-Marguerite
St-Roch
Vallière
Prairie
St-Nicolas
St-Paul
Lacroix

L'ÎLOT
DES PALAIS

Pl. du
Marché-du-
Vieux-Port

Bassin
Louise

Côte Dinan

VIEUX-QUÉBEC-BASSE-VILLE

Richelieu
McMahon
Rue du Palais
de l'Arsenal

MUSÉE DES
AUGUSTINES

CENTRE CATHERINE-
DE-ST-AUGUSTIN

St-André

St-Paul

OLD PORT
INTERPRETATION
CENTRE

VIEUX-
PORT

ARC HISTORIQUE
NATIONAL DE
L'ARTILLERIE

St-Olivier
St-Stanislas
St-Angèle
Elgin

Charlevoix
Couillard

MUSÉE
BON PASTEUR

Christie
Ferland

St-Antoine

Sous-le-Cap

NAVAL MUSEUM
OF QUEBEC

LE CAPITOLE
DE QUÉBEC

St-Jean

McWilliam
Cook

Garneau
Ste-Famille rie de l'Université
Hamel
Ste-Famille

des Remparts
du Fort

VIEUX-QUÉBEC

AGORA DU
VIEUX-PORT

Côte
Kent
Dauphine

D'Auteuil

St-Angèle

Ste-Anne

Côte de la Fabrique
B.Q. Chauveau

HÔTEL
DE VILLE

Rue des Jardins
B.Q. St-Jean

SÉMINAIRE
DE QUÉBEC

Buade

BASILIQUE
NOTRE-DAME

de la Barricade

St-Pierre

St-Antoine

Dalhousie

Prince de Galles

Bell

MUSÉE DE LA
CIVILISATION

PARC DE
L'ESPLANADE

St-Ursule

Patrick

Donnacona

COUVENT DES
URSULINES

CATH. OF
THE HOLY
TRINITY

QUÉBEC
EXPERIENCE

MUSÉE
DU FORT

Pl.
d'Armes

PARC
MONTMORENCY

Port-Dauphin

Sault-au-Matelot

Côte de la Montagne

Notre-Dame

du Porche

du Marché
Finlay

PLACE
ROYALE

CHALMERS-WESLEY
UNITED CHURCH

St-Louis

NOTRE-DAME-DU-
SACRÉ-CŒUR
PARC DU
CAVALIER-
DU-MOULIN

Mont-Carmel

CHÂTEAU
FRONTENAC

des Carrières

Sous-
le-Fort

MAISON DU
CHEVALIER

du Marché-
Champlain

QUARTIER
PETIT- CHAMPLAIN

Ste-Geneviève

des Grisons
de la Porte

du Petit-Champlain

SAINT-LAURENT

Côte de la Citadelle

D'Auteuil

D'Auteuil

Av St-Denis

Bl Champlain

to Lévis

LA CITADELLE

FLEUVE

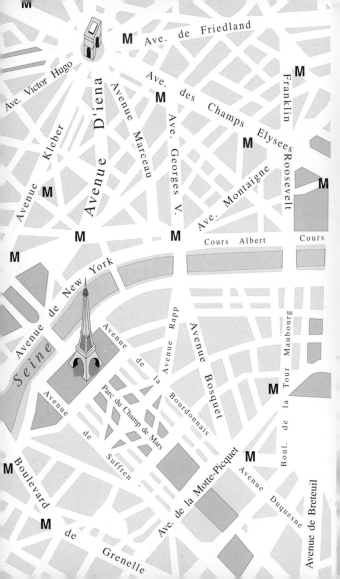